Infiltration

TAYLOR R. MARSHALL

INFILTRATION

THE PLOT TO DESTROY THE CHURCH FROM WITHIN

Manchester, New Hampshire

Cover design by Perceptions Design Studio.

Cover photo © Shutterstock.

Crisis Publications
Box 5284, Manchester, NH 03108
1-800-888-9344

www.CrisisMagazine.com

Library of Congress Cataloging-in-Publication Data

Names: Marshall, Taylor, author.
Title: Infiltration : the plot to destroy the Church from within / Taylor R. Marshall.
Description: Manchester, New Hampshire : Crisis Publications (an imprint of Sophia Institute Press), [2019] | Includes bibliographical references and index.
Identifiers: LCCN 2019014274 | ISBN 9781622828463 (hardcover : alk. paper)
Subjects: LCSH: Catholic Church—History—Modern period, 1500- | Modernist-fundamentalist controversy. | Catholic traditionalist movement.
Classification: LCC BX1397 .M29 2019 | DDC 282.09/03—dc23 LC record available at https://lccn.loc.gov/2019014274

To my eight children, the next generation
of warriors for Christ and His Church

Contents

Appendices

Foreword

In *Infiltration: The Plot to Destroy the Church from Within*, Taylor Marshall touches on a topic that is deliberately ignored today. The issue of a possible infiltration of the Church by forces outside her does not fit into the optimistic picture that Pope John XXIII and particularly the Second Vatican Council unrealistically and uncritically drew of the modern world.

In the last sixty years, there has been a continuously growing hostility toward the Divine Person of Jesus Christ and His claim to be the sole Redeemer and Teacher of humankind. This hostility of the allegedly "nice," "tolerant," "optimistic" modern world expresses itself in slogans such as "We don't want Christ to reign over us"; "We want to be free from any demanding doctrinal truth or moral law"; and "We will never acknowledge a Church that will not unconditionally accept the mindset of the modern world."

This hostility has reached its peak in our day. Not a few high-ranking members of the Catholic Church's hierarchy have not only yielded to the relentless demands of the modern world; they are, with or without conviction, actively collaborating in the implementation of its principles in the daily life of the Church in all areas and on all levels.

Many wonder how it could happen that the Church's doctrine, morals, and liturgy have been disfigured to such a large extent.

How is it that there remains very little difference between the predominant spirit in the life of the Church in our days and the mindset of the modern world? The modern world, after all, is inspired by the principles of the French Revolution: the absolute freedom of man from any divine revelation or commandment; the absolute equality that abolishes not only any social or religious hierarchy but even differences between the sexes; and a brotherhood of man so uncritical that it even eliminates any distinction on the basis of religion.

It would be dishonest and irresponsible only to state the facts of the Church's current internal crisis, and to deal with the symptoms. We must examine the very roots of the crisis, which, to a decisive extent, can be identified (as Taylor Marshall has done in this book) as an infiltration of the Church by the unbelieving world, and especially by Freemasons – an infiltration that, by human standards, could effectively succeed only through a long, methodical process.

As Pope Leo XIII noted when he opened the secret Vatican Archives, in researching and exposing historical facts – even if they are compromising and troubling – the Church has nothing to fear. This book reveals significant historical roots of the current global crisis in the Church and throws light on many otherwise puzzling events of the past.

Because of the lack of sufficient resource materials and since the relevant Vatican Archives are still closed to researchers, some issues considered in this book (such as the circumstances surrounding the death of Pope John Paul I) must remain as hypotheses. Other arguments presented here, however, point to the existence of a kind of ominous red thread which systematically runs through the history of the past century-and-a-half of the Church's history.

Foreword

The Church of Christ has always and will always be persecuted; she will always be infiltrated by her enemies. The question is always only about the extent of such an infiltration, and this is determined by the degree of vigilance exercised by those in the Church who are designated as "watchmen," which is the literal meaning of the word *episcopos*—that is, bishop. The highest watchman in the Church is the Roman pontiff, the supreme shepherd both of the bishops and of the faithful. The first infiltration in the Church happened with the apostate apostle Judas Iscariot. Since then, there have been in the Church intruders – priests, bishops, and even in very rare cases, popes – whom Our Lord called "wolves in sheep's clothing."

It is noble and meritorious to sound the alarm when robbers and other intruders are secretly breaking into the house and poisoning the food of its inhabitants. In the past fifty years, such an alarm has been sounded several times by courageous bishops, priests, and lay faithful. Those in responsible offices in the Church, however, have not paid due attention to those alarms, and so the intruders – wolves in sheep's clothing – have been able to wreak havoc, undisturbed, in the house of God, the Church.

With devastation and confusion in the Church now in full public view, it is time to expose the historical roots and the perpetrators of this harm. It may help many in the Church to wake up out of their lethargy and to stop acting as if everything is just fine. Taylor Marshall's book is a significant contribution to the work of raising awareness of this situation and taking preventive actions and countermeasures in the future.

Saint Augustine gave us the following realistic yet consoling description of the truth that the Church will be always persecuted:

> Many a time have they fought against me from my youth up (Ps. 128:1).... The Church is of ancient birth.... At one time, the Church was in Abel only, and he was fought against by his wicked ... brother Cain (Gen. 4:8). At one time, the Church was in Enoch alone: and he was taken from the unrighteous (Gen. 5:24). At one time, the Church was in the house of Noah alone, and endured all who perished by the flood, and the ark alone swam upon the waves, and escaped to shore (Gen. 6–8). At one time, the Church was in Abraham alone, and we know what he endured from the wicked. The Church was in his brother's son, Lot, alone, and in his house, in Sodom, and he endured the iniquities and perversities of Sodom until God freed him from among them (Gen. 13–20). The Church also began to exist in the people of Israel. She endured Pharaoh and the Egyptians.... We come unto our Lord Jesus Christ: the Gospel was preached in the Psalms. For this reason, lest the Church wonder now, or lest anyone ... who wishes to be a good member of the Church wonder, let him hear his Mother the Church saying to him, "Marvel not at these things, my son: *Many a time have they fought against me from my youth up, but they could not prevail over me*. (*Enarr. in Ps.* 128)

Even the most perfidious plot to destroy the Church from within will not succeed. Hence, our Mother the Church will answer with the voice of her innocent children, of her pure young men and virgins, of her fathers and mothers of families, of her courageous and knightly lay apostles and apologists, of her chaste and zealous priests and bishops, of her religious sisters and especially of her cloistered nuns, the spiritual gems of the Church: "They could not prevail over me!" *Christus vincit! Christus regnat! Christus imperat!*

+ Athanasius Schneider
Auxiliary Bishop of the
Archdiocese of Saint Mary in Astana
April 11, 2019

Acknowledgments

I would like to thank my wife, Joy Marshall; my parents; and all my readers, students, listeners, and viewers. I am grateful to His Excellency Athanasius Schneider, O.R.C., for reading the manuscript and for writing the foreword. Also, a special thanks to Charlie McKinney, John Barger, Charles A. Coulombe, and Rev. D. Christensen for reading the manuscript and for their advice.

Infiltration

1

The Smoke of God and the Smoke of Satan

Why did Pope Benedict XVI resign the papacy on 28 February 2013? And why did lightning strike the Vatican on the night he announced it? Was it prompted by scandal at the Vatican Bank? Was it a sex scandal tainting the highest cardinals? Was it a doctrinal crisis? All these questions and doubts coalesce when we acknowledge a substantiated and corroborated fact: Satan uniquely entered the Catholic Church at some point over the last century, or even before that. For over a century, the organizers of Freemasonry, Liberalism, and Modernism infiltrated the Catholic Church in order to change her doctrine, her liturgy, and her mission from something supernatural to something secular.

Catholics are increasingly aware of a climate change in the Catholic Church. Some point to the controversial pontificate of Pope Francis. Others highlight the confusion surrounding the surprise resignation of Pope Benedict XVI in 2013. Some are convinced that John Paul II was not who we thought him to be. Most agree that the Second Vatican Council, the Novus Ordo Mass, and the pontificate of Paul VI brought monumental confusion to the Catholic Church. But does the fall of the first domino begin in 1962 with the opening of Second Vatican Council?

I argue that the root of the problem extends back to an agenda put in play more than one hundred years before Vatican II. It is an agenda to replace the supernatural religion of the crucified and resurrected Jesus Christ with the natural religion of humanism and globalism. It echoes the primeval choice of Adam and Eve to make themselves divine by grasping at the fruits of nature, rather than kneeling in reception of the supernatural fruit of divine grace. Lucifer also rebelled against God. In his pride, he sought to ascend to the throne of God, not by sharing in the supernatural life of God, but by digging deep into his own nature and reaching for the stars—and thereby falling into the abyss of hell. Supernaturalism—relying on God who is above the natural—is Catholicism. Naturalism—relying on our created nature without the aid of God—is Satanism.

The Catholic Church is in crisis because the enemies of Christ plotted organized efforts to place a pope for Satan on the Roman Chair of Saint Peter. The enemies of Christ from Nero to Napoleon eventually discovered that to attack or murder the pope only creates sympathy and martyrs. It is a failed strategy in every era. So instead, they sought quietly to place one of their own in the papal shoes. It would require decades, even a century, to create the seminaries, the priests, the bishops, the cardinal electors, and then even the pope or popes themselves—but it would be worth the wait. It has been a slow, patient plan to establish a Satanic revolution with the pope as puppet.

If you do not believe that Satan exists, put down this book. Moreover, if you believe that the Catholic Church can be purified merely by updated rules, policies, and canonical procedures, you'll find little promise in the historical diagnosis and proposed cure found in this book. Saint Paul stated: "For we are not contending against flesh and blood, but against the principalities, against the powers, against the world rulers of this present darkness, against the spiritual hosts of wickedness in the heavenly places" (Eph.

6:12). The crisis of the Catholic Church relates to the intrusion of these "rulers of this present darkness," and she can only be purified by sanctified warfare against the demonic.

In a homily for Holy Mass on the feast of Saint Peter and Saint Paul (29 June 1972) and in commemoration of the ninth anniversary of being crowned as Bishop of Rome, Pope Paul VI lamented: "We would say that, through some mysterious crack—no, it's not mysterious; through some crack, the smoke of Satan has entered the Church of God. There is doubt, uncertainty, problems, unrest, dissatisfaction, confrontation."[1] This testimony of Paul VI acknowledged not merely that the Catholic Church had experienced secularization but that the smoke of Satan himself had entered the Church through a crack. What is this satanic smoke?

In Sacred Scripture, the word "smoke" is used about fifty times. In almost every case, the word refers to the liturgical worship of Israel's God through the smoke of incense and the smoke of animal sacrifice as "sweet-smelling sacrifice" (Sir. 38:11). In one case, "smoke" is even used for the exorcism of a demon: "And when the demon smelled the odor he fled to the remotest parts of Egypt, and the angel bound him" (Tob. 8:3). When Isaiah mystically enters the heavenly house of God, he makes particular mention that "the house was filled with smoke" (Isa. 6:4). Lastly, the book of Revelation details the plumes of smoke within the heavenly Holy of Holies: "The smoke of the incense rose with the prayers of the saints from the hand of the angel before God" (Rev. 8:4). Scripture, then, universally associates smoke with the worship and presence of God. Why, then, does Pope Paul VI speak of the smoke of Satan?

[1] *Insegnamenti di Paolo VI* (Città de Vaticano: Tipografia Poliglotta Vaticana, 1972), vol. X, p. 707.

Although smoke is nearly always a sign of holiness, sacrifice, and worship, in the book of Revelation, we find a handful of exceptions. We repeatedly observe how Satan mimics God, just as the Egyptian magicians copycatted the miracles of Moses. For example, Revelation presents a perverted satanic trinity of the devil, an antichrist king, and a false prophet. In place of a Holy and Virginal Church wedded to Christ, Satan establishes the Whore of Babylon riding the antichrist. In like manner, we observe sacred incense smoke in the eighth chapter of Revelation, and then immediately we read of the demonic smoke of Satan in the ninth chapter:

> I saw a star fallen from heaven to earth, and he was given the key of the shaft of the bottomless pit; he opened the shaft of the bottomless pit, and from the shaft rose smoke like the smoke of a great furnace, and the sun and the air were darkened with the smoke from the shaft. Then from the smoke came locusts on the earth, and they were given power like the power of scorpions of the earth. (Rev. 9:1–3)

This is the "smoke of Satan" to which Pope Paul VI referred in 1972. Satan is the "star fallen from heaven to earth." Just as Simon received a new name (Peter) and received the "keys of the kingdom of heaven" (Matt. 16:19), so also the devil received a new name (Satan) and received a "key of the shaft of the bottomless pit." Both Peter and Satan received new names and the power of keys. Satan is, therefore, the pope of the damned. That Satan is the *papa* or father of the damned can be discerned from the warning of Christ to the Pharisees, "You are of your father the devil."[2]

[2] "You are of your father the devil, and your will is to do your father's desires. He was a murderer from the beginning, and has

The Catholic office of pope goes back to Simon Peter. After Christ asks the apostles, "Who do you say that I am?" Simon answers, "You are the Christ, the Son of the living God" (Matt. 16:15–16). Christ then promises to Simon the Davidic office of steward or prime minister by changing his name:

> Blessed are you, Simon Bar-Jona! For flesh and blood has not revealed this to you, but my Father who is in heaven. And I tell you, you are Peter, and on this rock I will build my church, and the powers of death shall not prevail against it. I will give you the keys of the kingdom of heaven, and whatever you bind on earth shall be bound in heaven, and whatever you loose on earth shall be loosed in heaven. (Matt. 16:17–19)

The successors of Saint Peter are those *papas* or "popes" who succeed Saint Peter as bishops of the city of Rome. To understand fully how the "smoke of Satan" entered the Catholic Church before 1972 under Pope Paul VI, we must begin with the infestation of the Catholic Church by institutional naturalism and this leads us to the year of Our Lord 1859.

---

nothing to do with the truth, because there is no truth in him. When he lies, he speaks according to his own nature, for he is a liar and the father of lies" (John 8:44).

2

Alta Vendita: Satan's Revolution in Tiara and Cope

The Pope, whoever he may be, will never come to the secret societies. It is for the secret societies to come first to the Church, with the aim of winning them both. The work which we have undertaken is not the work of a day, nor of a month, nor of a year. It may last many years, a century perhaps, but in our ranks the soldier dies, and the fight continues.

—Freemasonic Permanent Instruction of the *Alta Vendita*

The Frenchman Jacques Crétineau-Joly had a fiery faith and entered the seminary only to discern that he did not have a vocation to the priesthood. He had been a philosophy professor and attempted poetry but found his talent in research and writing. In 1846, Crétineau-Joly published an exhaustive six-volume history of the Jesuits titled *The Religious, Political, and Literary History of the Society of Jesus* (*Histoire religieuse, politique et littéraire de la Compagnie de Jésus*). In 1859, with approval and encouragement from Pope Pius IX, he published his most important book *The Roman Church in the Face of Revolution* (L'Église romaine en face de la Révolution).

The Roman Church in the Face of Revolution was an explosive work that claimed that anti-Catholic secret societies would no longer attack the Church from without but would infiltrate her from within. The plot was detailed in a secret document acquired from the highest lodge in Italy, the *Alta Vendita* of the Carbonari. The Italian Carbonari, or "charcoal makers," were a secret society aligned with secret societies in France, Spain, Portugal, and Russia. These Freemasonic lodges shared common goals, such as a hatred for Catholicism and monarchy. The Italian Carbonari held a unique posture of hatred because, for them, the chief Italian monarch also happened to be the Catholic pope. Pope Pius IX had written the encyclical *Qui pluribus* in 1846 directly against the growing influence of the Carbonari.

Sometime before 1859, the Catholic Church acquired a secret document titled *The Permanent Instruction of the Alta Vendita* detailing how they will eventually take over the papacy. The Italian Carbonari met in secret in lodges, which they called *venditas*, or "shops." The chief lodge or *vendita* was the "high shop" or *alta vendita*. This document was thus a guiding document for the "high shop" of the Carbonari. Crétineau-Joly exposed the thesis of the *Alta Vendita*, and the Irish priest Monsignor George Francis Dillon subsequently took it up.

The Protestant Reformation of 1517 had obliterated European Christendom. As Protestantism splintered and weakened, there was a naturalistic desire for a new world order united around "*liberté, égalité, fraternité*." Beginning in 1717, the establishing of this new world order would be accomplished by forming a new organized "religion" through secret societies throughout Europe.

From 1717 forward, the chief enemy of the Catholic Church was Freemasonry. The oldest Freemason fraternities seem to derive from the medieval guilds of stonemasons. During the Reformation, however, these masonic lodges took on the form of subversive secret societies with occult rites and gnostic philosophy.

Occult Freemasonry likely derives from the Rosicrucian or "Rose Cross" rites popularized in Protestant regions of Germany. The founding document of Rosicrucian mysticism is *Fama Fraternitatis Rosae Crucis* (1614), written by the gnostic alchemist Michael Maier (1568–1622). This document pretends to be written by a certain man named "Father Brother C.R.C." or "Christian Rosa Crux" who was born in 1378 and allegedly lived 106 years. This pretended founder is typically referred to as Christian Rosenkreuz. He traveled to the East and acquired secret wisdom from Zoroastrianism, Sufism, Kabbalah, and gnostic teachers. Most traditions identify Christian Rosenkreuz as an Albigensian heretic. The core of Rosicrucianism is mystical parables and morality rites or liturgies that teach occult lessons for the enlightened. The central mystery is alchemy, or the belief that one can create gold from lower substances. This is the heresy of naturalism—manipulating nature to produce something above nature—just as Satan attempted to transcend his nature in order to become God.

After the Reformation of 1517 left a vacuum in Europe, Freemasonry organized a new universal "catholic church" instituted to unite man in naturalism, rationalism, and the universal brotherhood. The strategy of Rosicrucianism and Freemasonry is to arrange secret societies to subvert the current (Catholic) order and replace it with an enlightened order in which all religions are approximations of the truth—all religions become allegorical and equal. The Catholic Church is the *Vetus Ordo Saeculorum*—the Old Order of the World. Freemasonry is the *Novus Ordo Saeculorum*—the New Order of the World.

Freemasonry is the organized attempt to achieve what Lucifer attempted and what Adam and Eve tried. It is the temptation to alchemy—to transform lead into gold. Lucifer, Adam, and Eve attempted to transform their good natures into divine natures. Similarly, the Freemasons deny the unique Incarnation of Jesus Christ and reject the idea of sin and the need for Christ to die and rise again for human salvation. Consequently, there is no grace, no sacraments, and no Church—human nature alone is sufficient for humanity's happiness. It is the theological error that nature is neither healed nor perfected by grace. Rather, nature is divine. Creation is divine, and we must seek occult illumination to see the new world order of nature as divine.

Not surprisingly, Freemasonry always thrived where Protestantism took root first. Scotland (Presbyterianism), England (Anglicanism), and Germany (Lutheranism) are the traditional centers of European Freemasonry. Similarly, Protestant America also became infected by Freemasonry, especially in the Protestant Southern United States.

Following Rosicrucianism, Freemasonry worships the "Great Architect of the Universe," who is both god and the natural universe. Former members of Freemasonry have revealed that the "Great Architect of the Universe" is, in fact, Satan.

Formally organized Freemasonry originated in 1717, two hundred years after the 1517 Reformation. It grew out of the anti-Catholicism, Deism, and rationalism of its time. Reason, not faith, was prized by this epoch, and the Freemasonic lodges proliferated. Organized religion was rejected in favor of the sentiment that all religions are equally grasping for the unknown "Great Architect of the Universe." This is why the Freemason Benjamin Franklin tithed to all the religions and denominations in his day. This is also why Freemasons enshrine the scriptures of all religions on their altar: the Holy Bible, the Koran, the Vedas, the Zend-Avesta, the Sohar, the Kabbalah, the Bhagavad Gita, and the Upanishads. They are, for the Freemason, all equally true and all equally false. They are, for the Freemason, merely the kindergarten sketches of children picturing God.

Since organized religions are accepted equally, the mode of divine knowledge is reason, not faith, baptism, preaching, Eucharist, liturgy, or priesthood—and certainly not the papacy. Humanity does not need faith—it needs more reason. This is the fallout from Martin Luther's assertion of religious authority from Scripture alone. This principle made every man the private and final judge of theological doctrine. Private subjective reason sneaked in by this back door left open unwittingly by Luther.

The Catholic Church excommunicated any Catholic who joined Freemasonry, because it is a religion of all religions. Although it is a secret society, it makes no secret about seeking a new world order in which all religions are honored and treated as equally true. In its pursuit of equality, it also desires the equal distribution of human property.

Now that we have established the historical and philosophical background of Freemasonry, we can return to the *Alta Vendita* and the new strategy of the nineteenth-century Carbonari. Written pseudonymously by Piccolo Tigre or "Little Tiger," *The Permanent Instruction of the Alta Vendita* boldly details precisely how the papacy will be won over to Freemasonic philosophy and beliefs, and its central tenet cannot be repeated too often:

> The Pope, whoever he may be, will never come to the secret societies. It is for the secret societies to come first to the Church, with the aim of winning them both. The work which we have undertaken is not the work of a day,

> nor of a month, nor of a year. It may last many years, a century perhaps, but in our ranks the soldier dies, and the fight continues.[3]

Here the *Alta Vendita* grants that their project may take a century. The Little Tiger then goes on to explain how the papacy will be acquired:

> Now then, in order to secure to us a Pope according to our own heart, it is necessary to fashion for that Pope a generation worthy of the kingdom of which we dream. Leave on one side old age and middle life, go to the youth, and, if possible, even to children.

The Little Tiger explains how the youth will be seduced over time through the corruption of families, books, poems, colleges, gymnasiums, universities, and seminaries. Next, the Catholic clergy will be seduced and corrupted:

> The reputation of a good Catholic and good patriot will open the way for our doctrines to pass into the hearts of the young clergy and go even to the depths of convents. In a few years the young clergy will have, by the force of events, invaded all offices. They will govern, administer,

[3] This quote and all quotes from the *Alta Vendita* can be found in the *Permanent Instruction of the Alta Vendita* by Piccolo Tigre. Reproduced in English translation in the lecture by Right Rev. Mgsr. George Dillon, D.D., at Edinburgh in October 1884, about six months after the appearance of Pope Leo XIII's famous encyclical letter, *Humanum genus*, on Freemasonry. A few changes were made by Dr. Taylor Marshall to update the language and spelling to modern standards. The full text is found in the back of this book.

> and judge. They will form the Council of the Sovereign. They will be called upon to choose the Pontiff who will reign.

Once the corrupted young clergy become cardinals and elect a pope "according to our heart," many obstacles will remain in the way:

> and that Pontiff, like the greater part of his contemporaries, will be necessarily imbued with the Italian and humanitarian principles which we are about to put in circulation. It is a little grain of mustard which we place in the earth, but the sun of Justice will develop it even to be a great power, and you will see one day what a rich harvest that little seed will produce. In the way which we trace for our brethren there are found great obstacles to conquer, difficulties of more than one kind to surmount. They will be overcome by experience and by wisdom.

The Little Tiger next rejoices over the outcome of a Freemasonic naturalistic Pope reigning on the Chair of Saint Peter:

> The goal is so beautiful that we must put all sails to the wind in order to attain it. If you want to revolutionize Italy, look for the Pope whose portrait we have just drawn. Do you want to establish the reign of the chosen ones on the throne of the Whore of Babylon? Let the clergy march under your banner, while they naively believe they are marching under the banner of the Apostolic Keys.
>
> Do you want to wipe out the last vestige of the tyrants and oppressors? Cast out your nets like Simon Bar-Jona! Cast them deep into the sacristy, the seminaries, and monasteries, rather than at the bottom of the sea. And

> if you do not rush things, we promise you a catch more miraculous than this!
>
> The fisherman of fish became a fisherman of men. You, too, will fish some friends and lead them to the feet of the Apostolic See. You will have preached revolution in tiara and cope, preceded under the cross and the banner, a revolution that will need only a little help to set the quarters of the world on fire.

The plan of the Little Tiger doesn't include pamphlets, guns, bloodshed, or even political elections. It requires a step-by-step infiltration, first of the youth, next of the clergy, and then, as time passes, of those youth and clergy who become cardinals and then the pope.

Pope Gregory XVI originally acquired the *Alta Vendita* document, which places its composition likely within the years of his pontificate from 1831 to 1846. In 1832 he issued the encyclical *Mirari vos* on liberalism and religious indifferentism. The document is written against "the insolent and factious men who endeavored to raise the standard of treason." Pope Gregory XVI writes against what appears to be a French Revolution being fostered from *within* the Catholic Church. In *Mirari vos*, he addresses and condemns seven current errors invading the hearts of Catholics:

1. "The abominable conspiracy against *clerical celibacy*" (no. 11)
2. "Anything contrary to the *sanctity and indissolubility of honorable marriage* of Christians" (no. 12)
3. "*Indifferentism*. This perverse opinion is spread on all sides by the fraud of the wicked who claim that it is possible to obtain the eternal salvation of the soul by the profession of any kind of religion, as long as morality is maintained." (no. 13)

4. "The erroneous proposition which claims that *liberty of conscience* must be maintained for everyone." (no. 14)
5. "The *freedom to publish* any writings whatsoever and disseminate them to the people . . . for we read that the Apostles themselves burned a large number of books" (nos. 15–16)
6. "*Attacks on the trust and submission due to princes*; the torches of treason are being lit everywhere" (no. 17)
7. "The plans of those who desire vehemently to *separate the Church from the State*, and to break the mutual concord between temporal authority and the priesthood" (no. 20)

Catholics living in our time may be shocked to observe popes in our day advocating polar opposites of these condemnations laid down in 1832. Current papal and Conciliar documents, and canon law make room for clerical marriage, divorce and remarriage, liberty of conscience over the objective moral law, freedom of the press, political rebellion, and the complete separation of the Church from the State. Between the pontificate of Gregory XVI and our time, the plot of the *Permanent Instruction of the Alta Vendita* has taken deep root indeed.

Gregory's successor Pope Pius IX encouraged Jacques Crétineau-Joly to publish the text of the *Alta Vendita* in full in 1859. The plot of placing "our doctrines in the hearts of the young clergy and the monasteries" was no doubt on the mind of Pope Pius IX when he issued his *Syllabus of Errors* in 1864, which explicitly attacked the eighty errors of Freemasonry and the Carbonari, divided into ten sections:

1. Against pantheism, naturalism, and absolute rationalism (propositions 1–7)
2. Against moderate rationalism (propositions 8–14)

3. Against indifferentism and latitudinarianism (propositions 15–18)
4. Against socialism, communism, secret societies, Bible societies, and liberal clerical societies (a general condemnation, unnumbered)
5. Defense of the temporal power in the Papal States, which were overthrown six years later (propositions 19–38)
6. Relationship of civil society to the Church (propositions 39–55)
7. On natural and Christian ethics (propositions 56–64)
8. Defense of Christian marriage (propositions 65–74)
9. Civil power of the sovereign pontiff in the Papal States (propositions 75–76)
10. Against liberalism in every political form (propositions 77–80)

The Freemasons were fighting for the pantheistic deification of human beings—just as Satan had fought for the pantheistic deification of angelic beings. And once again, that preternatural war would come to earth. In just a few short years, the Freemasons would accomplish the overthrow of the political independence of the papacy and Pope Leo XIII would mystically see demons gathering upon Rome.

3

Our Lady of La Salette

The Successor of Saint Peter was not the only one concerned about the infiltration of the Catholic Church. In 1846, the Blessed Virgin Mary appeared in an apparition to two children at La Salette, France. Five years later, Pope Pius IX formally approved the apparition of Our Lady of Salette and its two "secrets." The two children were Maximin Giraud (age eleven) and Mélanie Calvat (age fourteen), who lived in the eight-hundred-person town of La Salette in Southeastern France. Returning from the mountain where they had been tending the cows of Mélanie's neighbor, the two children saw a beautiful lady weeping bitterly on Mount Sous-Les-Baisses.

There, the Blessed Virgin sat unceremoniously with her elbows on her knees, weeping into her hands. She wore a high headdress composed of various roses, a silver robe, a gold apron, white shoes, and a golden crucifix hung from a chain around her neck. Roses were also on the ground at her feet. While crying, she spoke to the children in their French dialect of Occitan. The message of Our Lady of La Salette concerned reverence for the Holy Name of God and rest from work on Sunday. She warned them of the impending potato famine that struck Ireland and France in 1846 and 1847. She then revealed a secret to each of the two children, ascended the hill, and disappeared.

The local bishop, Philibert de Bruillard of Grenoble, interviewed the children and found their story worthy of belief. Cardinal Bonald, the archbishop of Lyon, however, remained skeptical. The cardinal insisted that the children reveal each of their secrets. Mélanie agreed to do so only if the text of her secret would be carried directly to the pope. In agreement with this condition, the bishop of Grenoble sent two representatives to Rome carrying the two secrets of Our Lady, which they presented to Pius IX on 18 July 1851.

Maximin Giraud became a seminarian but never reached ordination to the priesthood; he died before turning forty on 1 March 1875. Mélanie Calvat became a nun at the age of twenty (taking the name Sister Mary of the Cross) with the Sisters of Providence and then transferred to the Sisters of Charity.

Mélanie's words became controversial in the compromise between Napoleon III (nephew of Napoleon Bonaparte) and the bishops of France. She revealed that the Blessed Virgin Mary had warned her of a Freemasonic plot to overturn the Catholic Church in France. Eager to remove this visionary from French politics, the hierarchy allowed her to transfer to an English Carmelite convent in 1855.

For five years in England, she spoke of prophecies and things to come. The local English bishop forbade her from speaking, so she returned to France and joined a convent at Marseille. Her identity was found out, and she shuffled through a few convents before leaving for Naples in 1867. In Naples, she wrote down her secret and a rule for a religious community of men called the Order of the Apostles of the Last Days, and another for women called the Order of the Mother of God. Mélanie met privately with Pope Leo XIII to discuss these orders, but nothing came of them. When she died in Naples, the local people were shocked to learn that the seer of La Salette had been living incognito in their midst.

What is the secret of Our Lady of La Salette that was given to Mélanie? She first wrote down the secret in 1851, and it was sealed and sent to Pope Pius IX—after which it was archived in the Holy Office in Rome. Mélanie wrote it down a second time 1873 and published this second version in 1879 as a booklet bearing the imprimatur of Bishop Salvatore Luigi Zola of the diocese of Lecce, Italy. The title of this booklet is *Apparition of the Blessed Virgin on the Mountain of La Salette*.

Mélanie's original 1851 version had been archived, lost, and forgotten since the late 1800s. In 1999, however, it was rediscovered in the archives of the Holy Office and published.[4] Only since 1999 have we been able to compare the two versions side by side. The 1851 archived version and the 1879 published version follow the same themes (persecution of the pope, apostasy, the destruction of Paris and Marseille, the birth of the antichrist from a nun, etc.), but the 1879 is much longer and more precise and contains details that are not found the other version.

The Holy Office censured the 1879 version almost immediately after its publication because it predicted the future apostasy of Rome. In 1923, it was placed on the *Index of Forbidden Books*. Most people today assume that the archived 1851 version is the pure, pristine, and true version, whereas the 1879 published

[4] Father Michel Corteville discovered Mélanie's original written secret of 1851 in the archives of the Holy Office in 1999. The 1851 version conforms in essence to her published 1879 version, but it lacks the phrases "Rome will lose faith and become the seat of the Antichrist," and "There will be an eclipse of the Church." In 2000 at the Angelicum, Father Michel Corteville defended his doctoral thesis in theology, entitled *Discovery of the Secret of La Salette*.

edition was falsified and sensationalized by Mélanie in her adult life. But why would Mélanie corrupt and falsely expand a secret she received from the Blessed Virgin Mary?

Those who reject the 1879 version, with its account of Rome as the seat of the antichrist, claim that Mélanie either lost her mind or that she bore malice toward the Catholic Church, so she created an embellished version of her secret. Yet we read that she died humbly, receiving the sacraments, and professing the Catholic Faith. Those who knew her testified to her sanctity and fidelity. Even Pope Pius X admired her and suggested her beatification after her death.

Mélanie was not insane, and she did not bear false witness about the words of the Mother of God. We can conclude, then, that the 1851 and 1879 versions are both equally true and do not invalidate one another, any more than the differing details in Saint Matthew's Gospel refute the authenticity and truth of Saint Mark's Gospel. The 1851 version states that the antichrist will be born of a nun. The 1879 version states the antichrist will be born of a *Hebrew* nun. Differences such as this do not discredit the more detailed 1879 version. Moreover, we know that the 1851 version was written down twice in 1851, and the first draft was rejected and destroyed. Some tampering did occur in 1851 as well.

We also know that in 1851, when the original version was approved and sealed, the girl Mélanie was suffering intimidation by a cardinal, a bishop, inquisitors, and theologians. The 1851 version, therefore, may not have been the exhaustive version, but simply the gist of Our Lady's secret to satisfy the cardinal commanding Mélanie. Moreover, in a letter to Abbé Combe, Mélanie also speaks of "the vision that I had in the moment when the Blessed Virgin was speaking of the resurrection of the dead."[5] That Mélanie received a vision as the Virgin spoke is often overlooked. In this author's opinion, the 1879 version incorporates both the message and the vision, whereas the 1851 contains a truncated version of the message.

I believe that both versions are valid (both versions are included in the appendix of this book), and thus I here reprint the most interesting passages from the 1879 edition. Firstly, Our Lady condemns the evil priests of the Catholic Church:

> The priests, ministers of my Son, the priests, by their wicked lives, by their irreverence and their impiety in the celebration of the holy mysteries, by their love of money, their love of honors and pleasures, the priests have become cesspools of impurity. Yes, the priests are asking vengeance, and vengeance is hanging over their heads. Woe to the priests and to those dedicated to God who by their unfaithfulness and their wicked lives are crucifying my Son again! The sins of those dedicated to God cry out to Heaven and call for vengeance, and now vengeance is at their door, for there is no one left to beg mercy and forgiveness for the people. There are no more generous souls, there is no one left worthy of offering a stainless sacrifice to the Eternal for the sake of the world.[6]

[5] Recorded by Abbé Gilbert-Joseph-Émile Combe, who edited *Le secret de Mélanie* (Lyon, France, 1904), 29–30. In another place, Mélanie referred to both a seen vision and an audible message: "*dans la vision et dans l'audition*" (G.J.E. Combe, *Le secret de Mélanie bergère de la Salette et la crise actuelle* (Rome, 1906), 118-119. Abbé Combe also records: "before the eyes of her intelligence which she called sight (*vue*), that is, the vision that accompanied the words that she heard," in Combe, *Le secret de Mélanie* (1906), 144.

[6] Mélanie Calvat, *Apparition of the Blessed Virgin on the Mountain of La Salette* (Lecce, Italy: 1879), 2.

Our Lady of La Salette then praises Pope Pius IX and condemns Napoleon III:

> May the Vicar of my Son, Pope Pius IX, never leave Rome again after 1859; may he, however, be steadfast and noble; may he fight with the weapons of faith and love. I will be at his side. May he be on his guard against Napoleon: he is two-faced, and he wishes to make himself Pope as well as Emperor. God will soon draw back from him. He is the mastermind who, always wanting to ascend further, will fall on the sword he wishes to use to force his people to be raised up.[7]

Our Lady names 1864 as the year in which Satan and his demons will be unleashed from hell; 1864 marks the publication of the *Syllabus of Errors*, in which Pope Pius IX condemns liberalism, rationalism, and socialism.

> In the year 1864, Lucifer together with many demons will be unloosed from hell; they will put an end to faith little by little, even in those dedicated to God. They will blind them in such a way, that, unless they are blessed with a special grace, these people will take on the spirit of these angels of hell; several religious institutions will lose all faith and will lose many souls.... All the civil governments will have one and the same plan, which will be to abolish and do away with every religious principle, to make way for materialism, atheism, spiritualism, and vice of all kinds.[8]

Our Lady then turns to the end of the world and describes the advent of the antichrist upon the earth:

[7] Ibid., 7

[8] Ibid., 11

> It will be during this time that the Antichrist will be born of a Hebrew nun, a false virgin who will communicate with the old serpent, the master of impurity, his father will be B.[9] At birth, he will spew out blasphemy; he will have teeth; in a word, he will be the devil incarnate. He will scream horribly, he will perform wonders, he will feed on nothing but impurity. He will have brothers who, although not devils incarnate like him, will be children of evil. At the age of twelve, they will draw attention upon themselves by the gallant victories they will have won; soon they will each lead armies, aided by the legions of hell.[10]
>
> The seasons will be altered, the earth will produce nothing but bad fruit, the stars will lose their regular motion, the moon will only reflect a faint reddish glow. Water and fire will give the earth's globe convulsions and terrible earthquakes, which will swallow up mountains, cities, etc.[11]
>
> Rome will lose faith and become the seat of the Antichrist.[12]

Mélanie's booklet received much resistance in Rome, presumably because it condemned wicked priests so violently and stated, "Rome will lose faith and become the seat of the Antichrist." In 1880, the Holy Office restricted the book, but it was reprinted repeatedly in France and Italy into the 1900s.[13] Yet Pope Pius

9 Here "B" is usually assumed to be "bishop." This means that the antichrist is not the son of Satan but born naturally of an unholy union between a nun and a bishop.

10 Calvat, *Apparition*, 26.

11 Ibid., 27.

12 Ibid., 28.

13 The Holy Office, under Pope Benedict XV, placed a reprinting of the 1879 version of the secret on the *Index of Forbidden Books* on 9 May 1923.

X seems to have given her his approbation, when, having read the biography of Mélanie, he exclaimed to the bishop of Altamura, "*La nostra Santa!*" and proposed to open the cause for her beatification. Despite the controversy surrounding her 1879 publication, Mélanie Calvat confirmed the claim of Cardinal Manning, who stated:

> The apostasy of the city of Rome . . . and its destruction by the Antichrist may be thought so new to many Catholics, that I think it well to recite the text of theologians of greatest repute. First, Malvenda, who writes expressly on the subject, states as the opinion of Ribera, Gaspar Melus, Viegas, Suarez, Bellarmine, and Bosius, that Rome shall apostatize from the faith, drive away the Vicar of Christ, and return to its ancient paganism.[14]

The war against the Vicar of Christ and the apostasy of Rome had just begun. And according to Mélanie, it began with satanic rage in 1864.

[14] Henry Edward Cardinal Manning, "The Present Crises of the Holy See Tested by Prophecy," reprinted in *The Pope and the Antichrist* (Sainte-Croix du Mont, France: Tradibooks, 2007), 75.

4

Attack on the Papal States in 1870

When this corruption has been abolished, then eradicate those secret societies of factious men who, completely opposed to God and to princes, are wholly dedicated to bringing about the fall of the Church, the destruction of kingdoms, and disorder in the whole world. Having cast off the restraints of true religion, they prepare the way for shameful crimes.

—Pope Pius VIII, *Traditi humilitati*

Napoleon Bonaparte once taunted a Catholic cardinal by threatening: "Your Eminence, are you not aware that I have the power to destroy the Catholic Church?" To which the cardinal quipped: "Your Majesty, we Catholic clergy have done our best to destroy the Church for the last eighteen hundred years. We have not succeeded, and neither will you."

From the time of Nero Caesar to the time of Napoleon Bonaparte, the enemies of Christ sought to destroy His Catholic Church by an outward attack of persecution. In every century, these attacks yielded a stronger Church, which confirmed the testimony of Tertullian: "The blood of the martyrs is the seed of the Church."[15]

Nero killed Peter and Paul, and the Church in Rome grew. Diocletian implemented the grandest persecution of Christians,

[15] Tertullian, *Apologeticus*, 50.

and within decades the Roman Empire became majority Christian, even producing the first baptized emperor. It seems to have taken eighteen hundred years for the enemies of the Church to realize that the Catholic Church cannot be destroyed by outward attacks. She must be infiltrated and compromised from within. Persecution by the sword only filled the world with cathedrals and basilicas erected to the honor of the martyrs.

Then, as Judas had betrayed Christ, so the Catholic Church would soon be betrayed by a kiss. The 1800s and 1900s would see the Church attacked by Judas priests from within her own ranks.

The moral and financial corruption of contemporary Catholicism begins not with the Second Vatican Council, as some Catholics naively insist, but rather with the fall of the Papal States under Pope Pius IX in 1870.

Before we can appreciate the way in which the internal attacks on the Church were launched, we must appreciate the origin and role of the Papal States in protecting the papal office. From the time Constantine moved his capital to Constantinople in A.D. 330, the pope in Rome maintained de facto political autonomy in Rome. The kings of the Franks formally ratified the pope's political autonomy five hundred years later.

In 751, Pope Zachary crowned Pepin the Short as "King of the Franks" in order to replace the Merovingian king Childeric III. Pope Zachary's successor, Pope Stephen II, extended the privileges by also granting King Pepin the title "Patrician of the Romans." King Pepin expressed his gratitude by defeating the Lombards in 754 and transferring their geographical properties to Pope Stephen II and his successors. These new "Papal States" were denoted in Latin as *Status Ecclesiasticus*, or the "the Church

Pope Pius IX, 1877

State," wherein the pope was both spiritual pastor and temporal governor.

In 781, King Pepin's son Charlemagne confirmed the Papal States as the Duchies of Rome, Ravenna, the Pentapolis, parts of the Duchy of Benevento, Tuscany, Corsica, Lombardy, and a number of Italian cities. The favors and gratitude were mutual when Pope Leo III crowned Charles Magnus, or Charlemagne, as he is commonly known, as Holy Roman Emperor on Christmas in 800. This Frankish-Roman arrangement yielded two important kingdoms. There would be an official Papal State that would protect the popes from political invasion by means of geographic insulation around Rome; and there would be a "Holy Roman Empire" that would serve as an allied security guard to protect the Papal State.

From 754 until 1870, the pope of Rome was both the spiritual pontiff and the temporal ruler of the Papal States. Famously, Pope Boniface VIII carried two swords in procession to signify his authority over both the spiritual realm of the Church and the temporal realm of the Papal States. On 18 November 1302, Pope Boniface VIII issued the papal bull *Unam sanctam*, in which he claimed that the pope's twofold authority derives from the "two swords" kept by Saint Peter at the Last Supper:

> "I tell you, Peter, the cock will not crow this day, until you three times deny that you know me." He said to them, "But now, let him who has a purse take it, and likewise a bag. And let him who has no sword sell his mantle and buy one. For I tell you that this scripture must be fulfilled in me, 'And he was reckoned with transgressors'; for what is written about me has its fulfilment." And they said, "Look, Lord, here are two swords." And he said to them, "It is enough." (Luke 22:34, 36–38).

This became known as the "two swords" theory, and it remained in place until 1798, when troops commanded by Napoleon dissolved the Papal States. The next year, Pope Pius VI died in exile. His successor, Pius VII, was elected in Venice and crowned in a rush with a famous papier-mâché papal tiara. Napoleon allowed Pius VII to return to Rome and restored the Papal States to the pope in 1800—a fitting millennial anniversary of the pope's crowning Charlemagne. Napoleon seized the Papal States in 1809, however, and the Congress of Vienna did not return them to the pope until 1814.

From 1814 until 1870, the Papal States were in danger. In 1859, Pope Pius IX ordered that every Low Mass of the Catholic Church within the Papal States end with three Hail Marys, the Salve Regina, a versicle and response, and a collect for the protection of the Church. In February 1849, a Roman Republic was declared, and Pope Pius IX fled Rome. In 1860, Emperor Napoleon III seized much of the Papal States but protected Rome. But with the outbreak of the Franco-Prussian War, Napoleon III withdrew and left Rome vulnerable. King Victor Emmanuel II offered the pope protection. Pope Pius IX refused. Italy declared war against the pope on 10 September 1870. Papal Rome fell on 20 September 1870 after a few hours' siege. The Kingdom of Italy offered the pope the use of the Vatican and an annual budget of 3.25 million liras. Italy denied the pope's sovereignty but granted him the right to send and receive ambassadors. Pope Pius IX resolutely rejected this offer. He refused to recognize the new kingdom and excommunicated King Victor Emmanuel II and the Italian parliament for their sacrilegious usurpation.

This was the definitive terminus of the Papal States—the end of a 1,116-year temporal rule of the pope (754 to 1870). Pope Pius IX declared himself a prisoner in the Vatican. He saw the attack not merely as political but as demonic.

5

Pope Leo XIII Sees Demons Gather on Rome

As early as 1859, Pope Pius IX decreed that a series of prayers be recited after all Low Masses within the Papal States. Priests and laity were to kneel and pray the Hail Mary three times, followed by the Salve Regina, and then a prayer for the Church.[16] The reason for the additions to the Holy Mass is the topic of a conspiracy theory, but in this case, it is a papally acknowledged "conspiracy" of "Socialism and Communism" addressed directly by Pope Pius IX in his encyclical *Nostis et nobiscum*:

> But if the faithful scorn both the fatherly warnings of their pastors and the commandments of the Christian Law recalled here, and if they let themselves be deceived by the present-day promoters of plots, deciding to work with them in their *perverted theories of Socialism and Communism*, let them know and earnestly consider what they are laying up for themselves. The Divine Judge will seek vengeance on the day of wrath. Until then, no temporal

[16] This 1859 prayer for the Church was composed of four orations taken from the *Missa B. Mariae Virginis*, the *Missa pro remission peccatorum*, the *Missa pro pace*, and the *Missa pro inimicis*.

> benefit for the people will result from their *conspiracy*, but rather new increases of misery and disaster. For man is not empowered to establish new societies and unions which are opposed to the nature of mankind. If these *conspiracies* spread throughout Italy there can only be one result: if the present political arrangement is shaken violently and totally ruined by reciprocal attacks of citizens against citizens by their wrongful appropriations and slaughter, in the end some few, enriched by the plunder of many, will seize supreme control to the ruin of all."[17]

Those conspiracies of which Pius IX spoke came to pass, as we have seen, in 1870, but his direct successor, Pope Leo XIII mystically observed an apparition revealing an infiltration deeply demonic and now settling upon Rome itself. Leo XIII identified this satanic infiltration as being accomplished by "secret societies" that foster demonic worship and rebellion. In his 1886 encyclical *Quod multum*, he refers to this infiltrating work:

> It is enough to recall rationalism and naturalism, those deadly sources of evil whose teachings are everywhere freely distributed. We must then add the many allurements to corruption: the opposition to or open defection from the Church by public officials, *the bold obstinacy of secret societies*, here and there a curriculum for the education of youth without regard for God.[18]

[17] Pope Pius IX, Encylical on the Church in the Papal States *Nostis et nobiscum* (8 December 1849), no. 25, emphasis added.

[18] Pope Leo XIII, Encyclical on the Liberty of the Church *Quod multum* (22 August 1886), no. 3.

Pope Leo XIII, ca. 1898

Pope Leo XIII would also lament that this "conspiracy" has not remained distant: "By way of conspiracies, corruptions, and violence, it has finally come to dominate Italy and even Rome."[19] In view of this new demonic infestation, Leo XIII in 1886 added to the Low Mass a newly composed prayer to Saint Michael, imploring the archangel to help in battle against the devil. It is the same prayer to Saint Michael that we are familiar with today:

> Saint Michael the Archangel, defend us in battle. Be our protection against the wickedness and snares of the Devil. May God rebuke him, we humbly pray, and do thou, O

[19] Pope Leo XIII, Encyclical on Freemasonry *Custodi di quella fede* (8 December 1892), no. 3.

> Prince of the heavenly hosts, by the power of God, cast into hell Satan and all the evil spirits, who prowl about the world seeking the ruin of souls. Amen.[20]

The prayers after Low Mass arranged by his predecessor Pope Pius IX were essentially Marian in scope. Why, then, did Pope Leo XIII feel compelled to add this apocalyptic prayer to Saint Michael against "Satan and all the evil spirits, who prowl about the world seeking the ruin of souls"? In 1931, Monsignor Carl Vogl (1874–1941) related the following legend about the origin of this prayer:

> A rather peculiar circumstance induced Pope Leo XIII to compose this powerful prayer. After celebrating Mass one day he was in conference with the Cardinals. Suddenly he sank to the floor. Several doctors were summoned, and one found no sign of a pulse—the very life seemed to have ebbed away from the fragile and aging body. Suddenly he recovered and said, "What a horrible vision I have been shown!" He saw the ages to come, the seductive powers and ravings of the devils against the Church in every land. But Saint Michael appeared in the moment of greatest distress and cast Satan and his cohorts back into the abyss of hell. Such was the occasion that caused Pope Leo XIII to prescribe this prayer for the universal Church.[21]

[20] *Sáncte Míchael Archángele, defénde nos in proélio, cóntra nequítiam et insídias diáboli ésto præsídium. Ímperet ílli Déus, súpplices deprecámur: tuque, prínceps milítiæ cæléstis, Sátanam aliósque spíritus malígnos, qui ad perditiónem animárum pervagántur in múndo, divína virtúte, in inférnum detrúde. Ámen.*

[21] Carl Vogl, *Weiche Satan!* (Altötting: Geiselberger, 1931), 31–32. This translation of the German quote derives from Kevin

Critics point out that Monsignor Vogl's account in 1931 is forty-five years removed from Leo's composition of the prayer to Saint Michael and his inclusion of it in Low Masses in 1886. The fact that Pope Leo XIII added a specific prayer to Saint Michael for "our protection against the wickedness and snares of the devil" need not require a mystical apparition to the Holy Father.

Nevertheless, a certain Cardinal Giovanni Battista Nasalli Rocca di Corneliano (1872–1952) testified that he had repeatedly received precisely the same story from Pope Leo XIII's personal secretary Monsignor Rinaldo Angeli (1851–1914):

> "Who prowl about the world" has a historical explanation, which has been shared numerous times by the Holy Father's most faithful secretary, who was very close to him through most of his pontificate, Monsignor Rinaldo Angeli.
>
> Pope Leo XIII truly had a vision of demonic spirits, who were gathering on the Eternal City [Rome]. From that experience—which he shared with the Prelate and certainly with others in confidentiality—comes the prayer which he wanted the whole Church to recite. This was the prayer which he recited (we heard this many times in the Vatican Basilica) with a strong powerful voice, which resonated in an unforgettable way in the universal silence beneath the vaults of the most important temple of Christianity.
>
> Not only that, but he wrote a special exorcism, which is found in the *Rituale Romanum* with the title *Exorcismus in Satanam et angelos apostaticos*. The Pontiff recommended to the bishops and priests that these exorcisms be recited often

---

Symonds, *Pope Leo XIII and the Prayer to St. Michael* (Boonville, NY: Preserving Christian Publications, 2018), 8.

> in their dioceses and in their parishes by priests who had received the proper faculties from their ordinaries. However, to set a good example, he recited it himself frequently throughout the day. In fact, another prelate familiar with the Pontiff used to tell us that even on his walks through the Vatican Gardens, he would take a small book—worn from much use—from his pocket and recite his exorcism with fervent piety and deep devotion. The small book is still preserved by a noble family in Rome, whom we know well.[22]

The account given by the personal secretary of Pope Leo XIII adds the "historical explanation" that the pope saw "a vision of demonic spirits, who were gathering on the Eternal City." The pope's secretary notes that Leo XIII not only added the prayer to Saint Michael at the end of Low Mass, but also that he composed a more lengthy exorcism prayer in 1890 to be used by bishops and priests throughout the world. This is the testimony of the pope's secretary—the man closest to the heart, thoughts, and words of Pope Leo XIII on these matters.

The Alleged Conversation between God and Satan

The demonic apparition to Pope Leo XIII was embellished with apocryphal details shortly after this time. In 1947, Father Domenico Pechenino recounted that Pope Leo XIII was assisting at a second Mass after having celebrated Holy Mass himself. This version claims that the pope gazed at something above the head of the priest celebrant and then rushed away from the chapel to

[22] Translated by Bryan Gonzalez and found in *Pope Leo XIII and the Prayer to St. Michael* by Kevin Symonds (Boonville, NY: Preserving Christian Publications, 2018), 27–28.

his private study, where he immediately composed the prayer to Saint Michael. Father Pechenino then adds a provocative detail to the story, reporting that Pope Leo XIII saw Satan himself during the Mass:

> This is what happened. God had shown Satan to the Vicar of His Divine Son on earth, just like he did with Job. Satan was bragging that he had already devastated the Church on a large scale. In fact, these were tumultuous times for Italy, for many nations in Europe, and a bit around the world. The Freemasons ruled, and government hadn't become docile instruments. With the audacity of a boaster, Satan put a challenge to God:
>
> "And if you gave me a little more freedom, you could see what I would do for your Church!"
>
> "What would you do?"
>
> "I would destroy it."
>
> "Oh, that would be something to see. How long would it take?"
>
> "Fifty or sixty years."
>
> "Have more freedom, and the time you need. Then we'll see what happens."[23]

This account in 1947 is the first known report that Satan and God conversed about the timing of the destruction of the Church, and that God assigned a time period for Satan to attempt his coup. Should we trust this story?

Father Pechenino's version relates that this Leonine vision happened "a little time after 1890." This is not altogether accurate, since the prayer to Saint Michael for Low Mass was assigned

[23] Symonds, *Pope Leo XIII*, 46.

in 1886 and the longer Saint Michael exorcism was published in 1890. So we know right away that the details by Pechenino are not entirely trustworthy.

Another issue with his "Dialogue with Satan" account is that it seems to be derived from the visions of Blessed Anne Catherine Emmerich (1774–1824), who, in her *Detached Account of the Descent into Hell*, states the following:

> God Himself had decreed this, and I was likewise told, if I remember correctly, that he will be unchained (*freigelassen*) for a time fifty or sixty years before the year of Christ 2000. The dates of many other events were pointed out to me which I do not now remember; but a certain number of demons are to be let loose much earlier than Lucifer, in order to tempt men, and to serve as instruments of the divine vengeance.

Emmerich (who predates Pechenino by a century) refers specifically to the unchaining of Satan for "fifty or sixty years." If, however, Pechenino was ignorant of Emmerich, we have a providential agreement of two separate sources—namely, that Satan will be loosed for the last "fifty or sixty years" of the twentieth century. There are historical and theological problems with the dialogue account of Pechenino. Nevertheless, we shall discover substantiated examples of infiltration within the Catholic Church beginning in the 1940s and 1950s—conforming to Emmerich's vision of Satan being "unchained" in the final "fifty or sixty years" of the twentieth century. Before we observe the weeds crowding Our Lord's field, we must first understand how the heretical seeds of Modernism were planted in the Church at the turn of the century.

6

Infiltration of the Church by Secret Societies and Modernism

Everyone should avoid familiarity or friendship with anyone suspected of belonging to Masonry or to affiliated groups. Know them by their fruits and avoid them. Every familiarity should be avoided, not only with those impious libertines who openly promote the character of the sect, but also with those who hide under the mask of universal tolerance, respect for all religions, and the craving to reconcile the maxims of the Gospel with those of the revolution. These men seek to reconcile Christ and Belial, the Church of God and the state without God.

—Pope Leo XIII, *Custodi di quella fede*

Three years after Pope Leo XIII's vision of the demons gathering on Rome, a statue of Giordano Bruno of Nola was erected in Rome at the Campo de' Fiori. Giordano Bruno was a Dominican friar who publicly preached and denied the Catholic doctrines on the Blessed Trinity, the divinity of Christ, the virginity of Mary, Eucharistic transubstantiation, and the eternity of hell. He also seemed to teach pantheism, reincarnation, and that *all* religions lead to the divine. Bruno was condemned by the Holy Office and executed in 1600. It was the Freemasons who erected this statue of Bruno in Rome as a sign of their false philosophy and their ambition to gain influence over papal Rome.

Pope Leo XIII spoke against the "erection of the statue to the renowned apostate of Nola" in his 1890 encyclical *Dall'alto dell'Apostolico*. The pope recognized the erection of the memorial as "carried out by the Freemasons" and as "an insult to the Papacy." It was a theological symbol of the Freemasonic *Alta Vendita*: let the Catholic priest be the one who sows the seed of Freemasonic ideals. Bruno was the mascot for their infiltration. The writers of the *Alta Vendita* wanted eventually to elect a pope in the mold of Giordano Bruno of Nola: pantheistic, naturalistic, relativistic, and universalistic. The *Alta Vendita* hoped for a pope who would unflinchingly teach that the plurality and diversity of religions are expressions of the wise and divine will of God, who created all human beings. But that would take more than a century to achieve.

Pope Leo XIII died in 1903 after having published eighty-eight encyclicals, including twelve on the Rosary and four against Freemasonry.[24] After his Requiem Mass, sixty-two of the sixty-four living cardinals met in Rome to elect the next Successor of Saint Peter. Of the two missing, one was ill and the other was still traveling by ship from Australia. Pope Leo XIII had lived so long that only one of those living cardinals had voted in the previous papal election.

The favored candidate for pope was the Sicilian cardinal Mariano Rampolla. Cardinal Rampolla, like Leo XIII, approved the Third Republic of France and tolerated republicanism. For this reason, Cardinal Rampolla had been a favorite of Leo XIII

[24] *Humanum genus* (1884), *Dall'alto dell'Apostolico Seggio* (1890), *Custodi di quella fede* (1892), and *Inimica vis* (1892).

and his heir apparent. Reports on the first ballots yielded twenty-nine votes for Rampolla, sixteen votes for Girolamo Maria Gotti, and ten votes for Giuseppe Sarto.[25] The number of cardinal votes needed for the election of a pope at that time was forty-two. The gridlock between these three candidates would require a compromise.

After three ballots, the Polish Cardinal Jan Puzyna de Kosielsko of Kraków delivered the imperial veto of Emperor Franz Joseph against the election of Cardinal Rampolla. This move officially obstructed Rampolla's election to the papacy. The imperial veto, or *ius exclusivae* (right of exclusion), is a privilege afforded the recognized Christian emperor to exclude a cardinal from being elected as pope. This imperial right of exclusion had been used no fewer than ten times since 1644. The privilege extends back to the Eastern Roman emperors. For example, when Pope Pelagius II died of the plague on 7 February 590, the clergy of Rome elected Pope Gregory the Great shortly thereafter. After this papal election, however, there was a delay in his installation in Rome while they waited for the *iussio* from the emperor in Constantinople. Once the imperial approbation was received, Pope Gregory was installed as bishop of Rome on 3 September 590—after a papal interregnum of some seven months.

This balance between emperor and pope existed with the Byzantine Christian emperors of the 600s and continued with the Holy Roman emperors in the West. By 1903, the right of papal veto belonged to Emperor Franz Joseph of Austria, who exercised it accordingly against Cardinal Rampolla. Outraged by this act of imperial intervention, Cardinal Rampolla denounced

[25] David V. Barret, "Ballot Sheets from 1903 Conclave to Be Sold at Auction," *Catholic Herald*, 2 June 2014.

it as "an affront to the dignity of the Sacred College." The cardinals in support of Rampolla flaunted the imperial veto and again gathered twenty-nine votes for Rampolla on the next ballot, but runners-up flipped positions with twenty-one for Sarto and nine for Gotti. The cardinals began to recognize that the fragile papacy, without the Papal States and entering a more secularized century, would require the allegiance of Emperor Franz Joseph. Their votes turned more and more to Cardinal Sarto, who took the lead on the fifth ballot and won the papal election on the seventh ballot with fifty votes, which gained him more than the forty-two votes required. Initially, Sarto declined, but after being pressed by the cardinals, he accepted the election.

Giuseppe Melchiorre Cardinal Sarto (1835–1914) took the papal name Pius X, signaling that his papacy would continue the rigid policies of Pope Pius IX before him. Pope Pius X gave his first Urbi et Orbi papal blessing facing into the interior of Saint Peter's, *with his back to the secularized city of Rome*. This act symbolized his opposition to secular Italian rule over Rome and his demand for the return of the Papal States. Six months later, he issued an apostolic constitution forever banning the imperial veto in papal election and placed an automatic excommunication on any monarch seeking to impose a veto on a papal conclave.

A lesser known fact is that Pope Pius X, not Pope John Paul II, is the first ethnically Polish pope—both his parents were Polish immigrants to Italy. He was the second of ten children and grew up very poor. He studied Latin with the parish priest and received clerical tonsure at age fifteen so that he could pursue seminary formation and ordination to the priesthood.

When he was twenty-three years old, Sarto was ordained a priest. At the age of forty-nine he was appointed bishop of Mantua by Pope Leo XIII and consecrated by Cardinal Lucido Parocchi, Bishop Pietro Rota, and Bishop Giovanni Maria Berengo. Sarto received a papal dispensation because he lacked a doctorate. Pope Leo XIII appointed him both cardinal and patriarch of Venice at age fifty-eight in 1893. Ten years later, he would be pope.

Pope Pius X was a man of impeccable doctrine and personal sanctity. After his death and during the process of his canonization, the appointed "devil's advocate," who was charged with discovering anything disordered in his life, could present only two known "faults" of Pius X: he smoked one cigarette daily, and his daily Low Mass was sometimes shorter than twenty-five minutes. These were the only arguments against his canonization as a saint.

Pope Pius X is celebrated for promoting frequent Communion among the laity, and for lowering the canonical age of First Communion from age twelve to age seven.[26] He loved the sacred liturgy as "participation in the most holy mysteries and in the public, official prayer of the church."[27] The pope favored traditional Gregorian chant and warned that "the employment of the piano is forbidden in church, as is also that of noisy or frivolous instruments such as drums, cymbals, bells and the like."[28]

His greatest contribution to the Catholic Church was his adamantine resolve against the heresy of Modernism. Catholic theologians of the 1800s had pressed the limits of Catholic orthodoxy by following rationalism and the Protestant critical approach to Sacred Scripture. Pope Leo XIII had written against

[26] Pius X lowered the age to the age of reason in his decree *Quam singulari* (1910).

[27] Saint Pius X, *Tra le sollecitudini*.

[28] Ibid., 19.

Pope Pius X

this as Liberalism, but Pope Pius X identified the movement as "Modernism."

Pius X recognized that Freemasonry would not square off openly against Catholicism but would undermine her from within *with ideas*. He at once identified this internal Freemasonic attack as "Modernism," the naturalism of Freemasonry with a Catholic veneer that justifies itself by appealing to the "evolution of dogma."

The Modernist heresy seeks to *reinterpret* biblical history, as well as Catholic philosophy, theology, and liturgy, through the modern prism of rational science and post-Enlightenment philosophy. At first, this might sound admirable. One might ask, "Should not the Catholic Faith acculturate herself to the modern world in order to make the Faith more compelling? Didn't Paul quote non-Christian philosophers? Didn't Augustine employ Platonism? Didn't Thomas Aquinas reconcile Aristotle? Why not try to reconcile Kant, Hegel, or even Nietzsche with Catholicism?" The Apostles, Church Fathers, and Scholastics "plundered the Egyptians" and often employed the writings, thoughts, and analogies of the pagans before them.

Modernism, however, came into existence *after* the rejection of the Catholic intellectual tradition. Socrates lived before Christ. His philosophical system was not against Christianity *per se*. It was pre-Christian. The same is true for Platonists, Aristotelians, and most Stoic thinkers.

But the philosophy of Kant or Hegel is purposefully post-Christian and seeks to replace the Catholic Faith with something better and new. Hence, Modernism tries to do the impossible: it seeks to reinterpret Catholicism within a modern system that already rejects Christianity.

The features of Modernism, according to Pius X, are threefold. The first feature is the critical analysis and rational "demythologizing" of Sacred Scripture. For Modernists, the Bible is an important collection of legends redacted by powerful people to communicate a message. The existence of Noah, Abraham, Moses, and David is brought under suspicion. Even the four Gospels are questioned for their accounts of miracles. Following the presumed naturalism of Freemasonry, Modernism rejects anything truly supernatural. For example, when Our Lord Jesus Christ multiplies the loaves and fishes, it is really the "miracle of sharing." Nothing supernatural happens to increase the amount of consumable food. Christ's driving out demons, the Modernist explains, is a symbolic story of bringing psychological peace to troubled people. Jesus' walking on water is just a literary way to depict Him overcoming worldly troubles. When Christ tells

His Apostles, "This is my body," He is asking them to remember Him. Bread doesn't become anything supernatural. Everything has a natural explanation.

The second feature of Modernism is secularism and universal fraternity. Saint Thomas Aquinas rightly taught that grace heals and elevates nature. The order of reality is that the supernatural reigns over the natural. With the Modernist denial of the supernatural, the secular and the political become primary. The concepts of beatitude and salvation are reinterpreted as secular or political goals. This reduces the clergy to political activists and demotes the pope to merely an inspiring "coach" to the secular nations. It is such a separation of Church and state that the Church no longer even has relevance in the public sphere. Religion is private.

The third plank of Modernism is the rejection of what Catholics had known as the good (morals), the true (doctrine), and the beautiful (aesthetics). The tight system of original sin, venial sin, mortal sin, and being forgiven and healed through redemption in Christ is abandoned. Moral relativism is promoted. Modernists say that doctrine must always be "pastoral," not "true." And the gorgeous art, statuary, architecture, and music of the Catholic Church is cast aside for the pedestrian, modern, and useful.

Any Catholic living in the third millennium will immediately identify the remains of Modernism still rotting the Catholic Church. Scripture is not read at all or is explained away in homilies. How many times have you heard, "Matthew didn't really write this" or "Paul didn't actually write this"? The pope and the cardinals are generally reduced to cheerleaders for globalism, migration, and the redistribution of goods. Catholic morality has declined. Heresy is preached from the pulpit. And once-glorious churches have been renovated to remove statuary from the sanctuary in favor of their bare utility as "worship spaces."

In July 1907, the Holy Office published *Lamentabili sane exitu*, which condemned sixty-five Modernist propositions. Most of those propositions were taken from the writings of the suspect priests Father George Tyrrell, S.J., and Father Alfred Loisy.

When people ask, "What happened to the Jesuits?" one might aptly reply "Father Tyrrell." George Tyrrell was an Irish Anglican convert to Catholicism who joined the Jesuits. He made a reputation for himself by rejecting the Scholastic tradition of Saint Thomas Aquinas. Tyrrell openly taught that reason did not apply to the dogmas of the Catholic Faith. This assertion condemns not only Thomas Aquinas, but the entire medieval consensus of faith and reason. Instead, he defended "the right of each age to adjust the historico-philosophical expression of Christianity to contemporary certainties, and thus to put an end to this utterly needless conflict between faith and science which is a mere theological bogey."[29]

This claim of Tyrrell captures the Modernist prejudice that Christianity needs to be reconformed to each and every age, and especially to our modern time. Tyrrell's theology was seen as outrageous, even for the Jesuits, and he was dismissed from the Society of Jesus for his heretical beliefs in 1906—one year before *Lamentabili sane exitu* was issued.

Pope Pius X followed up in September 1907 with his anti-Modernist encyclical *Pascendi dominici gregis*, in which he described Modernism as the "synthesis of all heresies." Father Tyrrell published two critical letters against *Pascendi* in the *Times* and

[29] *Autobiography and Life of George Tyrell: Life of George Tyrell from 1884 to 1909* (New York: Longman, Green, 1912), 185.

was subsequently suspended and excommunicated. He was later denied Catholic burial because he refused to abjure his Modernist beliefs.

In 1908, Father Alfred Loisy was also excommunicated for Modernism. Loisy substantially agreed with Tyrrell. The boldness of Loisy's Modernism is manifest by his own admission: "Christ has even less importance in my religion than he does in that of the liberal Protestants: for I attach little importance to the revelation of God the Father for which they honor Jesus. If I am anything in religion, it is more pantheist-positivist-humanitarian than Christian."[30]

Pope Pius X's motu proprio *Sacrorum antistitum* required all Catholic bishops, priests, and teachers to take an anti-Modernist oath. This was the formal and public means by which Pius X would expose Modernists among the clergy and in seminaries and universities.[31] An unofficial group of monitoring theologians called the *Sodalitium Pianum*, or "Fellowship of Pius," was tasked with reporting anyone who taught Modernist doctrines. Regarding the covert Modernist clergy, Pius X said, "For they should be beaten with fists. In a duel, you don't count or measure the blows, you strike as you can."[32]

To correct doctrine and establish the Catholic Church in orthodoxy further, Pius X decreed a catechism class in every parish on earth. In 1908, he issued the 115-page *Catechism of Pius X* for doctrinal instruction in parishes. He required that in marriages

[30] Alfred Loisy, *Mémoires pour servir à l'histoire religieuse de notre temps* (Paris: E. Nourry, 1930–1931), II, 397.

[31] This oath remained in force until 1967, when Pope Paul VI abolished it.

[32] John Cornwell, *Hitler's Pope: The Secret History of Pius XII* (New York: Penguin, 2008), 37.

between Catholics and non-Catholics, the non-Catholic spouses must promise to allow the children to be raised Catholic. He gave bishops greater oversight over seminaries and called for regional seminaries. He also called for the first universal codified Code of Canon Law, which would not be completed until after his death and then promulgated by his successor Pope Benedict XV in 1917 as the Pio-Benedictine Code of Canon Law.

Theologically, Pius X followed Pope Leo XIII's ardent enthusiasm for Thomism, but politically he was much more conservative. Pius X was a hardliner against the secular state of Italy and broke off diplomatic relations with France over it. He opposed trade unions that were not Catholic, and he told Italian Catholics that they could never vote for Socialists. One month before he died, Pope Pius X approved the request of Cardinal James Gibbons for the construction site of the National Shrine of the Immaculate Conception in Washington, D.C. He suffered heart trouble after the outbreak of World War I and died on 20 August 1914.

The World War I Conclave

The Papal Conclave of 1914 met eleven days after the death Pope Pius X. Prior to that, a Bosnian Serb Yugoslav nationalist named Gavrilo Princip assassinated the Austro-Hungarian heir Archduke Franz Ferdinand in Sarajevo on 28 June 1914. That July crisis divided Europe into two coalitions consisting of Britain, France, and Russia allied in opposition against Germany, Austria-Hungary, and Italy. The conclave of 1914 brought together cardinals from all the opposing alliances and nations.

Fifty-seven cardinals participated and voted. Eight cardinals were not able to attend due to illness or distance—such as the two American cardinals and the Canadian cardinal who arrived too late to vote. The papal conclave lasted four days and consisted of ten ballots. Three cardinals were initially favored. Domenico Cardinal Serafini was the moral successor to Pius X. He was an archconservative and desired to pursue the anti-Modernist protocols of Pius X. Opposite him was the liberal Pietro Cardinal Maffi of Pisa. Standing between Serafini on the right and Maffi on the left was the compromise candidate: Giacomo Cardinal della Chiesa of Bologna.

The three cardinals were equally supported. By the fifth ballot, the liberal Maffi lost support and left the election to Serafini and della Chiesa. Maffi's supporters switched to della Chiesa, and on the tenth ballot della Chiesa gained the two-thirds majority. There was a further compilation because della Chiesa had won the two-thirds majority by only one vote, and the pious cardinal Rafael Merry del Val noted that if della Chiesa had voted for himself, the election was invalid. When they checked the ballots, it was shown that della Chiesa had not voted for himself. The election stood.

Cardinal della Chiesa, elected at the young age of fifty-nine, took the name Benedict XV. He was known as *Il Piccoletto*, or "the little man," and the white papal cassock had to be quickly hemmed to fit him. He immediately declared that the Holy See remained neutral in World War I, which he called "the suicide of Europe."

The war had disrupted Catholic missionary work throughout the world. Pope Benedict XV sought to revitalize the missions. In 1917, he promulgated the Code of Canon Law initiated by his predecessor, Pius X. He canonized Saint Joan of Arc and Saint Margaret Mary Alacoque. He approved the feast of Mary, Mediatrix of All Graces by authorizing a Mass and office under this title for the dioceses of Belgium. Most importantly, Pope Benedict continued the fight against Modernism in his *Ad beatissimi*

Pope Benedict XV, ca. 1915

Apostolorum. He also upheld the excommunications of Modernists by Pius X, despite the initial allegations that he was a theological moderate. Pope Benedict XV died of pneumonia on 22 January 1922.

His pontificate is known not so much for his leadership as for what happened during his reign. Toward the end of the war, from 13 May to 13 October 1917, apparitions of Our Lady occurred in Fatima, Portugal. Theologians and historians have connected the pastoral letter of Pope Benedict XV on 5 May 1917 to the beginning of the Fatima apparitions eight days later. In this letter, the pope formally added the title "Our Lady of Peace" to the Litany of Loreto and asked for an end to World War I through the intercession of the Blessed Virgin Mary:

> Our earnestly pleading voice, invoking the end of the vast conflict, the suicide of civilized Europe, was then and has remained ever since unheard. Indeed, it seemed that the dark tide of hatred grew higher and wider among the belligerent nations, and drew other countries into its frightful sweep, multiplying ruin and massacre. Nevertheless our confidence was not lessened.... To Mary, then, who is the Mother of Mercy and omnipotent by grace, let loving and devout appeals go up from every corner of the earth–from noble temples and tiniest chapels, from royal palaces and mansions of the rich as from the poorest hut–from blood-drenched plains and seas. Let it bear to Her the anguished cry of mothers and wives, the wailing of innocent little ones, the sighs of every generous heart: that Her most tender and benign solicitude may be moved and the peace we ask for be obtained for our agitated world.[33]

It is providential and miraculous that eight days later, the visions of Fatima began, *and* on that same day Pope Benedict XV consecrated Eugenio Pacelli as a bishop. Pacelli would go on to become Pope Pius XII and, as such, would serve as *the* pope of Fatima.

[33] Pope Benedict XV, Letter of 27 April 1915.

7

Our Lady of Fatima

The events at Fatima mark the most important Marian apparition in the history of the Catholic Church and lead up to the largest witnessed miracle in the history of humanity, second only to the parting of the Red Sea under Moses. The story began in 1916, when nine-year-old Lúcia dos Santos and her cousins Francisco and Jacinta Marto were herding sheep at the Cova da Iria near the parish of Fatima, Portugal. They were visited three times by an angel who introduced himself in this way:

> Do not be afraid. I am the Angel of Peace. Pray with me." He knelt, bending his forehead to the ground. With a supernatural impulse we did the same, repeating the words we heard him say: "My God, I believe, I adore, I hope, and I love Thee. I ask pardon for those who do not believe, do not adore, do not hope, and do not love Thee." After repeating this prayer three times the angel rose and said to us: "Pray in this way. The Hearts of Jesus and Mary are ready to listen to you."[34]

[34] Except where otherwise noted, the narrative and quotations are derived from the memoirs of Sister Lúcia de Jesus Rosa dos Santos, which can be found in Louis Kondor, ed., *Fátima in Sister Lúcia's Own Words* (Fatima: Secretariado dos Pastorinhos, 1976).

It is notable that during World War I, Pope Benedict XV added "Our Lady of Peace" to the Litany of Loreto, and this angel calls himself the "Angel of Peace." A second time, the angel appeared and exhorted them to pray: "What are you doing? You must pray! Pray! The hearts of Jesus and Mary have merciful designs for you. You must offer your prayers and sacrifices to God, the Most High."

When the children asked what sacrifices they should make, the angel explained: "In every way you can offer sacrifice to God in reparation for the sins by which He is offended, and in supplication for sinners. In this way you will bring peace to our country, for I am its guardian angel, the Angel of Portugal. Above all, bear and accept with patience the sufferings God will send you."

During third and final visit, the angel taught the children to pray this prayer:

> Most Holy Trinity, Father, Son and Holy Spirit, I adore Thee profoundly, and I offer Thee the Most Precious Body, Blood, Soul, and Divinity of Jesus Christ, present in all the tabernacles of the world, in reparation for the outrages, sacrileges, and indifferences by which He is offended. And by the infinite merits of His most Sacred Heart and the Immaculate Heart of Mary, I beg the conversion of poor sinners.

Then the angel offered the Eucharistic host and chalice to the children, saying, "Eat and drink the Body and Blood of Jesus Christ, terribly outraged by the ingratitude of men. Offer reparation for their sakes and console God." Then he disappeared, and they never saw him again.

The First Apparition of Fatima

Just as these visions ended with the Blessed Sacrament, so they resumed almost eight months later on the feast of the Blessed

Lúcia Santos, Jacinta and Francisco Marto, 1917

Sacrament: 13 May 1917. On that morning, the three children passed the parish church of Fatima and walked north to the slopes of the Cova to graze their sheep as they played in the field. They ate their packed lunches and decided to pray the Rosary. The three children had adopted a quick version of the Rosary in which they said only the first few words of each prayer. After finishing their abbreviated Rosary, they saw lightning and prepared to return home. As they drove the sheep home, they saw another flash of lightning and then saw on a short holm oak tree a lady dressed in white "shining brighter than the sun, giving out rays of clear and intense light, just like a crystal goblet full of pure water when the fiery sun passes through it. We stopped, astounded by the apparition. We were so near that we were in the light that encircled her, or which she radiated, perhaps a meter and a half away." The Lady wore a pure white mantle down to her feet, trimmed with gold. The rosary beads in her hands shone like stars, with its crucifix the most radiant gem of all.

The Lady tenderly addressed the children: "Please don't be afraid of me; I'm not going to harm you."

Lúcia responded, "Where are you from?"

"I come from heaven."

"And what do you want of me?"

The Lady explained, "I want you to return here on the thirteenth of each month for the next six months, and at the very same hour. Later I shall tell you who I am, and what it is that I most desire. And I shall return here yet a seventh time."

"And shall I go to heaven?"

"Yes, you will," answered the Lady.

"And Jacinta?"

"She will go, too."

"And Francisco?"

"Francisco, too, my dear, but he will first have many Rosaries to say."

For a moment the Lady looked at Francisco with compassion. Lúcia then remembered some friends who had died: "Is Maria Neves in heaven?"

"Yes, she is."

"And Amelia?"

"She is in purgatory."

"Will you offer yourselves to God, and bear all the sufferings He sends you? In atonement for all the sins that offend Him? And for the conversion of sinners?"

"Oh, we will, we will!"

"Then you will have a great deal to suffer, but the grace of God will be with you and will strengthen you."

Lúcia said that "as the Lady pronounced these words, she opened her hands, and we were bathed in a heavenly light that appeared to come directly from her hands. The light's reality cut into our hearts and our souls, and we knew somehow that this light was God, and we could see ourselves embraced in it. By an interior impulse of grace we fell to our knees, repeating in our hearts: 'O Holy Trinity, we adore Thee. My God, my God, I love Thee in the Blessed Sacrament.'"

The children remained kneeling in the flood of this wondrous light, until the Lady spoke again, mentioning the war in Europe, which the pope had prayed about eight days before, but of which they had little knowledge.

"Pray the Rosary every day, to bring peace to the world and an end to the war."

Lúcia recorded later: "After that she began to rise slowly in the direction of the east, until she disappeared in the immense distance. The light that encircled her seemed to make a way amidst the stars, and that is why we sometimes said we had seen the heavens open."

Lúcia instructed the other two children to keep this vision a secret. However, seven-year-old Jacinta later told all to her mother, who patiently listened but gave it little credence. Her brothers and sisters piped in with their questions and jokes. Quite touchingly, only her father accepted the story as true. He is memorialized as the first believer in Fatima.

The mother of Lúcia was not as believing. She worried that her daughter was lying and blaspheming. She demanded that Lúcia recant, and when she would not, she dragged Lúcia before their parish priest, Father Ferreira. Lúcia stood firm in her belief that a heavenly Lady in white had visited her.

Meanwhile the children prepared for their next appointment, on 13 June 1917.

The Second Apparition of Fatima

The Lady had told them to come to the holm oak tree at the same time on the thirteenth day of each month. The thirteenth of June fell on the feast of Portugal's most famous saint, Anthony of Padua (who was born in Lisbon, Portugal, but died in Padua, Italy). Lúcia's mother hoped that the parish festivities would distract the three children from the suspicious apparition scheduled for this day.

At noon, the children walked to the place where the Lady had appeared previously. There they found a small, curious crowd awaiting them. After praying the Rosary with Jacinta and Francisco and the other people who were present, the children saw again the lightning nearing them and then the Lady on the holm oak, exactly as in the previous month.

"Please tell me, Madam, what is it that you want of me?" Lúcia asked.

"I want you to come here on the thirteenth of next month. I want you to continue saying the Rosary every day. And after each one of the mysteries, my children, I want you to pray in this way: 'O my Jesus, forgive us our sins, save us from the fires of hell. Lead all souls to heaven, especially those who are most in need.' I want you to learn to read and write, and later I will tell you what else I want of you."

"Will you take us to heaven?"

"Yes, I shall take Jacinta and Francisco soon, but you will remain a little longer, since Jesus wishes you to make me known and loved on earth. He wishes also for you to establish devotion in the world to my Immaculate Heart."

"Must I remain in the world alone?"

"Not alone, my child, and you must not be sad. I will be with you always, and my Immaculate Heart will be your comfort and the way which will lead you to God."

Lúcia explains what happened next:

> The moment she said the last words, opening her hands, she transmitted to us, for the second time, the reflection of that intense light. In it we felt we were submerged in God. Jacinta and Francisco seemed to be in that part of the light which was rising to Heaven, and I in the part spreading over the earth. In front of the palm of Our Lady's right hand was a heart encircled with thorns, which appeared to pierce it. We understood it was the Immaculate Heart of Mary offended by the sins of mankind, craving reparation. Once again, the Lady departed to the east and disappeared into heaven. The people did not see the Lady, but some said they saw the light or lightning.

The Third Apparition and the Secret of Fatima

Now that the apparitions were being widely discussed, the local pastor of Fatima began to intervene and express his concern that the apparitions might in fact be demonic. Lúcia's pastor's disapproval discouraged her so much that she was reluctant to go for the third appointment on July 13. Nevertheless, she attended with Jacinta and Francisco at noon of that day, where a large crowd had gathered. They saw the flash of light, and the Lady appeared on the holm oak.

"Lúcia, speak," Jacinta instructed. "Our Lady is talking to you."

"Yes?" said Lúcia. She spoke humbly, asking pardon for her doubts with every gesture, and to the Lady: "What do you want of me?"

"I want you to come back here on the thirteenth of next month. Continue to pray the Rosary every day in honor of Our

Lady of the Rosary, to obtain the peace of the world and the end of the war, because only she can obtain it."

"Yes, yes. I would like to ask who you are, and if you will do a miracle so that everyone will know for certain that you have appeared to us."

"You must come here every month, and in October I will tell you who I am and what I want. I will then perform a miracle so that all may believe."

Thus assured, Lúcia began to place before the Lady the petitions for help that so many had entrusted to her. The Lady said gently that she would cure some, but others she would not cure.

"And the crippled son of Maria da Capelinha?"

"No, neither of his infirmity nor of his poverty would he be cured, and he must be certain to say the Rosary with his family every day."

Another case recommended by Lúcia to the Lady's assistance was a sick woman from Atouguia who asked to be taken to heaven.

"Tell her not to be in a hurry. Tell her I know very well when I shall come to fetch her. Make sacrifices for sinners, and say often, especially while making a sacrifice: 'O Jesus, this is for love of Thee, for the conversion of sinners, and in reparation for offenses committed against the Immaculate Heart of Mary.'"

> As Our Lady spoke these words, she opened her hands once more, as she had during the two previous months. The rays of light seemed to penetrate the earth, and we saw as it were a sea of fire. Plunged in this fire were demons and souls in human form, like transparent burning embers, all blackened or burnished bronze, floating about in the conflagration, now raised into the air by the flames that

issued from within themselves together with great clouds of smoke, now falling back on every side like sparks in huge fires, without weight or equilibrium, amid shrieks and groans of pain and despair, which horrified us and made us tremble with fear. (It must have been this sight which caused me to cry out, as people say they heard me do). The demons could be distinguished by their terrifying and repellent likeness to frightful and unknown animals, black and transparent like burning coals. Terrified and as if to plead for succor, we looked up at Our Lady, who said to us, so kindly and so sadly:

> You have seen hell, where the souls of poor sinners go. It is to save them that God wants to establish in the world devotion to my Immaculate Heart. If you do what I tell you, many souls will be saved, and there will be peace.
>
> This war will end, but if men do not refrain from offending God, another and more terrible war will begin during the pontificate of Pius XI. When you see a night that is lit by a strange and unknown light[35] you will know it is the sign God gives you that He is about to punish the world with war and with hunger, and by the persecution of the Church and the Holy Father.
>
> To prevent this, I shall come to the world to ask that Russia be consecrated to my Immaculate Heart, and I shall ask that on the first Saturday of

[35] The historical occurrence of this miraculous light is explained subsequently in the chapter about Pope Pius XII.

> every month Communions of reparation be made in atonement for the sins of the world. If my wishes are fulfilled, Russia will be converted and there will be peace; if not, then Russia will spread her errors throughout the world, bringing new wars and persecution of the Church; the good will be martyred and the Holy Father will have much to suffer; certain nations will be annihilated. But in the end my Immaculate Heart will triumph. The Holy Father will consecrate Russia to me, and she will be converted, and the world will enjoy a period of peace. In Portugal the faith will always be preserved.

The vision of hell and the consecration of Russia are the first and second parts of the secret of Fatima. The controversial third part, which followed, was so horrific and terrible that it could not be revealed until 1960. We shall return to the third part of the secret of Fatima at length, but for now we shall continue the narrative of 13 July as reported by Lúcia.

"Remember, you must not tell this to anyone except Francisco. When you pray the Rosary, say after each mystery: 'O my Jesus, forgive us our sins, save us from the fires of Hell. Lead all souls to heaven, especially those who are most in need.'"

"Is there anything more that you want of me?"

"No, I do not want anything more of you today."

As in previous months, the Lady rose toward the east into the sky.

The family, the neighbors, and the priest tried to get the three children to reveal the threefold secret of the Lady, but the children kept their promise to the Lady. For this reason, the apparition of 13 July 1917 continues to be the most controversial.

Lúcia kept the Threefold Secret until 1941, when she wrote down the first and second parts. It is best to see the Secret of Fatima as one united secret with three interrelated parts, but, for convenience's sake, we will refer to those parts as the First Secret, the Second Secret, and the Third Secret. So in 1941, Lúcia revealed the First Secret about the vision of Hell, and the Second Secret about the consecration and conversion of Russia to the Immaculate Heart.

In October 1943 the Bishop ordered Lúcia under obedience to put the Third Secret into writing, which she hesitated to do because of its shocking contents. On 2 January 1944, Our Lady of Fatima appeared to Lúcia and gave her permission to write down the Third Secret but to have it sealed until 1960, because "it will be clearer then." Lúcia then wrote the secret down and sealed it in an envelope the next day. This sealed envelope would in 1955 be transferred to Rome and wait to be opened by Pope John XXIII in 1959. To this controversy we will return.

The Fourth Apparition of Fatima

By August, the three children were reaching celebrity status and gaining the negative attention of the clergy and politicians. On 11 August 1917, an intervention was staged to force the children to reveal their secret and fess up to lying. The children refused to recant. So the local mayor, Arturo Santos, a Freemason and anti-Catholic, devised a plot to take the children into custody.

Before the three children made their way to the Cova on the thirteenth of August, Santos offered them the prestigious favor of riding in his automobile to the site. The Ford Model T had debuted in America in 1908 with a limited release in Britain and France in 1911. Even by 1917, the sight of an automobile was still rare in rural Portugal. The mayor offered a ride in his automobile to transport the children safely through the crowds. These growing crowds testify to the enthusiastic regional interest in the Fatima visionaries by August 1917.

The three children took the bait and climbed into the Freemason's automobile with their parents. Mayor Santos drove them to the church to visit the parish priest before driving to the Cova. Once at the church, Mayor Santos abandoned the parents and drove the three children to his district headquarters in Vila Nova de Ourém, nine miles away. Here he attempted to bribe the children, and when that didn't succeed, he threatened to lock them away in prison with other criminals. Finally, he threatened them with death. Lúcia was ten years old. Francisco was nine, and Jacinta was seven. Despite their age, they stood firm against the mayor and his threats.

Meanwhile, back at the Cova, the lightning flashed as it had before, but, as before, the crowds did not see the Lady in white on the holm oak. Without the children present, the crowd dispersed in confusion. To the sorrow of their parents, the three children remained in custody for two days. They were released on the feast of the Assumption of Mary, August 15, when they were driven back to Fatima and dropped off on the steps of the church. Since it was a feast day, the church was full, and everyone saw that Mayor Santos had kidnapped the three children.

On the nineteenth of August, Lúcia, her brother John, and Francisco were tending sheep in a different area, where the Angel of Peace had appeared to them in 1916. Toward the end of the day, Lúcia sensed the presence of Our Lady. She bribed her brother John with some pennies to fetch Jacinta. When Jacinta finally arrived, the Lady in white appeared to them.

"What do you want of me?"

"Come again to the Cova da Iria on the thirteenth of next month, my child, and continue to say the Rosary every day. In the last month I will perform a miracle so that all may believe."

"What are we to do with the offerings of money that people leave at the Cova da Iria?"

"I want you to have two ardors [litters to carry statues] made, for the feast of Our Lady of the Rosary. I want you and Jacinta to carry one of them with two other girls. You will both dress in white. And then I want Francisco, with three boys helping him, to carry the other one. The boys, too, will be dressed in white. What is left over will help towards the construction of a chapel that is to be built here."

Lúcia then asked for the cure of some sick people.

"Some I will cure during the year. Pray, pray very much. Make sacrifices for sinners. Many souls go to hell, because no one is willing to help them with sacrifice." Having said that she departed to the east.

The Fifth Apparition of Fatima

By September of 1917, the national press had picked up the story of the three visionary children. The Freemasons and the secular press had conspired to ridicule the monthly visions as examples of Catholic ignorance. On 13 September, more than thirty thousand curious people gathered in the Cova to pray the Rosary and to wait for the Lady to appear to the three children.

"What do you want of me?" said Lúcia to the Lady, whom she could see but that the crowds could not.

The Lady answered her, "Continue the Rosary, my children. Say it every day that the war may end. In October, Our Lord will come, as well as Our Lady of Sorrows and Our Lady of Mount

Carmel. Saint Joseph will appear with the Child Jesus to bless the world. God is pleased with your sacrifices, but He does not want you to wear the cords to bed. Keep them on during the day."

"I have the petitions of many for your help. Will you assist a little girl who is deaf and dumb?"

"She will improve within the year."

"And the conversions that some have asked to have brought about? The cures of the sick ones?"

"Some I will cure, and some I will not. In October I will perform a miracle so that all may believe."

The Lady rose and disappeared into the eastern heavens and Lúcia called out to the crowd, "If you wish to see her: Look! Look!"

The Sixth Apparition of Fatima

Rain poured all night and into the morning of the thirteenth of October. The ground was soaked, and curious pilgrims made their way to the Cova tramping through the mud. Fifty thousand to seventy thousand spectators came on foot, on animal, by carriage, and even by automobile to the Cova. By now, a trestle had been raised over the little holm oak where the Lady would stand and speak to the children. Six months ago, the three children received their first apparition there alone with their rosaries and sheep. Now they were surrounded by gawkers—both pious and skeptical. After the Rosary at noon, the Lady appeared.

Lúcia asked, "What do you want of me?"

"I want a chapel built here in my honor. I want you to continue saying the Rosary every day. The war will end soon, and the soldiers will return to their homes."

"Yes. Yes. Will you tell me your name?"

"I am the Lady of the Rosary."

"I have many petitions from many people. Will you grant them?"

"Some I shall grant, and others I must deny. People must amend their lives and ask pardon for their sins. They must not offend our Lord anymore, for He is already too much offended!"

"And is that all you have to ask?"

"There is nothing more."

Lúcia then describes how the Lady rose toward the east and turned her palms toward the sky. The dark clouds blocking the sun's rays opened, and light burst forth with the sun spinning like a disk of silver.

"Look at the sun!"

The 50,000 to 70,000 spectators observed the sun spinning and dancing in the sky.

Meanwhile, the three children saw a magnificent apparition in the sky that corresponded to the Joyful, Sorrowful, and Glorious Mysteries of the Rosary. First, they beheld Saint Joseph with the Child Jesus and Our Lady robed in white with a blue mantle, beside the sun. Saint Joseph and the Child Jesus seemed to bless the world, for they traced the Sign of the Cross with their hands. This is remarkable because it reveals Saint Joseph as having a priestly power of blessing, along with our High Priest, Jesus Christ.

This initial apparition disappeared, and the three children next saw a sign corresponding to the Sorrowful Mysteries. Lúcia said, "I saw Our Lord and Our Lady. It seemed to me to that it was Our Lady of Sorrows. Our Lord appeared to bless the world in the same manner as Saint Joseph had done." This apparition then disappeared.

Last of all, Lúcia alone saw the Lady once more, this time resembling Our Lady of Mount Carmel. The depiction of Our Lady of Mount Carmel signifies the glorious Queenship of Mary, since her devotees enroll as her visible subjects by wearing the Holy Scapular.

This public miracle for the crowds and the private apparitions for Lúcia, Francisco, and Jacinta brought the Fatima apparitions to an end, with one exception. Our Lady would return to the Cova for a seventh and final visit in 1920 before Lúcia left for boarding school. The Lady would come to urge her to dedicate herself wholly to God, which would later be fulfilled when Lúcia consecrated herself as a Carmelite nun.

Secular and Freemasonic newspapers published the fact of the Miracle of the Sun. Many were converted back to Christ in the Catholic Church. Numerous books have chronicled the articles and personal testimonies made by eyewitness accounts. All agree that everyone present saw the sun moving and spinning. Colors of yellow, red, blue, purple, and white, the rainbow, or mother-of-pearl were reported. Many explained that it seemed that the sun rose and then appeared to fall upon them. Many shouted, "We are going to die." The muddy ground dried. The wet clothing of the people dried by a heat that lasted for ten minutes. The crowed cried out in joy and in fear. Some shouted, "A miracle! A miracle!"

Alfredo da Silva Santos of Lisbon was a firsthand witness to the Miracle of the Sun:

> We made our arrangements and went in three motor cars on the early morning of the 13th. There was a thick mist, and the car which went in front mistook the way so that we were all lost for a time and only arrived at the Cova da Iria at midday by the sun. It was absolutely full of people, but for my part I felt devoid of any religious feeling. When Lúcia called out: "Look at the sun!" the whole multitude

> repeated: "Attention to the sun!" It was a day of incessant drizzle but a few moments before the miracle it stopped raining. I can hardly find words to describe what followed. The sun began to move, and at a certain moment appeared to be detached from the sky and about to hurtle upon us like a wheel of flame. My wife—we had been married only a short time—fainted, and I was too upset to attend to her, and my brother-in-law, João Vassalo, supported her on his arm. I fell on my knees, oblivious of everything, and when I got up, I don't know what I said. I think I began to cry out like the others. An old man with a white beard began to attack the atheists aloud and challenged them to say whether something supernatural had occurred.[36]

Father Ignacio Lorenco said he saw the miracle from eleven miles away:

> I was only nine years old at this time, and I went to the local village school. At about midday we were surprised by shouts and cries of some men and women who were passing in the street in front of the school. The teacher, a good, pious woman, though nervous and impressionable, was the first to run into the road, with the children after her.
>
> Outside, the people were shouting and weeping and pointing to the sun, ignoring the agitated questions of the schoolmistress. It was the great Miracle, which one could see quite distinctly from the top of the hill where my village was situated—the Miracle of the Sun, accompanied by all its extraordinary phenomena.

[36] Andrew Apostoli, *Fatima for Today: The Urgent Marian Message of Hope* (San Francisco: Ignatius Press, 2010), 131.

O MILAGRE DE FÁTIMA

Varios aspectos do povo ajoelhado e orando no momento de descobrir o sol e de se dar o fenomeno que tanto impressionou a multidão.

(Carta a alguem que pede um testemunho insuspeito).

Quebrando um silencio de mais de vinte anos e com a invocação dos longinquos e saudosos tempos em que convivemos n'uma fraternal camaradagem, iluminada então pela fé comum e fortalecida por identicos propositos, escreves-me para que te diga, sincera e minuciosamente, o que vi e ouvi na charneca de Fátima, quando a fama de celestes aparições congregou n'aquele desolado ermo dezenas de milhares de pessoas mais sedentas, segundo creio, de sobrenatural do que impelidas por mera curiosidade ou receosas de um logro... Estão os catolicos em desacordo sobre a importancia e a significação do que presencearam. Uns convenceram-se de que se tinham cumprido prometimentos do Alto; outros acham-se ainda longe de acreditar na incontroversa realidade de um milagre. Foste um crente na tua juventude e deixaste de sel-o. Pessoas de familia arrastaram-te a Fátima, no vagalhão colossal d'aquele povo que ali se juntou a 13 de outubro. O teu racionalismo sofreu um formidavel embate e queres estabelecer uma opinião segura socorrendo-te de depoimentos insuspeitos como o meu, pois que estive lá apenas no desempenho de uma missão bem dificil, tal a de relatar imparcialmente para um grande diario, *O Seculo*, os factos que diante de mim se desenrolassem e tudo quanto de curioso e de elucidativo a eles se prendesse. Não ficará por satisfazer o teu desejo, mas decerto que os nossos olhos e os nossos ouvidos não viram nem ouviram coisas diversas, e que raros foram os que ficaram insensiveis á grandeza de semelhante espectaculo, unico entre nós e de todo o ponto digno de meditação e de estudo ..

* * *

O que ouvi e me levou a Fátima? Que a Virgem Maria, depois da festa da Ascenção, aparecera a tres crianças que apascentavam gado, duas mocinhas e um zagalete, recomendando-lhes que orassem e prometendo-lhes aparecer ali, sobre uma azinheira, no dia 13 de cada mez, até que em outubro lhes daria qualquer sinal do poder de Deus e faria revelações. Espalhou-se a nova por muitas leguas em redondeza; voou, de terra em terra, até os confins de Portugal, e a roma-

355

Page from Ilustração Portuguesa, 29 October 1917, showing the crowd looking at the Miracle of the Sun

I feel incapable of describing what I saw and felt. I looked fixedly at the sun, which seemed pale and did not hurt the eyes. Looking like a ball of snow revolving on itself, it suddenly seemed to come down in a zigzag,

> menacing the earth. Terrified, I ran and hid myself among the people, who were weeping and expecting the end of the world at any moment.
>
> Near us was an unbeliever who had spent the morning mocking at the simpletons who had gone off to Fatima just to see an ordinary girl. He now seemed to be paralyzed, his eyes fixed on the sun. Afterwards he trembled from head to foot and lifting his arms fell on his knees in the mud, crying out to our Lady.
>
> Meanwhile the people continued to cry out and to weep, asking God to pardon their sins. We all ran to the two chapels in the village, which were soon filled to overflowing. During those long moments of the solar prodigy, objects around us turned all the colors of the rainbow. We saw ourselves blue, yellow, and red. All these strange phenomena increased the fears of the people. After about ten minutes the sun, now dull and pallid, returned to its place. When the people realized that the danger was over, there was an explosion of joy, and everyone joined in thanksgiving and praise to our Lady.

The churches of Portugal were filled, and the bishops recognized this Miracle of the Sun. Pope Benedict XV, by his papal invocation of the Blessed Virgin Mary, received a divine response, and he recognized this to some extent. In a letter dated 29 April 1918 to the Portuguese bishops, he referred to the occurrences at Fatima as "an extraordinary aid from the Mother of God," but he seems to have taken little formal interest in these apparitions in Fatima. The apparition of Our Lady of Fatima would not be approved as "worthy of belief" until 1930 during the papacy of his successor Pope Pius XI.

8

Conclave of 1922: Pope Pius XI

The Secret Societies, which by their nature are ever ready to help the enemies of God and of the Church—be these who they may—are seeking to add fresh fires to this poisonous hatred, from which there comes no peace or happiness of the civil order, but the certain ruin of states.

—Pope Pius XI, *Caritate Christi compulsi*

The conclave of 1922 began eleven days after Pope Benedict XV died of pneumonia on 22 January 1922. There were sixty living cardinals, but only fifty-three participated. Three were sick, and one could not make the trip from Rio de Janeiro. The two American cardinals and one Canadian cardinal arrived too late to vote (as had happened in the conclave that elected Benedict XV). Several cardinals insisted that the conclave should wait for these non-European cardinals, but they were ignored.

The conclave of 1922 was the most gridlocked of the twentieth century. Whereas the previous three conclaves had elected a supreme pontiff in three days or less, this conclave lasted five days with fourteen ballots. The two factions aligned with two previous pontificates. The former were stalwart anti-Modernists, the "Irreconcilable Party." They revered Pope Pius X and favored his secretary of state, Cardinal Merry del Val (who had been dismissed by Pope Benedict XV). The latter were the progressive party who favored the more conciliar approach of Pope Benedict XV. They supported Pietro Cardinal Gasparri, who had served as secretary of state under Benedict XV.

A Roman proverb says, "Whoever enters the conclave as 'pope' leaves the conclave as cardinal." That is, the men most supported initially usually do not attain the two-thirds majority needed for papal election. In 1922, the two parties were evenly divided and could not attain the required majority. When it became clear after three days of voting that neither Merry del Val nor Gasparri would win, Gasparri approached Achille Cardinal Ratti as a possible compromise candidate and offered to send his supporters to Ratti. Cardinal Gaetano de Lai allegedly said to Cardinal Ratti "We will elect Your Eminence if Your Eminence will promise that you will not choose Cardinal Gasparri as your secretary of state."[37] Cardinal Ratti rebuffed him saying, "I hope and pray that among so highly deserving cardinals the Holy Spirit selects someone else. If I am chosen, it is indeed Cardinal Gasparri whom I will take to be my Secretary of State."[38] In this way, Cardinal Ratti showed himself to be an ally to Cardinal Gasparri and the legacy of Pope Benedict XV.

The followers of Cardinal Merry del Val in the legacy of Pope Pius X sought to attain the majority, but Cardinal Ratti won the election on the fourteenth ballot with thirty-eight votes on 6

[37] David I. Kertzer, *The Pope and Mussolini: The Secret History of Pius XI and the Rise of Fascism in Europe* (Oxford, UK: Oxford University Press, 2014), 15.

[38] Thomas J. Reese, *Inside the Vatican: The Politics and Organization of the Catholic Church* (Cambridge, MA: Harvard University Press, 1996), 94.

February 1922. Surprisingly, Ratti took the name not of Benedict but of the opposition by choosing Pius XI. When asked why he chose the name Pius, he replied that "he wanted a Pius to end the Roman question[39] which had begun under a Pius."[40] In this way, he subtly rebuked the hardliner legacy of both Pope Pius IX and Pope Pius X.

Some of the conservative cardinals and followers of Cardinal Merry del Val begged the new Pope Pius XI not to give the Urbi et Orbi blessing from the balcony of Saint Peter's Basilica. The omission of this blessing had become a symbolic protest against the secular state of Italy and a sign of the pope's imprisonment in the Vatican. Pope Pius XI responded to them, "Remember, I am no longer a cardinal. I am the Supreme Pontiff now."[41] Pope Pius XI began by giving the Urbi et Orbi blessing facing the people; he was the first pope to do so since the fall of the Papal States in 1870. This indicated that he would, in fact, retreat from the firm position of Pius IX, Leo XIII, and Pius X. He would accommodate the modern secular state of Italy and surrender the temporal claims of the papacy. Much to the disappointment of the conservative cardinals, Pope Pius XI immediately appointed Cardinal Gasparri as his secretary of state—just as he had promised in the conclave.

Pope Pius XI was a mountaineer and a scholar. Ordained a priest in 1879, he gave his life to studying medieval manuscripts. His passion was the Ambrosian Library of Milan, where he edited and published an edition of the Ambrosian Rite Missal particular to Milan. He went on to become vice prefect of the Vatican

[39] The dispute regarding the temporal power of the popes.

[40] "Cardinal Ratti New Pope as Pius XI," *New York Times*, 7 February 1922.

[41] Ibid.

Pope Pius XI, 1939

Library (1914–1915) and then prefect of the Vatican Library (1915–1919). He spent his vacations climbing mountains and had ascended the Matterhorn and Mont Blanc.

He published thirty-one encyclicals proclaiming Catholic orthodoxy. He published an encyclical promoting the study of Saint Thomas Aquinas, *Studiorum ducem* in 1923. He established the feast of Christ the King in 1925 and promoted the Social Reign of Christ the King. In 1928, he rejected the idea that Christian unity could be attained by a federation of Christian denominations, teaching instead that all Christians must enter the one true (Catholic) Church. He also prohibited Catholics from joining interfaith bodies and conferences.

In 1930, after the Church of England allowed artificial means of contraception, Pope Pius XI issued *Casti connubii*, which praised

Christian marriage and condemned artificial contraception in no uncertain words: "Any use whatsoever of matrimony exercised in such a way that the act is deliberately frustrated in its natural power to generate life is an offense against the law of God and of nature, and those who indulge in such are branded with the guilt of a grave sin."[42]

To commemorate the fortieth anniversary of Pope Leo XIII's *Rerum novarum*, he published *Quadragesimo anno*, condemning socialism as intrinsically evil and unrestrained capitalism as contrary to human dignity.

All previous popes had refused to recognize or compromise with the state of Italy. Pope Pius XI was determined to find a solution. Italy's prime minister Benito Mussolini was also eager to reach an agreement with the pope. Mussolini offered the following terms to Pope Pius XI:

- Vatican City State (108.7 acres within the Vatican walls) would receive sovereignty as an independent nation in return for the Vatican's relinquishing its claim to the former territories of the Papal States.
- Pius XI would be recognized as sovereign of this Vatican City State.
- Catholicism would be recognized as the sole religion of Italy.
- Italy would pay salaries to priests and bishops.
- Civil recognition would be given to church marriages (previously the Kingdom of Italy required that couples had to have a civil ceremony).
- Catholic instruction would take place in the public schools.

[42] Pius XI, Encyclical *Casti connubii* (December 31, 1930), no. 56.

- The Italian state would have a veto power over selection of its bishops.
- Italy would pay the Vatican 1,750 million lira (about $100 million) for the seizures of church property since 1860.

This was a bad deal, but Pope Pius XI took the bait. He agreed to the Lateran Treaty in 1929. Mussolini bought the Catholic Church for a cheap price: $100 million and some concessions that could and would be later revoked. Imagine the happy grin of Mussolini when the deal went through with Pope Pius XI and was subsequently ratified by the Italian parliament. Sadly, this compromise of 1929 undermined Pius XI's teaching in 1925 that Christ is King over the political realm.

In retrospect, the Lateran Treaty looks more like a bribe and less like a covenant based on Catholic principles. Since the pope was no longer at odds with the Italian state, Pope Pius XI explained that the Leonine Prayers would remain but would be prayed for a new purpose: "to permit tranquility and freedom to profess the faith to be restored to the afflicted people of Russia."[43] The axis of evil had shifted from Rome to Moscow. This was appropriate because Our Lady had warned in 1917 of the errors of Russia, and Moscow implemented a new anti-Christian campaign in 1929 in which the destruction of churches peaked around 1932.

I personally believe that Pope Pius XI acted in goodwill, but that he did, in fact, sign a deal with the devil in the person of Benito Mussolini. Pope Pius X and his saintly secretary of state, Cardinal Merry Del Val (to whom is attributed the Litany of

[43] *Indictam ante* of 30 June 1930, in *Acta Apostolicae Sedis* 22 (1930): 301.

Humility), had the right approach against Modernism and the right approach against the Freemasonic Kingdom of Italy. The 1929 Lateran Treaty opened the floodgates to demonic influence in the world, as we shall see.

9

Communist Infiltration of the Priesthood

He will set up a counter church which will be the ape of the Church, because he, the Devil, is the ape of God. It will have all the notes and characteristics of the Church, but in reverse and emptied of its divine content. It will be a mystical body of the Antichrist that will in all externals resemble the mystical body of Christ.

—Archbishop Fulton J. Sheen[44]

The Freemasons and Socialists persecuted Christianity ruthlessly in Mexico, Spain, and Russia during the pontificate of Pope Pius XI. Pius XI appointed Berlin's nuncio Eugenio Pacelli (future Pius XII) to work secretly on diplomatic arrangements between the Vatican and the Soviet Union. This approach yielded failure. Pius XI is largely seen as abandoning the Cristeros, who fought for the Catholic Church in the Cristeros War in Mexico (1926–1929). During the Spanish Civil War (1936–1939), priests, monks, and nuns were brutally attacked, churches were sacked, and believers were tortured. Former Communist agent Bella Dodd later explained, "During the Spanish War the Communist

[44] Fulton J. Sheen, *Communism and the Conscience of the West* (Indianapolis: Bobbs-Merrill Company, 1948), 24–25.

Party was able to use some of the best talent of the country against the Catholic Church by repeating ancient appeals to prejudice and by insinuating that the Church was indifferent to the poor and was against those who wanted only to be free."[45] As a result, the Freemasonic-Communist Spanish government appropriated all church properties and schools. In 1937, Pius XI endorsed a third way against both Communism and Fascism in his encyclical *Divini Redemptoris*, which did nothing to stop the emerging power of the Communist Soviets nor the Fascists in Italy, Germany, and Spain. Pius XI died on 10 February 1939. On 1 September 1939, Nazi Germany would invade Poland and launch World War II. Between those two dates, Pope Pius XII was elected.

Unbeknownst to Pius XI, the Communists were not simply attacking Catholic government and monarchs. Beginning in the 1930s, the Russians began secretly to infiltrate Catholic seminaries to plant their own Communist men as priests and eventually as bishops, cardinals, and even pope. Recall the advice of the Carbonari Freemasons who, as early as the 1840s, were recommending the following strategy: "So, in order to secure a pope according to our heart, it is a task first of all to form for this pope a generation worthy of the kingdom that we desire. Leave aside old and mature men, and go instead to youth, and, if possible, even to children."[46] The planned goal of the enemies of Christ since the 1800s was eventually to "secure a

45 Bella V. Dodd's testimony in United States House Committee on Un-American Activities, *Investigation of Communist Activities in Columbus, Ohio* (Washington, D.C.: U.S. Government Printing Office, 1953), 1741–1777.

46 *Alta Vendita*, 7.

pope according to our heart," and that entailed planting their own as seminarians.

Bella Dodd testified before the United States House Committee on Un-American Activities Committee in 1953 about the subversive ways in which Communists try to infiltrate American institutions. She originally converted to Communism "because only the Communists seemed to care about what was happening to people in 1932 and 1933.... They were fighting hunger and misery and Fascism then, and neither the major political parties nor the churches seemed to care. That is why I am a Communist." Having lived as a Communist agent in America, she later renounced her Communism under the spiritual direction of Archbishop Fulton J. Sheen and returned to Catholicism in 1952. Dodd testified before a committee of the House of Representatives that, in the late 1920s and all during the 1930s, Communist agents in the United States followed directives from Moscow. One such order from Russia was to destroy the Catholic Church from within by planting Communist Party members in seminaries and in diocesan positions.

Dodd testified that "in the 1930s we put eleven hundred men into the priesthood in order to destroy the Church from within, and that right now they are in the highest places in the Church."[47] She was not claiming to have worked alone but worked with a group of Communists who sought to infiltrate not only the Catholic priesthood but also the American public school system, as is stated openly in the *Alta Vendita*: "Leave

[47] Bella Dodd, "Lecture at Fordham University in 1953," recorded audiotape; lecture referenced in C. P. Trussell, "Bella Dodd Asserts Reds Got Presidential Advisory Posts," *New York Times*, March 11, 1953.

aside old and mature men, and go instead to youth, and, if possible, even to children." As a former Communist agent in America, her testimony echoes perfectly the strategy mapped out in the *Alta Vendita*.

A second former Communist, African-American agent Manning Johnson, also testified before the United States House Committee on Un-American Activities in 1953 regarding Russian Communists infiltrating the Catholic priesthood:

> Once the tactic of infiltration of religious organizations was set by the Kremlin ... the Communists discovered that the destruction of religion could proceed much faster through infiltration of the [Catholic] Church by Communists operating within the Church itself.... In the earliest stages it was determined that with only small forces available to them, it would be necessary to concentrate Communist agents in the seminaries. The practical conclusion drawn by the Red leaders was that these institutions would make it possible for a small Communist minority to influence the ideology of future clergymen in paths conducive to Communist purposes. This policy of infiltrating seminaries was successful beyond even Communist expectations.[48]

Here we have sworn testimony by former Communist agents that the Kremlin was strategically placing their own men in American and European seminaries so as to infiltrate the Catholic

[48] Manning Johnson's testimony in United States House Committee on Un-American Activities, *Investigation of Communist Activities in the New York City Area* (Washington, D.C.: U.S. Government Printing Office, 1953), 2278.

priesthood and that it was "successful beyond even Communist expectations"—all before 1953. In other words, long before the Second Vatican Council (1962–1965), the Communists had their own men in the seminaries, in the priesthood, and in the episcopate. Bella Dodd revealed that four of their infiltrated priests had attained the level of cardinal.

In 1967 or 1968, just before Dodd's death, she was interviewed by the scholar Dietrich von Hildebrand and his wife, Alice, in New Rochelle, New York. Alice von Hildebrand recounted their conversation:

> DIETRICH VON HILDEBRAND: I fear the Church has been infiltrated.
>
> BELLA DODD: You fear it, dear professor; I know it! When I was an ardent Communist, I was working in close contact with four cardinals in the Vatican working for us; and they are still very active today.
>
> DIETRICH VON HILDEBRAND: Who are they? My nephew Dieter Sattler is a German stationed at the Holy See.[49]

"But Bella, who was under the spiritual guidance of Archbishop Sheen, declined to give him this information," Alice Von Hildebrand explained.[50]

[49] "Alice von Hildebrand Sheds New Light on Fatima," *One Peter Five*, May 12, 2016.

[50] Ibid. In 1973, a book entitled *AA-1025* was published, purporting to be the memoirs of a Communist who had infiltrated the Church and brought about many of the unfortunate changes in the Church that followed Vatican II. As its front matter includes a disclaimer saying that it is only a "dramatized presentation," many have contested its authenticity, so I have not included here materials from it.

Who were these active Vatican cardinals?

We can construct a limited pool of cardinals by noting that Dodd was active since the 1930s and that she converted in 1952. Moreover, these cardinals were "active" as late as 1966 or 1967. These historical restrictions yield only twenty-six possible cardinals who could be the four Communist cardinals claimed by Dodd:

- Krikor Bedros XV Aghagianian
- Benedetto Aloisi Masella
- Clemente Micara
- James Charles McGuigan
- Carlos Carmelo de Vasconcelos Motta
- Norman Thomas Gilroy
- Francis Joseph Spellman
- Jaime de Barros Câmara
- Enrique Pla y Deniel
- Josef Frings
- Ernesto Ruffini
- Antonio Caggiano
- Thomas Tien Ken-sin
- Augusto Álvaro da Silva
- Pietro Ciriaci
- Maurice Feltin
- Carlos María Javier de la Torre
- Giuseppe Siri
- James Francis Louis McIntyre
- Giacomo Lercaro
- Stefan Wyszynski
- Benjamín de Arriba y Castro
- Fernando Quiroga y Palacios
- Paul-Émile Léger

- Valerian Gracias
- Alfredo Ottaviani

Some of these cardinals, such as Siri and Ottaviani, can be removed from consideration due to their orthodoxy. Among the most likely would be Cardinal Spellman (reputed sodomite and ecclesial patron of the young Theodore McCarrick), Cardinal Lercaro (the leading liberal candidate for pope in the 1963 conclave that went to Cardinal Montini instead), and Cardinal Frings (important German leader at Vatican II and sponsor of the young Joseph Ratzinger).

Another case of infiltration involves the mysterious contents of a left-behind briefcase. In 1975, Archbishop Annibale Bugnini left his briefcase unattended in a Vatican conference room. Bugnini was the chief architect of the Novus Ordo Mass, published in 1969 and 1970, and we shall thoroughly cover his influence over Pius XII and Paul VI in the pages to come. Suffice it here to state that Bugnini was an infiltrated priest and a Freemason. A Dominican priest discovered the unattended briefcase and opened it, in order to discover the identity of its owner. Inside he found documents addressed "to Brother Bugnini," with "signatures and place of origin [that] showed that they came from dignitaries of secret societies in Rome."[51] This became a scandal in Rome and Pope Paul VI was forced to send his chief liturgist and recently minted archbishop to Iran as pro-nuncio, a surprising and obvious demotion and exile. Respected theologian Father Brian Harrison also testifies to the veracity of the discovery of Bugnini's Freemasonic documents: "An internationally known churchman of unimpeachable integrity has also told me that he

[51] Piers Compton, *The Broken Cross: The Hidden Hand in the Vatican* (Australia: Veritas Publications, 1984), 61.

heard the account of the discovery of the evidence against Bugnini directly from the Roman priest who found it in a briefcase which Bugnini had inadvertently left in a Vatican conference room after a meeting."[52] When the Italian Masonic Registry was released in 1976, Annibale Bugnini's name was found on the Masonic register along with his Freemasonic codename, "Buan."[53] He had joined the Masonic Lodge on the feast of Saint George, 23 April 1963. This was less than two months before the death of John XXIII.

Clearly, high-ranking priests and bishops before and during Vatican II were infiltrated Freemasons. The testimonies provided by Bella Dodd and Manning Johnson, along with the guilt and expulsion of Archbishop Annibale Bugnini, reveal that infiltration of the Catholic clergy had been accomplished before and after 1940. Yet before examining the Second Vatican Council, we must return to the historical timeline leading up to the election of Pope Pius XII and then Pope John XXIII after him.

[52] Father Brian Harrison, "A Response to Michael Davies' Article on Archbishop Bugnini," AD2000.com, June 1989.

[53] *Most Asked Questions about the Society of Saint Pius X* (Kansas City, MO: Angelus Press), 26.

10

1939 Papal Conclave: Pius XII

Pope Pius XI had stipulated that the College of Cardinals wait longer in order to allow the cardinals from North and South America to arrive in Rome for the election of the pope. He said that the conclave should wait as long as eighteen days in expectation of their American brothers. For the first time in a long time, every single living cardinal participated in the conclave of 1939—all sixty-two of them.

Eugenio Cardinal Pacelli was the undisputed choice, and he won on the first day of voting, on the second ballot. As mentioned previously, Pacelli had been consecrated a bishop on 13 May 1917, the very day that Our Lady of Fatima first appeared to the three children. Pius XI had made subtle indications that he desired Pacelli to succeed him. Cardinal Pacelli was the camerlengo, or papal chamberlain, and oversaw the election. When elected, he accepted by saying, "*Accepto in crucem*" (I accept it as a cross). He took the name Pope Pius XII "as a sign of gratitude towards Pius XI."[54]

Pope Pius XII was born as Eugenio Maria Giuseppe Giovanni Pacelli in 1876. His family had deep roots in the *nobiltà nera*, or

[54] Joseph Brosch, *Pius XII: Lehrer der Wahrheit* (Trier: Kreuzring, 1968), 45.

Pope Pius XII, 1950

"black nobility"—those deriving from the aristocratic Roman families that sided with the pope against the invasion of Rome in 1870.[55] His grandfather, Marcantonio Pacelli, had been undersecretary in the Papal Ministry of Finances, and then secretary of the interior under Pope Pius IX from 1851 to 1870. His grandfather was also partly responsible for the founding of the newspaper *L'Osservatore Romano* in 1861. His father, Filippo Pacelli, had served as the dean of the Roman Rota, and his brother, Francesco Pacelli, served as a canon lawyer negotiating the Lateran Treaty of 1929 between Pope Pius XI and Benito Mussolini.

[55] After the Lateran Treaty in 1929, the black nobility received dual citizenship in Italy and Vatican City. Pope Paul VI abolished the status and honors of the black nobility in 1968.

Pius XII was raised in Rome and within the corridors of the papal court. Their family attended Mass at the Chiesa Nuova. It was here that the young Eugenio made his First Communion and served as an altar boy to the Oratorian priests. He seems to have received special dispensations in the seminary, due to his family's prestige in the papal court. For example, his fellow seminarians were ordained together in the Basilica of Saint John Lateran, but Pacelli was ordained a priest privately on Easter Sunday 1899 in the personal chapel of a family friend, the vicegerent of Rome, Monsignor Paolo Cassetta. His first priestly assignment was curate at the family's parish, Chiesa Nuova. In 1901, Pope Leo XIII personally asked Pacelli to deliver condolences on behalf of the Holy Father to King Edward VII of England after the death of Queen Victoria.

Pacelli was already an international man when he earned his doctorate in 1904, writing his dissertation on the nature of concordats and the function of canon law when a concordat falls into abeyance. In 1908, he accompanied Cardinal Merry del Val to London, where he met Winston Churchill. In 1911, he represented the Holy See at the coronation of King George V. On 24 June 1914, just four days before Archduke Franz Ferdinand of Austria was assassinated in Sarajevo, Pacelli and Cardinal Merry del Val were present, representing the Holy See, when the Serbian Concordat was signed.

As mentioned previously, Pope Pius X died that same year on 20 August. His successor, Pope Benedict XV, as he promised, appointed as secretary of state Cardinal Gasparri, who chose Pacelli as his undersecretary. In 1915, Pacelli traveled to Vienna in negotiations with the Emperor Franz Joseph I of Austria regarding Italy.

Pope Benedict XV appointed Pacelli nuncio to Bavaria in 1917, consecrating him as titular archbishop of Sardis in the

Sistine Chapel on 13 May 1917. Since there was no nuncio to Prussia or Germany, Pacelli effectively became the ambassador of the Holy See to all the German Empire, where he met with King Ludwig III and Kaiser Wilhelm II. It was during this time that he was joined by Mother Pascalina Lehnert—a Bavarian nun who would serve him for the rest of his life as his housekeeper and secretary. Mother Pascalina serves as our primary source for the personal life and details of the life of Pacelli, both before and after he became Pope Pius XII.

In Germany Pacelli was threatened repeatedly, and once at gunpoint, according to Mother Pascalina. The pope officially appointed Pacelli as nuncio to Germany in 1920. For the next decade, Pacelli would watch with disgust as Nazi beliefs emerged. He made forty-four speeches as apostolic nuncio to Germany, and forty of them spoke against Nazism.[56] Due to his placement in Germany, Pacelli also became the de facto nuncio to Russia during the 1920s. Through unofficial and secret negotiations, he negotiated food shipments and relief to Catholics in Russia, until Pope Pius XI ordered off all talks with Moscow in 1927.

After Pope Pius XI signed the Lateran Treaty and settled the "Roman Question," he recalled Pacelli to Rome and named him a cardinal before Christmas of 1929. Pope Pius XI then raised Cardinal Pacelli to cardinal secretary of state—the highest post in the Church, second only to the pope. Since the Vatican had been deprived of international political status since the fall of the Papal States in 1870, the new Vatican City State created in 1929 meant that Pacelli, as secretary of state, would need to reestablish the lost ties. He visited Franklin Roosevelt and

[56] David G. Dalin and Joseph Bottum, *The Pius War: Responses to the Critics of Pius XII* (Lanham, MD: Lexington Books, 2010), 17.

reestablished official diplomatic relations with the United States. Having served so long in Germany during the 1920s, he had the unique role of warning the world of the growing Nazi threat of the 1930s, especially after 1933, when Adolf Hitler was appointed chancellor. With Pacelli's help, Pope Pius XI issued an encyclical in German, *Mit brennender Sorge*, which condemned Nazism as inhuman and pagan in ideology. It was smuggled into Germany and secretly delivered to each Catholic church so that priests could read it aloud to the faithful on Palm Sunday of 1937.

Observing the world torn apart by alliances and impending war, Cardinal Pacelli lamented that the dangers prophesied by Our Lady Fatima were about to come to pass:

> I am concerned by the Blessed Virgin's messages to Lúcia of Fatima. Mary's persistence about the dangers that menace the Church is a divine warning against the suicide of altering the Faith, in Her liturgy, Her theology, and Her soul.... I hear all around me innovators who wish to dismantle the Sacred Chapel, destroy the universal flame of the Church, reject her ornaments, and make her feel remorse for her historical past.
>
> A day will come when the civilized world will deny its God, when the Church will doubt as Peter doubted. She will be tempted to believe that man has become God. In our churches, Christians will search in vain for the red lamp where God awaits them. Like Mary Magdalene, weeping before the empty tomb, they will ask, "Where have they taken Him?"[57]

[57] Some doubt this quote, but it is found in Georges Roche and Philippe Saint Germain, "*Pie XII devant l'Histoire*" (1972), 52.

It was well established that Pacelli was the uncontested candidate for the papacy after Pius XI, and Pacelli knew it. As he looked toward the future, perhaps he foresaw the attacks against Mother Church and against "Her liturgy, Her theology, and Her soul." What's more startling is that he seems to have foreseen the removal of the tabernacles from the Church, so that the faithful would look in vain for the red lamp signifying the Real Presence of Christ our Lord. "The Church will doubt as Peter doubted."

11

Pius XII as the Pope of Fatima

Therefore the whole and entire Catholic doctrine is to be presented and explained: by no means is it permitted to pass over in silence or to veil in ambiguous terms the Catholic truth regarding the nature and way of justification, the constitution of the Church, the primacy of jurisdiction of the Roman Pontiff, and the only true union by the return of the dissidents to the one true Church of Christ."

—Pope Pius XII, Instruction *On the "Ecumenical Movement"*

There seems to be only one apparent error in the message of Fatima. The Lady in white told Lúcia, "The war is going to end, but if people do not cease offending God, a worse one will break out during the Pontificate of Pius XI." Pius XI died on 10 February 1939, and World War II didn't officially begin until the German invasion of Poland on 1 September 1939—during the Pontificate of Pius XII. Was Lúcia wrong about the beginning of World War II?

Lúcia did not release this information until 1941, so she could have easily fudged or corrected the mistake. One might argue, however, that the "worse war" foretold by Our Lady of Fatima did begin prior to 1939, when Germany annexed Austria and made claims over parts of Czechoslovakia in 1938, during the pontificate of Pius XI. The chess pieces were already moved into position.

Regardless of the precise trigger date, Pope Pius XII is known as the pope of Fatima and the pope of World War II. Pius XII was devoted to Our Lady of Fatima and understood that his episcopal consecration occurred in conjunction with her first apparition on the same day of 13 May 1917. Lúcia revealed the First and Second Secrets of Fatima in 1941 and Pope Pius XII took notice of the Second Secret, which described both an "unknown light" and the consecration of Russia:

> This war is going to end but if people do not cease offending God, a worse one will break out during the Pontificate of Pope Pius XI. When you see a night illumined by an unknown light, know that this is the great sign given you by God that He is about to punish the world for its crimes, by means of war, famine, and persecutions of the Church and of the Holy Father. To prevent this, I shall come to ask for the Consecration of Russia to my Immaculate Heart, and the Communion of reparation on the First Saturdays. If my requests are heeded, Russia will be converted, and there will be peace; if not, she will spread her errors throughout the world, causing wars and persecutions of the Church. The good will be martyred; the Holy Father will have much to suffer; various nations will be annihilated. In the end, my Immaculate Heart will triumph. The Holy Father will consecrate Russia to me, and she shall be converted, and a period of peace will be granted to the world.[58]

Regarding the "unknown light," something like the aurora borealis appeared on the night of 25–26 January 1938. From 8:45 p.m. until 1:15 a.m. these northern lights oddly extended

[58] Apostoli, *Fatima for Today*, 71.

as far south as Spain, Austria, and Portugal, where Lúcia herself witnessed them as a sign. Pope Pius XI in Rome was rumored to have seen the "unknown light," as well. The *New York Times* of 26 January 1938 reported:

> The Aurora Borealis, rarely seen in Southern or Western Europe, spread fear in parts of Portugal and lower Austria tonight while thousands of Britons were brought running into the streets in wonderment. The ruddy glow led many to think half the city was ablaze. The Windsor Fire Department was called out thinking that Windsor Castle was afire. The lights were clearly seen in Italy, Spain, and even Gibraltar. The glow bathing snow-clad mountain tops in Austria and Switzerland was a beautiful sight, but firemen turned out to chase nonexistent fires. Portuguese villagers rushed in fright from their homes fearing the end of the world.

A little over a year later, Pope Pius XI died, on 10 February 1939, and Pope Pius XII was elected on 2 March 1939. But it was too late: "When you see a night illumined by an unknown light, know that this is the great sign given you by God that He is about to punish the world for its crimes, by means of war, famine, and persecutions of the Church and of the Holy Father."

While World War II burned through the world "for its crimes," Pope Pius XII attempted to obey the Blessed Virgin of Fatima. In 1942, he performed the Fatima consecration to the Immaculate Heart of Mary for the entire world. This would set the pattern for many more papal consecrations to the Immaculate Heart of Mary that would not specify Russia in their formulas. This has given rise to decades of debate over the consecration of Russia. Does "consecrating the world" properly "consecrate Russia" in the way that Our Lady of Fatima asked?

An analogy might be helpful in answering this dispute. If a father asked the pope to bless his terminally ill son, and the pope replied, "Yes, I will be happy to do this blessing. I bless all the children in the world *in nomine Patris, et Filii, et Spiritus Sancti.*" Did the pope bless the man's sick son? Yes, he did bless the boy, but in a general mode and not in a specific mode. And there is a key difference. The Catholic Church, in her blessings and liturgy, requires specificity in her rites. A priest may not baptize several people simultaneously with a bucket of water or a hose. Each person must be baptized individually. When the priest consecrates the Eucharist, he consecrates only those hosts on the corporal—not those nearby in the sacristy. In exorcism, a specific person is exorcised, not a group.

The instructions given by the Blessed Mother at Fatima to Lúcia regarded a specific consecration of Russia, and not a general consecration of the world.[59] And yet, on the following dates, popes have refrained from doing so because of the great pressure that Russia placed on Europe and on the Catholic Church beginning in the 1940s and up through our own time:

- Pius XII on 31 October 1942
- Paul VI on 21 November 1964
- John Paul II on 13 May 1982

[59] Concerning this request, Sister Lucia told Professor William Thomas Walsh during a 15 July 1946 interview: "What Our Lady wants is that the Pope and all the bishops in the world shall consecrate Russia to her Immaculate Heart on one special day. If this is done, she will convert Russia and there will be peace. If it is not done, the errors of Russia will spread through every country in the world." [Walsh:] "Does this mean, in your opinion, that every country, without exception, will be overcome by Communism?" [Lucia:] "Yes." William Thomas Walsh, *Our Lady of Fatima* (New York: Image Books, 1990), 221.

- John Paul II on 25 March 1984 with all the bishops
- Francis on 13 October 2013

All of these were general-mode consecrations of the world to the Immaculate Heart of Mary, and, as such, they were gracious, good, and beneficial to the Catholic Church and, by extension, to all humanity. "Remember, O most gracious Virgin Mary, that never was it known that anyone who fled to your protection, implored your help, or sought your intercession, was left unaided." And yet, it is not an exact papal consecration of Russia to the Immaculate Heart.

There is one and only one papal consecration in the history of the Catholic Church that comes close to meeting the specific consecration of Russia to the Immaculate Heart, and it is found in Pius XII's Apostolic Letter *Sacro vergente*, dated 7 July 1952. There, Pius XII recounts the thousand-year relationship of Rome with the Russian people, beginning with the missionary efforts of Saints Cyril and Methodius (on whose feast this letter was written), who were sent by Pope Adrian II to the Slavic peoples. Pius recounts the happy fellowship of Rome and Russia and mentions the relief provided (through his own mediation as Cardinal Pacelli) by Pope Benedict XV and Pope Pius XI. Without apology, he notes that Pius XI assigned the traditional Leonine Prayers after Low Mass to be prayed for "the unhappy conditions of religion in Russia." Then he specifically consecrates Russia to the Immaculate Heart:

> We, therefore, so that Our prayers may be more readily granted, and to give you a singular attestation of Our particular benevolence, as we a few years ago have consecrated the whole world to the Immaculate Heart of the virgin Mother of God, so now, so very special, *we consecrate all the peoples of Russia to the same Immaculate Heart, in the sure trust that with the most powerful patronage of the*

> *Virgin Mary the vows are fulfilled as soon as possible*, that we—that all the good ones—form for true peace, for a fraternal concord and for the due freedom to all and first of all to the church; so that, through the prayer that We raise together with you and with all Christians, the saving kingdom of Christ, which is the kingdom of truth and life, the kingdom of holiness and grace, the reign of justice, in all parts of the earth may triumph and steadily grow.[60]

Pius XII explicitly refers to the international consecration of all nations in 1942, and here in 1952 he renews it again, but this time for Russia specifically: "We consecrate all the peoples of Russia to the same Immaculate Heart, in the sure trust that with the most powerful patronage of the Virgin Mary the vows are fulfilled as soon as possible." This, in fact, appears to be a specific and precise papal consecration of Russia to the Immaculate Heart and in some way fulfills the request of Mary in 1917—but it did not include the participation of the bishops of the world. Hence, it does not fulfill the precise instructions of Our Lady.

Less than two months later, on 2 September 1952, Pope Pius XII sent Father Joseph Schweigl to Coimbra, Portugal, to interview Sister Lúcia in her convent about the Third Secret. On his return to the Russicum in Rome, Father Schweigl confided this to one of his colleagues: "I cannot reveal anything of what I learned at Fatima concerning the Third Secret, but I can say that it has two parts: One concerns the Pope. The other, logically—although I must say nothing—would have to be the continuation of the words 'In Portugal, the dogma of the Faith will always be preserved.'"[61]

60 Pius XII, *Sacro Vergente*, 9. Emphasis added.

61 Michael of the Holy Trinity, *The Whole Truth about Fatima*, vol. 3, *The Third Secret* (Buffalo, NY: Immaculate Heart Publishing, 1990), 710.

12

Communist Infiltration of the Liturgy

Unfortunately, the second half of the pontificate of Pius XII is not as brilliant as the first half. In 1948, Pius XII appointed the controversial priest Father Annibale Bugnini to the Commission for Liturgical Reform.

The commission was tasked with restoring the liturgy for the Mass of Holy Saturday, usually celebrated in the morning, to that of a Paschal Vigil celebrated into the night in anticipation of Easter the following morning. In A.D. 800, the Holy Saturday Mass was celebrated just before nightfall. By 1076, the Holy Saturday Mass was celebrated in the afternoon. By the 1500s, this Holy Saturday Mass with the triple candle, the paschal candle, and twelve readings was universally celebrated in the early morning of Holy Saturday. Pope Saint Pius V even decreed in his 1566 bull *Sanctissimus* that all priests were banned from celebrating the Holy Saturday Mass after noon.

Liturgists had long noted that the "Exultet" hymn, chanted by the deacon in the blessing of the paschal candle, spoke of the chant occurring in the nighttime:

> Therefore, the hallowing of this night putteth wickedness to flight, washeth away sins, and restoreth innocence to the fallen, and joy to the sorrowful; it banisheth hatred,

> and prepareth peace, and maketh sovereignties to yield. Therefore, in favor of *this night*, receive, O holy Father . . .

Since the liturgy itself is ancient and refers to the context as "this night," liturgists of the 1940s wanted to resituate the liturgy in the nighttime of Holy Saturday just before Easter Day. Previous theologians, such as Saint Thomas Aquinas and Saint Pius V, had defended the daytime celebration of Holy Saturday. The morning argument for Holy Saturday Vigil Mass was that fasting required an earlier time and that most laymen would not be able to attend a late-night Saturday Mass and a Sunday Morning Mass—since there was not yet any notion of fulfilling one's Sunday obligation with a Saturday-evening Vigil Mass. Interestingly enough, it was thought to be a "pastoral" concession to celebrate the Holy Saturday Mass on Saturday morning and not late on Saturday night. Traditional theologians also noted that the liturgy is full of "temporal rescheduling." Our Lord Jesus Christ celebrated the first Eucharist at night, but we almost universally celebrate it in the morning. The Last Supper was on Thursday, but our obligation is for Sunday. And so on.

The Liturgical Movement would hear none of it and wanted to resituate this Holy Saturday Mass as a late-night Paschal Vigil. But they immediately realized that this was not "pastoral" for laymen (which had been known for centuries). So, these liturgical innovators concluded that they would need to rewrite the entire Holy Saturday Mass to conform Holy Saturday to this nighttime slot.

Sadly, Pope Pius XII unwisely chose Father Annibale Bugnini to accomplish a "restoration" of something that never previously existed.

Annibale, whose name means "gift of Baal," was born in Civitella del Lago in Umbria in 1912. At age twenty-four, he was ordained a priest for the Congregation of the Mission. He earned his doctorate in sacred theology at the Pontifical University of Saint Thomas Aquinas (Angelicum) by defending his dissertation on the liturgy and the Council of Trent. He became the editor of *Ephemerides Liturgicae*, a Catholic journal dedicated to the Liturgical Movement, when he caught the attention of Pope Pius XII. Unbeknownst to Pope Pius XII, he was rumored to be a Freemason.

The revised Holy Saturday liturgy of 1951 turned into a revised Holy Week in 1955. And in 1956, Bugnini convinced Pius XII to allow concelebration, in which priests could celebrate Mass together in a group around the altar—a custom rarely practiced in the Roman Rite.[62] Already, Bugnini was at work on what others would later identify as "Protestantization" of the Catholic liturgy:

- Blessings (such as of palms) were reduced or eliminated.
- The priest prayed from the chair and not from the altar.
- The triple candle, representing the Blessed Trinity and the three Marys arriving at the tomb, was suppressed.
- The traditional folded chasubles and vesture were suppressed or simplified.
- The priest began to face more toward the people.
- Vernacular language was introduced.
- The number of lessons was reduced from twelve to four (to make the Paschal Vigil shorter for laypeople).

[62] In A.D. 619 the Council of Seville decreed that priests could not concelebrate Mass with a bishop present. An exception may have been made in Rome for cardinals to concelebrate with the Pope on feast days as late as the 1100s. Concelebration was allowed in the Roman Rite at the ordination of a priest so that the new priest concelebrated with the ordaining bishop, and similarly at the consecration of a bishop so that the newly consecrated bishop concelebrated with the consecrating bishop.

- The Litany of Saints was modified.
- Contrary to tradition, the laity were asked to kneel for the prayer for the Jews on Good Friday.
- Holy water was blessed in front of the people and not at the baptismal font.
- Renewal of baptismal vows was added (in the vernacular) so that the laity could "participate."
- Tenebrae was suppressed.
- Evening celebrations for Maundy Thursday and Holy Saturday were enforced.

Beyond Holy Week, Bugnini suppressed many of the octaves and vigils, abolished the First Vespers of many feasts, and made the "Dies Irae" optional at funeral Masses.

Clearly, this was no longer the ancient and received rite. The Holy Week liturgy in the Roman Rite is the *oldest* liturgy in the world, and Bugnini slashed it to pieces as an experiment. Those in the Liturgical Movement rejoiced about these "restorations" that restored nothing but time slots at the expense of the actual texts and rubrics of the ancient liturgies.

Worst of all, this inspired Bugnini and others to press for even more radical changes to the Mass itself. They called for the suppression of the prayers at the foot of the altar, the offertory prayers, the Last Gospel, and the Leonine Prayers. Everything was up for grabs.

The original 1951 Holy Saturday revision began merely as an "experiment," but it became the required norm. This set the agenda. Their modus operandi was to propose changes as an "experiment" and then press for the changes to be required under pain of sin. What became the *Novus Ordo Missae* of 1969–1970 arose from the seeds planted by Bugnini in Holy Week of 1955.

13

Woeful Illness of Pius XII: Three Crypto-Modernists

It's difficult to understand why Pope Pius XII softened in his later years and how he was ostensibly manipulated by the likes of Father Bugnini. His friends and acquaintances noted a drastic change in his personality beginning in 1954, when the pope succumbed to a serious case of gastritis. Photos reveal that Pope Pius XII deeply enjoyed the ceremony of the Roman Rite and enjoyed the pomp and glory of the papal liturgies. He is often depicted with his arms extended and jaw tilted upward. Perhaps the most glorious depictions of the papacy in human history are photos of Pius XII.

Yet beginning with his extreme illness in 1954, the pope eschewed the ceremonial of the Catholic Church. Unlike his younger self as nuncio in Germany and as a younger pope, he became reluctant about making decisions. Perhaps because of his poor health, he also avoided long liturgies and papal responsibilities. From 1955 to 1958, he succumbed to night terrors and hallucinations and seems to have resigned himself to death.

With the onset of illness, Pope Pius XII, on 17 May 1955, sent his trusted Cardinal Ottaviani, head of the Vatican's Holy Office, to interrogate Sister Lúcia concerning the sealed contents of the

Third Secret of Fatima. As a result of Ottaviani's interview with Lúcia, the Holy See asked Lúcia's bishop to transfer the Third Secret, still sealed in an envelope, to the Vatican in April 1957. Just before sending the Third Secret to the Vatican, Bishop John Venancio held the sealed envelope up to his lamp. He noted that the sealed envelope contained one sheet of paper with twenty-five lines of written text with ¾-centimeter margins on both sides. When the Third Secret came to the Vatican, it was placed in a safe in the papal apartments, as shown in a photograph in *Paris Match* magazine. Pius XII, as a good and obedient pope, did not open the sealed envelope but submitted to the inscription on the envelope that it should be opened in 1960.

Meanwhile, three clerics exercised immense influence over the dying Pius XII: Bugnini, Montini, and the German Jesuit Augustin Bea. These three crypto-Modernists used the final three years of the pontificate to hatch their plot for a new style of pope, a new council, and new liturgy. Pius XII had not appointed a cardinal secretary of state. He innovated by bifurcating the office of secretary of state and appointing Montini (future Pope Paul VI) as his interior Vatican City affairs secretary and Domenico Cardinal Tardini as his exterior foreign affairs secretary. In effect, it was Montini who ran the Holy See and the papacy from 1955 until the death of Pius XII in 1958. For example, Montini allowed the disgraced papal physician to enter the Papal apartment and photograph the dying Pius XII—photos he sold to newspapers for a profit.

Montini had a dark side, as demonstrated by his friendship with Saul Alinsky. In the late spring of 1958 (months before the death of Pius XII on 9 October 1958), Montini met three times with Jewish-American Leftist and Chicago infiltrator Alinsky through the arrangement of the French philosopher

Jacques Maritain. Maritain was a pseudo-Thomist who had penned the Modernist book *Integral Humanism* in 1935. In this book, Maritain proposed a "new form" of Christendom, rooted in his philosophical, political, and religious pluralism. In brief, it was a prototype for the ideals and goals of Vatican II. (Incidentally, Maritain was the ghost-writer of the *Credo of the People of God*, solemnly proclaimed by Pope Paul VI on 30 June 1968.)

In the mid-1940s, Jacques Maritain became Saul Alinsky's friend and collaborator. Alinksy had worked as a soft-socialist "community organizer" in Chicago since the 1940s, and he had made it his goal to establish fronts of social justice with Protestant and Catholic clergy. Dishonestly, Maritain canonized the agnostic Alinsky as a "practical Thomist."[63] Sadly, Maritain also encouraged Alinsky to publish his infamous infiltration manifesto *Rules for Radicals*, which was dedicated to "the first radical known to man who rebelled against the establishment and did it so effectively that he at least won his own kingdom—Lucifer."[64] So much for Alinsky as a "practical Thomist." The book later became the handbook for Chicago community organizers, especially for the future United States president Barack Obama. The thesis of Alinsky is that a perceived noble end always justifies the means, no matter how vicious or pernicious the means may be. Maritain praised *Rules for Radicals* as, "A great book, admirably free, absolutely fearless, radically revolutionary,"[65] and Maritain

[63] Bernard Doering, *The Philosopher and the Provocateur: The Correspondence of Jacques Maritain and Saul Alinsky* (Notre Dame: University of Notre Dame Press, 1994), xx.

[64] Saul Alinsky, *Rules for Radicals* (New York: Vintage Books, 1972), 4.

[65] Doering, *The Philosopher and the Provocateur*, 110.

received exclusive rights to the French translation. Regarding his admiration for Saul Alinsky, Maritain wrote:

> I see in the Western world no more than three revolutionaries worthy of the name—Eduardo Frei in Chile, Saul Alinsky in America, . . . and myself in France, who am not worth beans, since my call as a philosopher has obliterated my possibilities as an agitator. . . . Saul Alinsky, who is a great friend of mine, is a courageous and admirably staunch organizer of "people's communities" and an anti-racist leader whose methods are as effective as they are unorthodox.[66]

Maritain loved Alinsky; as a teacher to Montini, Maritain wanted Montini to meet Alinsky.

Before the first meeting between Alinksy and Montini in 1958, Maritain wrote to Alinsky assuring him of Montini's enthusiasm: "the new cardinal was reading Saul's books and would contact him soon."[67] Why was Cardinal Montini of Milan studying the books of a Jewish-American agnostic? Montini bore some interest in the ways of organized infiltration and revolution, because he wanted to meet Alinsky in person. We know that at least three personal meetings occurred between the two, because Alinksy says so in a letter to Maritain dated 20 June 1958: "I had three wonderful meetings with Montini and I am sure that you have heard from him since."[68] We don't know what was discussed

[66] Bernard Doering, "Jacques Maritain and His Two Authentic Revolutionaries," *Thomistic Papers* (Houston, TX: Center for Thomistic Studies, 1987), 96.

[67] P. David Finks, *The Radical Vision of Saul Alinsky* (New York: Paulist Press, 1984), 115.

[68] Doering, *The Philosopher and the Provocateur*, 79.

at these meetings, but the admiration between the two men was mutual. That same year, after the death of Pius XII, Alinsky wrote to a friend as follows: "No, I don't know who the next Pope will be, but if it's to be Montini, the drinks will be on me for years to come."[69] In other words, the author of the *Rules for Radicals* could think of no better "radical" pope than Montini. But Montini was not the only radical cardinal undermining the final days of ailing Pope Pius XII.

Since 1946, Pope Pius XII had fallen under the influence of his chosen confessor and spiritual director, Augustine Cardinal Bea, S.J., who, after the death of Pius XII, took as his personal secretary the young Irish priest Father Malachi Martin, S.J. Prior to Bea, the confessor of Pope Pius XII had been the stalwart Thomist theologian Michel-Louis Guérard des Lauriers, O.P., who had helped to write the 1950 dogmatic decree on the bodily Assumption of the Blessed Virgin Mary. For some reason, Pius XII removed his trusted Guérard des Lauriers and began confessing to and receiving spiritual direction from the Jesuit Cardinal Bea.

Cardinal Bea would reveal himself as a Modernist. He openly fought against the imposition of the anti-Modernist oath on clergy at Vatican II. He loved the new "ecumenism" and worked with unbridled determination to appease Jewish rabbis and intellectuals and to remove anything they deemed anti-Semitic from Catholic teaching and liturgy (he would later draft for the Second Vatican Council *Nostra aetate*—the controversial document on the new ecumenism). Bea also advocated the radical liturgical changes being suggested by Bugnini. In fact, Bea had produced a new "Bea Psalter," based on the Hebrew psalms, that would

[69] Finks, *The Radical Vision of Saul Alinsky*, 115.

effectively destroy Gregorian chant, based on the traditional Latin Psalter derived from the Greek Septuagint.

As in *The Lord of the Rings*, J. R. R. Tolkien depicted a dying Théoden, king of Rohan, as under the evil influence of Gríma Wormtongue and Saruman, so the dying Pius XII was truly under the spell of these three false friends: Bugnini, the liturgist; Montini, the secretary; and Bea, the confessor. Ill news is an ill guest. Like King Théoden, his relief would come not by Gandalf but by Gandolfo.

14

Mysterious Conclave of 1958

Pope Pius XII died at Castel Gandolfo on 9 October 1958. Earlier that week, he suffered extreme stomach pain, and his doctor tried unsuccessfully to pump his stomach. He was given Last Rites and prepared for death. The night before he died, he looked at the stars and said: "Look, how beautiful, how great is our Lord." At 3:52 a.m. he smiled, lowered his head, and died. Mother Pascalina recorded that the doctor stated: "The Holy Father did not die because of any specific illness. He was completely exhausted. He was overworked beyond limit. His heart was healthy, his lungs were good. He could have lived another 20 years, had he spared himself."[70]

The papal conclave of 1958 lasted from 25 to 28 October. Fifty-one of the fifty-three living cardinals participated. The two missing cardinals—József Mindszenty and Aloysius Stepinac—had been effectively banned from traveling to Rome by the Communists. Thirty-five votes would attain the two-thirds majority required for electing the pope.

The conservative cardinals supported Giuseppe Cardinal Siri of Genoa, who was young at the age of fifty-two. Siri also seemed to have been delegated by Pope Pius XII as his preferred successor.

[70] Pascalina Lehnert, *Ich durfte Ihm Dienen, Erinnerungen an Papst Pius XII* (Würzburg: Naumann, 1986), 91.

The liberal cardinals supported Giacomo Cardinal Lercaro of Bologna at the ideal age of sixty-seven. The compromise candidate was Angelo Cardinal Roncalli, patriarch of Venice, who possessed more than twenty-five years of international diplomatic service in Bulgaria, Turkey, and France. At the old age of seventy-seven, Cardinal Roncalli would be a short-term pope. Most agreed that Cardinal Siri or Cardinal Roncalli would exit the conclave as pope.

There were no ballots the first day, just discussions. On the second day, Sunday, 26 October 1958, after allegedly four ballots, white smoke billowed out from the chimney of the Sistine Chapel at 6 p.m., signaling the election of a pope. The white smoke continued for a full five minutes. Not only did the smoke signal a papal election, but the bells of Saint Peter's Basilica rang out to confirm it. Vatican Radio announced: "There can be absolutely no doubt. A pope has been elected." The Swiss Guard took their posts, and people gathered in the piazza of Saint Peter's to lay eyes on the new pope and receive his first benediction. The crowd waited for half an hour, and no pope appeared. Vatican Radio announced that a mistake had been made. The crowds dispersed. *Non habemus Papam*.

The legend is that Cardinal Siri was, in fact, elected that day and that he accepted the papacy, choosing (or proposing) the name Gregory XVII. Then there was an intervention by the French cardinals or an outside communication that harm would happen to Siri or his family. Other legends state that the Russians threatened "great destruction" if the anti-Communist Siri was elected. Former FBI consultant Paul L. Williams claims to have seen FBI documents asserting that Cardinal Siri was elected, but these documents either no longer exist or are still classified.[71] We

[71] Paul L. Williams, *The Vatican Exposed* (New York: Prometheus Books, 2003), 90–92.

will never know what happened on the second day of the conclave. The white smoke and bells testify that a pope was elected and that some mistake or misunderstanding occurred. Another version is that the camerlengo Cardinal Masella invalidated the election for some reason.

On the night of Monday, 27 October, a penumbral lunar eclipse appeared over Rome from 5:13 p.m. until 6:36 p.m. The next day, the cardinals elected Cardinal Roncalli, who appeared on the balcony of Saint Peter's as Pope John XXIII—the name of an antipope from the days of the Western Schism. In his old age, he was deemed a transitory pope, but he proved to be one of the most revolutionary popes in Catholic history.

15

Pope John XXIII Opens the Third Secret

The three persons of influence over the ill days of Pope Pius XII—Bugnini, Montini, and Bea—rose to prominence under Pope John XXIII. One of the Pope's first actions as pope in 1958 was to elevate Montini to cardinal.

On 25 January 1959—about three months after his election—Pope John XXIII, to the shock of *some* of the cardinals, announced his intention to call a general council. The secretary of state, Cardinal Tardini, and the newly made Cardinal Montini were enthusiastically supportive. Even more interestingly, the two eminent conservative cardinals Ruffini and Ottaviani supported the idea of a council to reform the Church.

On 17 August 1959, Pope John XXIII had the Third Secret brought to him where he was summering at Castel Gandalfo. Pope John opened the Third Secret of Fatima, even though Lúcia had instructed that it "be opened and read to the world either at her death or in 1960, whichever came first."[72] This is why Pope Pius XII, who had custody of the sealed envelope, had never opened it or read it.

[72] Joaquin Alonso, *La Verdad sobre el Secreto de Fatima* (Madrid: Centro Mariano, 1976), 46–47.

Pope John XXIII disobeyed the inscription. He opened it one year early.

When the sealed envelope arrived, Pope John hesitated and said, "I am waiting to read it with my confessor." We cannot be certain, but his confessor at this time may have been Monsignor Alfredo Cavagna.[73] The Portuguese translator was Monsignor Paulo Jose Tavarez of the Secretariat of State. Cardinal Ottaviani also read the Third Secret, either at this initial reading or later.

Afterward, John XXIII responded only: "This does not concern my pontificate," and, contrary to the instruction of Lúcia and the Blessed Virgin Mary said that it would *not* be published to the world in 1960. The pope, with optimistic hope for fellowship with the world, couldn't bring himself to endorse the ramblings of "prophets of doom." Pope John would silence the pessimistic apocalypse of the Fatima message.

On 8 February 1960, a Vatican press release stated that the Third Secret would not be published in 1960 as expected and ended with this: "Although the Church recognizes the Fatima apparitions, she does not desire to take responsibility for guaranteeing the veracity of the words the three shepherd children said the Virgin Mary had addressed to them." In other words, Pope John XXIII doubted the words of three children.

Cardinal Ottaviani related that Pope John XXIII filed away the Third Secret "in one of those archives which are like a very deep, dark well, to the bottom of which papers fall and no one is able to see them anymore."[74] This may be the reason why so

[73] "Confessor of John XXIII Dies," *New York Times*, May 1, 1970, 35.

[74] Alfredo Cardinal Ottaviani, "Allocution on 11 February 1967 at the Antonianum in Rome." Recorded in the Acta of the Pontifical International Marian Academy.

many assume that there are two parts or two versions of the Third Secret.

Does the Third Secret Have Two Parts?

There are three competing theories about the content of the Third Secret. One is that it is the apocalyptic text released by the Vatican in the year 2000. The second theory is that the text of 2000 is the first part, but that another one-page part exists or has existed. Third, there is the belief that the Third Secret was lost or destroyed in 1959 or 1960 by Pope John XXIII and that it will never be known.

Archbishop Loris Francesco Capovilla, private secretary to Pope John XXIII in 1959, claimed that he was present and saw Pope John XXIII break open the intact seal of the envelope in 1959 and read the Third Secret. Capovilla also stated that he himself read the Third Secret and that it matches the secret released by the Catholic Church in 2000.

The problem with Capovilla' s testimony is that Bishop John Venancio previously testified that the Third Secret was on one sheet of paper. Yet the Third Secret released in 2000 is on four sheets of paper. Moreover, we know from Lúcia's fourth memoir that the Third Secret begins, "In Portugal the dogma of the Faith will always be preserved." But the version of the Third Secret released in 2000 does not contain this phrase except in a footnote.

Furthermore, we know that the Third Secret of Fatima has two parts, one about the pope and one that regards the final words of the Second Secret: "In Portugal, the dogma of the Faith will always be preserved." As explained previously, Pope Pius XII ordered Father Joseph Schweigl to interview Sister Lúcia about the Third Secret in 1952. Father Schweigl said, "I cannot reveal anything of what I learned at Fatima concerning the Third Secret, but I can say that it has two parts: one concerns the pope. The other, logically—although I must say nothing—would have to be the continuation of the words 'In Portugal, the dogma of the Faith will always be preserved.'"[75]

This testimony by Father Schweigl gives rise to the belief of a two-part Third Secret: 3a and 3b. This conforms to the First and Second Secrets, since each of them has a complicated revelation followed by the Blessed Virgin Mary directly explaining what she means and desires. The same would be true of the Third Secret. There should be a vision or revelation followed by the Blessed Virgin Mary directly explaining the vision and what she desires.

The Third Secret document released by the Catholic Church in 2000 is four pages long, and it is about the suffering and murder of the pope. I reproduce here completely and precisely the Third Secret published by Cardinal Ratzinger on behalf of the Congregation for the Doctrine of the Faith on 26 June 2000:

> The third part of the secret revealed at the Cova da Iria-Fátima, on 13 July 1917.
>
> I write in obedience to you, my God, who command me to do so through his Excellency the Bishop of Leiria and through your Most Holy Mother and mine.
>
> After the two parts which I have already explained, at the left of Our Lady and a little above, we saw an Angel with a flaming sword in his left hand. Flashing, it gave out flames that looked as though they would set the world on fire, but they died out in contact with the splendor that Our Lady radiated towards him from her right hand. Pointing to the earth with his right hand, the Angel cried

[75] Michael of the Holy Trinity, *The Whole Truth about Fatima*, 710.

> out in a loud voice: 'Penance, Penance, Penance!' And we saw in an immense light that is God 'something similar to how people appear in a mirror when they pass in front of it' a Bishop dressed in White. "We had the impression that it was the Holy Father."
>
> Other bishops, priests, men, and women religious were going up a steep mountain, at the top of which there was a big Cross of rough-hewn trunks as of a cork-tree with the bark. Before reaching there, the Holy Father passed through a big city half in ruins; and half trembling with halting step, afflicted with pain and sorrow, he prayed for the souls of the corpses he met on his way. Having reached the top of the mountain, on his knees at the foot of the big Cross he was killed by a group of soldiers who fired bullets and arrows at him, and in the same way there died one after another the other bishops, priests, men, and women religious, and various lay people of different ranks and positions. Beneath the two arms of the Cross there were two Angels, each with a crystal aspersorium in his hand, in which they gathered up the blood of the Martyrs and with it sprinkled the souls that were making their way to God.[76]

The vision depicts an angel with fiery sword to the left of Our Lady calling out, "Penance. Penance. Penance." A "bishop in white" who is presumed to be the pope is then shot down, along with "bishops, priests, men, and women religious, and various

[76] The original Portuguese version and facsimile version of the four pages is available on the Vatican website, http://www.vatican.va/roman_curia/congregations/cfaith/documents/rc_con_cfaith_doc_20000626_message-fatima_en.html.

lay people." The vision is very difficult to interpret and lacks the statement "In Portugal, the dogma of the Faith will always be preserved."

This is the revelatory part of the Third Secret, or what I call Secret 3a. Yet there must be a second part of the Third Secret, as Schweigl says, in which the Blessed Virgin Mary explains what is meant by this vision. Furthermore, we know from Lúcia that it begins with "In Portugal, the dogma of the Faith will always be preserved." And to date, the Catholic Church has never released this one-page document of words by the Blessed Virgin Mary, beginning with "In Portugal . . ." This means that there is another section (Secret 3b) of the Third Secret of Fatima that is not yet public.

To substantiate the existence of a Secret 3b, there is an interview with Cardinal Ratzinger published in the 11 November 1984 edition of *Jesus* magazine. Cardinal Ratzinger claimed to have read the Third Secret and said that it is about "the importance of the Last Things" and about the "dangers threatening the faith and the life of the Christian and therefore of the world." Ratzinger further explained that "if it is not made public, at least for the time being, it is in order to prevent religious prophecy from being mistaken for a quest for the sensational."[77] And yet the version of the Third Secret released in 2000 contains nothing about the dangers threatening the faith of the Christian.

In an interview with Charles Fiore, Malachi Martin provided another account of the reading of the Third Secret. Martin claimed that while serving as secretary to Cardinal Bea, he happened upon this papal reading of the Third Secret in 1959: "I

[77] Michael of the Holy Trinity, *The Whole Truth about Fatima*, 822–823.

cooled my heels in the corridor outside the Holy Father's apartments, while my boss, Cardinal Bea, was inside debating with the Holy Father, and with a group of other bishops and priests, and two young Portuguese seminarians, who translated the letter, a single page, written in Portuguese, for all those in the room."[78] Here again we see that the Third Secret is on a "single page" and not four pages, as is the case of the Third Secret documents released in 2000.

Malachi Martin presents certain details that contradict our known facts about the initial reading by John XXIII. The initial reading happened at Castel Gandolfo. Martin places himself "in the corridor outside the Holy Father's apartment" back at the Vatican. Martin also refers to two Portuguese seminarians, whereas the official account has one Portuguese priest. Martin also places his exposure to the Third Secret in February 1960: "Early a.m., February 1960—before I read it, I had to take a vow not to reveal it. It would be a shock, no doubt, some would become very angry." Either Malachi Martin has invented a sensationalized version to place himself into the events, or he was present at a second reading that included Cardinal Bea and perhaps Cardinal Ottaviani (who seems to have read it later). Martin would not reveal what he claims to have read, but he did reply in this interview:

> I consider Fatima to be the key event in the declining fortune of the Roman Catholic organization for the near future of the Church in the third millennium, the defining event. In Rome there are men among the great with

[78] Audio recording by Brian Doran, "Malachi Martin: God's Messenger—In the Words of Those Who Knew Him Best," 11 August 2000.

strong wills, all their lives engaged in macro-government, not merely in religion, but in state. They would not touch this with a ten-foot pole. Pope John Paul II is an ardent supporter of a one world government. He wants to bring in his brand of Christianity, of course. To the UN he said, "I am a member of humanity." This is no longer Pius IX and Pius X, who said, "I am the vicar of Christ." Completely absent is the Kingship of Christ.

For reasons I have documented elsewhere, I do not trust Malachi Martin unreservedly, but his testimony does seem to conform to the words of those who had close access to Lúcia and to the Third Secret:

> The Secret of Fatima speaks neither of atomic bombs, nor nuclear warheads, nor Pershing missiles, nor SS-20's. Its content concerns only our faith. To identify the Secret with catastrophic announcements or with a nuclear holocaust is to deform the meaning of the message. The loss of faith of a continent is worse than the annihilation of a nation; and it is true that faith is continually diminishing in Europe.[79]

> Thus it is quite possible that in this intermediate period which is in question [the time after 1960], the text makes concrete references to the crisis of the Faith of the Church and to the negligence of the pastors themselves.
>
> —Father Joaquin Alonso, C.M.F., official Fatima archivist[80]

[79] Bishop Alberto Cosme do Amaral, public statement made in Vienna, Austria, on 10 September 1984.

[80] Michael of the Holy Trinity, *The Whole Truth About Fatima*, 687.

> It [the Third Secret] has nothing to do with Gorbachev. The Blessed Virgin was alerting us against apostasy in the Church.
>
> —Cardinal Silvio Oddi[81]

> In the Third Secret it is foretold, among other things, that the great apostasy in the Church will begin at the top."
>
> —Cardinal Mario Luigi Ciappi, O.P.[82]

The full Third Secret describes the great apostasy in the Church.

[81] Maike Hickson, "Cardinal Oddi on Fatima's Third Secret, the Second Vatican Council, and Apostasy," *One Peter Five*, 28 November 2017.

[82] "Alice von Hildebrand Sheds New Light on Fatima."

16

Vatican II — Modernism on Parade

Pope John XXIII opened the Second Vatican Council on 11 October 1962, saying, "The prophets of doom always talk as though the present in comparison to the past is becoming worse and worse. But I see mankind as entering upon a *new order* and perceive in this a divine plan."[83] It's worth noting that there were only three acknowledged contemporary Catholic prophets or seers at the time of Pope John XXIII: the three children of Fatima. Did Pope John have them in mind when he condemned the "prophets of doom"? Regardless, this opening statement displays the agenda of Freemasonry. Prophets of doom are condemned. The world isn't getting worse; it's getting better. And John XXIII says he sees "mankind as entering upon a new order."

Devout Catholics often defend Vatican II by saying that it was "hijacked," and that is certainly the case, but the question is when, and by whom. As will become clear, Pope John XXIII, and his favorites, Bugnini, Bea, and Montini, had already set the optimistic new order, or *novus ordo*, agenda. Bugnini would create the *novus ordo* liturgy; Bea would create *novus ordo* ecumenism

[83] From the address of Pope John XXIII on 11 October 1962 at the opening of Vatican Council II, italics added.

and primacy of conscience over dogma; and Montini would become the *novus ordo* pope.

Vatican II opened with more than two thousand bishops present, along with their periti (experts) and representatives from the Orthodox churches and Protestant communities. Two years had been spent preparing for the Council, in which about a dozen commissions worked to produce preliminary documents. The first act of the Council was to reject schemata, or drafts, from these preparatory sessions. New ones were created by new commissions. Pope John approved.

Alarmed by the sudden shift in direction, Archbishop Marcel Lefebvre met with two Brazilian bishops—Geraldo de Proença Sigaud of Diamantina and José Maurício da Rocha of Bragança Paulista—to form a resistance party of conservatives. Archbishop Lefebvre organized an informal steering committee that eventually became the Coetus Internationalis Patrum (CIP), or "International Group of Fathers," which was joined by Bishop Antonio de Castro Mayer of Campos, Brazil, and the Abbot of Solesmes, Jean Prou, OSB. The CIP grew to incorporate 250 bishops (and up to nine cardinals) from Canada, Chile, China, and Pakistan. Two hundred fifty bishops of the 2,400 bishops participating in Vatican II means that the CIP under Lefebvre had captured more than 10 percent of the Council's bishops.[84] The CIP became the thorn in the side of the Modernist agenda as the Council continued over the next two years.

[84] John O'Malley S.J., *What Happened at Vatican II* (Cambridge, MA: Harvard University Press, 2008), Kindle edition location 455.

Assembly of the Second Vatican Council, Saint Peter's Basilica, Rome

Having rejected the original preparations, the Council adjourned on 8 December 1962 so that the new commissions could prepare documents for the next session, in 1963. Pope John XXIII died on 3 June 1963, bringing a definitive cessation in the Second Vatican Council.

17

Conclave of 1963: Paul VI

The crypto-Modernists wanted the Second Vatican Council to proceed. The election of an anti-Council cardinal might end the council or severely change its agenda from John XXIII's prescription for "mankind as entering upon a *new order*." The conclave lasted from 19 to 21 June 1963 and was the largest conclave ever assembled. Papal elections had ranged from twelve to sixty cardinals. This conclave included eighty-two cardinal electors, of which eighty participated. Once again Cardinal Mindszenty was blocked by the Communists of Hungary and could not travel to Rome. And Cardinal Carlos María de la Torre of Quito, Ecuador, at eighty-nine years old, was too old and weak to make the journey to Europe.

The two leading cardinals going into the conclave were Siri and Montini. Cardinal Siri represented the old guard of Pope Pius XII and had spoken against the proposed reforms of the Second Vatican Council. Cardinal Montini, however, was openly associated with the agenda of John XXIII and an open advocate for the proposed reforms of the Council.

Pope John XXIII may have served a short pontificate, but he had busied himself stacking the College of Cardinals with his men. Of the eighty voting cardinals, forty-five had been selected by John XXIII (eight were appointed by Pius XI and twenty-seven by Pius XII). Fifty-six percent of the cardinals were appointees of Pope John. It seemed certain that the Second Vatican Council would resume under a cardinal of his choosing. It would be difficult for Cardinal Siri to capture the two-thirds majority over Cardinal Montini.

On the first day, as is customary, there was no voting. It is reported that the conservative cardinals formed one bloc around Siri to prevent the election of Montini. On the second day, after four ballots, there was still no pope. Allegedly, by the end of these first four ballots, Montini was only four votes short of the two-thirds majority. The next day, after the sixth ballot, white smoke emerged from the Sistine Chapel at 11:22 a.m. Cardinal Ottaviani (who had no doubt voted for Cardinal Siri), announced to the crowd the election of Cardinal Montini, who had taken the name Paul VI. To the disappointment of the crowds (and the world), Pope Paul VI did not give the traditional Urbi et Orbi blessing (to which is attached an indulgence just by hearing it), but instead gave the shorter blessing of a bishop. Pope Paul VI's first act as pope signified the direction for the rest of his pontificate: *aggiornamento*, or "updating."

18

Crypto-Modernism and *Nouvelle Théologie*

The first task of Pope Paul VI was to ensure that the Second Vatican Council would proceed as previously planned. He reduced the proposed schemata drafts to seventeen and set dates. To the shock of many cardinals, Pope Paul VI explained that he would invite lay Catholics and *non-Catholics* to participate in the Council. This had never happened previously, unless you count the presence of the emperor Constantine at the First Ecumenical Council of Nicaea.

Pope Paul VI advocated what came to be recognized as the *nouvelle théologie*, or "new theology." Beginning in the 1940s, when the vigilant policies of Pope Pius X against Modernism had been relaxed, Catholic theologians began to push the limits of rationalism and naturalism through dissimulation. They paraded their theology with a disdain for Scholasticism and a return (*ressourcement*) to the Church Fathers. They tended to prefer Origen and the Eastern Church Fathers. At root, theologians espousing the *nouvelle théologie* showed contempt for the bullet-point precision of Saint Thomas Aquinas.

The alarm was sounded as early as 1946 by the saintly and eminent Thomistic theologian Father Réginald Garrigou-Lagrange,

O.P., in his article "The New Theology (*Nouvelle Théologie*): Where Is It Going?"[85] Garrigou-Lagrange did not mince words. Theologians promoting the *nouvelle théologie* were leading to Modernism and unbelief, he said. He wrote that their appeal to *ressourcement* was dishonest. Bugnini later took a page from their game book and played the same trick. He claimed to resource and restore the ancient Roman Rite but ended up creating something entirely new—the *novus ordo*.

The so-called *ressourcement* or *nouvelle* theologians would become the prominent theologians of the 1960s under Pope Paul VI. They and their writings would become the intellectual foundation of the so-called spirit of Vatican II. They included the following:

- Pierre Teilhard de Chardin (French, Jesuit; died in 1955)
- Hans Urs von Balthasar (Swiss, Jesuit)
- Louis Bouyer (French, Oratorian)
- Henri de Lubac (French, Jesuit)
- Jean Daniélou (French, Jesuit)
- Jean Mouroux (French, diocesan)
- Joseph Ratzinger (German)
- Walter Kasper (German)
- Yves Congar (French, Dominican)
- Karl Rahner (German, Jesuit)
- Hans Küng (Swiss)
- Edward Schillebeeckx (Belgian, Dominican)
- Marie-Dominique Chenu (French, Dominican)

Most of these theologians were suspected of heresy during the Pontificate of Pius XII, especially Congar, Daniélou, de Lubac,

[85] Réginald Garrigou-Lagrange O.P., "La nouvelle théologie: où va-telle?" *Angelicum* 23 (1946): 126–145.

Küng, Rahner, and Schillebeeckx.[86] These theologians did not simply return to primitive Christianity; they obliterated the traditional Catholic distinction between grace and nature. They sought to make everything grace, and by doing so, they, in fact, reduced everything to the natural, so that the natural longings of every human became the means of salvation. Hence, all human nature itself is "open" to attaining salvation. This means that liturgy should be less supernatural and that other religions are "open" as means of salvation. This theology necessitated a new liturgy, a new ecumenism, and a new form of Catholicism. It was Freemasonic naturalism cloaked with quotations of the Church Fathers. The *nouvelle théologie* was a frontal attack on Thomas Aquinas and the Thomistic tradition represented by Garrigou-Lagrange.

Pope Pius XII's 1950 encyclical *Humani generis* is a direct criticism of *nouvelle théologie* and of Henri de Lubac in particular. De Lubac's influential *Surnaturel* of 1946 especially comes under attack in *Humani generis*. In *Surnaturel*, de Lubac claims that human nature is naturally ordered to supernatural fulfillment in the Beatific Vision and that the Scholastic teaching of pure nature in the human person is false and a corruption of the teaching of Saint Thomas Aquinas. *Humani generis* contradicts de Lubac and rightly teaches that rational persons (humans and angels) are not per se naturally oriented to supernatural beatitude. *Humani generis* is a rare case in the twentieth century when a Catholic theologian was refuted and corrected by a pope. It has long been rumored that Garrigou-Lagrange (a friend of Pope Pius XII) was the ghost writer of *Humani generis*. De Lubac

[86] Roberto de Mattei, *The Second Vatican Council: An Unwritten Story* (Fitzwilliam, NH: Loreto Publications, 2012), 188.

pulled the book and later corrected it and re-released it as *Le Mystère du surnaturel*.

After this encyclical in 1950, the battle was drawn between the traditional theologians who favored Thomas Aquinas, Scholasticism, and Pope Pius X (represented by Réginald Garrigou-Lagrange) and the *ressourcement* theologians (represented by Henri de Lubac).

Pope Pius XII not only sided with Garrigou-Lagrange in 1950; he also canonized Pope Pius X. This was another blow to the *ressourcement* camp. Yet, as reported above, Pius XII entered his long, debilitating illness around 1954. From that time, the influences of Bea, Bugnini, and Montini took over. Between 1954 and 1958 the *ressourcement* camp built their influence to elect John XXIII and then Paul VI.

19

Theological Infiltration of Vatican II

The engineers of Vatican II were Karl Rahner, Edward Schillebeeckx, Hans Küng, Henri de Lubac, and Yves Congar. All five men were held under suspicion of Modernism under Pius XII. Karl Rahner, S.J. had a greater influence than any other on the theology Vatican II—so much so that one might say that Vatican II is simply Rahnerianism. He led the German progressives at Vatican II and was accompanied by his two brilliant protégés, Father Hans Küng and Father Joseph Ratzinger. The Jesuit was prolific, and by the opening of the Council in 1962, he had written enough articles and books to fill five volumes. Cardinal Ottaviani attempted to convince Pius XII to excommunicate Rahner on three occasions, all to no avail.

His fortune flipped when John XXIII appointed Rahner as a peritus, or expert, at Vatican II, and he was accompanied by his friend Joseph Ratzinger. Rahner was charged with reframing the doctrine of the Church for modern times, and the result was the Rahnerian document *Lumen gentium*. Rahner introduced a new ecclesiology in which the Church of Christ is not *the* Catholic Church but rather "subsists in the Catholic Church."[87] This

[87] Second Vatican Council, Dogmatic Constitution on the Church *Lumen gentium* (21 November 1964), no. 8.

seems to contradict the teaching of Pope Pius XII in his 1943 encyclical *Mystici Corporis* that the Mystical Body of Christ and the Catholic Church are one and the same entity.

For Rahner, there are many "anonymous Christians." These are people of goodwill who may be professing Protestants, Jews, Muslims, Buddhists, Hindus, pagans, or even atheists. By their goodwill and openness to the transcendent, they, too, are saved and are related to the Church. For this reason, the Church only "subsists in" the Catholic Church. Beyond the Catholic Church is the wider "People of God," who include not just Catholics but all people of goodwill who profess other religions.[88] This theology opens the way for John XXIII's optimistic approach to the world and to the religious ecumenism of Vatican II. Rather than striving to convert all nations and people to Christ in the Catholic Church through baptism, Catholics would now accompany all people in their spiritual journeys. The Catholic Church became a pilgrim church calling not for conversion but for conversation. As Rahner taught, the Catholic Church was the *sacramentum mundi*—the "sacrament of the world." Pope Paul VI would pick up with this concept and favor the term "People of God." It remains a buzzword for theologians and popes even in our day.

Rahner was a student of the poisonous philosophy of Heidegger, and he saw only the existential present moment as counting. Hence, he reinterpreted all Christian doctrines in this light. Rahner said that Jesus died in history but that His

[88] This also finds its way into Eucharistic Prayer III: "To our departed brothers and sisters and to all who were pleasing to you at their passing from this life, give kind admittance to your kingdom."

Resurrection did not occur in historical time.[89] He saw the Resurrection of Christ as only an existential "vindication" by God. It's all very slippery, but it touches on how Rahner understands the Incarnation, the Resurrection, the founding of the Church, and Church history. He even posits that Christ is the one who is saved: "We are saved because this man who is one of us has been saved by God, and God has thereby made his salvific will present in the world historically, really and irrevocably."[90] Sadly, this flimsy theology is the backdrop for Vatican II and *Lumen gentium*.

Two other Jesuits would serve a key role in the two most controversial documents of the Council: *Dignitatis humanae* and *Nostra aetate*. *Dignitatis humanae*, the Second Vatican Council's Declaration on Religious Freedom, reframed Catholic teaching on religious liberty. The document was the brainchild of the German Jesuit Cardinal Bea but was crafted by the American Jesuit John Courtney Murray. It was promulgated at the last minute, on 7 December 1965—the day before Pope Paul VI officially closed the Second Vatican Council.

It is still debated whether *Dignitatis humanae* asserts a divinely granted right to believe a false religion. In Catholic moral theology, no one has a right to perform an evil. No one has a right to break the Ten Commandments, which include "Thou shalt have no other gods before me." Hence, the Hindu cannot appeal to a God-given right to worship his many gods. The worship of a false god is an intrinsic evil and never permitted by natural law and

[89] Karl Rahner, *Foundations of Christian Faith: An Introduction to the Idea of Christianity*, trans. William V. Dych (New York: Seabury Press, 1978), 264–277.

[90] Ibid., 284.

the Decalogue. A human person does not possess the "right" to procure an abortion or to worship Satan. Previously, Catholics had sought to grant religious liberty *for Catholics* and had merely tolerated other religions. But *Dignitatis humanae* seems to suggest that Catholics should work for the religious liberty of all (false) religions on equal footing with Catholicism.

Catholic history is full of stories of missionaries, such as Saint Boniface, who destroyed the sacred totem and idols of the pagans. Boniface did not recognize the dignity of German pagans who venerated the sacred oak—rather, he chopped it down with his own hands. After he preached faith and baptism in Christ to the pagans, the newly baptized converts built a church out of its wood. In a similar way, Saint Benedict went to Cassino, where country folk still worshipped Apollo at an ancient temple surrounded by a grove. "The man of God coming to that place broke the idol, overthrew the altar, burned the groves, and of the temple of Apollo made a chapel of St. Martin. Where the profane altar had stood, he built a chapel of St. John; and by continual preaching he converted many of the people there about."[91] The ancient saints and missionaries physically destroyed paganism with their own hands and preached Christ with their mouths.

The second hotly debated text of Vatican II is the Declaration on the Relation of the Church with Non-Christian Religions, titled *Nostra aetate*, in which "the Church examines more closely her relationship to non-Christian religions."[92] The document

[91] Pope Pius XII recounts this story of Saint Benedict in his Encyclical *Fulgens radiatur* (21 March 1947), no. 11.

[92] Second Vatican Council, Declaration on the Relation of the Church with Non-Christian Religions *Nostra aetate* (28 October 1965), no. 1.

was overseen by Cardinal Bea but drafted by Father Gregory Baum, who would later leave the priesthood and marry a close female friend, Shirley Flynn. Despite his heterosexual marriage, he was openly homosexual, admitting that he had loved another laicized priest in the 1980s. In his later years, he was an advocate for LGBT rights before dying in 2017. Hence, a man who ended as a proponent of gay rights was the mastermind behind this Vatican II document.

The document directly addresses the state of Jews, Muslims, Hindus, Buddhists, and all other non-Christian religions. It contains assertions that have been questioned, such as this: "In Hinduism, men contemplate the divine mystery."[93] How do polytheists contemplate the divine mystery? Do they do so in the same way as Catholic monks or angels in heaven? Regarding Buddhism, the document reads "Buddhism, in its various forms, realizes the radical insufficiency of this changeable world; it teaches a way by which men, in a devout and confident spirit, may be able either to acquire the state of perfect liberation, or attain, by their own efforts or through higher help, supreme illumination."[94] How is it that Buddhism "teaches a way by which men . . . may be able to acquire the state of perfect liberation"? Is that the state of perfection about which Saint Teresa of Avila speaks? Is it truly perfect liberation? And how do Buddhists attain "higher help [for] supreme illumination"? Is this the same illumination that the baptized receive through the sacraments, prayer, and penance?

Regarding Muslims, *Nostra aetate* reads: "The Church regards with esteem also the Moslems. They adore the one God, living

93 Ibid., no. 2.

94 Ibid.

and subsisting in Himself; merciful and all-powerful, the Creator of heaven and earth, who has spoken to men; they take pains to submit wholeheartedly to even His inscrutable decrees, just as Abraham, with whom the faith of Islam takes pleasure in linking itself, submitted to God."[95] Do Muslims adore the Trinity rightly, or do they merely aim their worship toward a philosophical God? Do they really "submit wholeheartedly to His inscrutable decrees"? Do they submit to the divine decree regarding baptism, monogamy, and Sunday obligation? These words are patently false or tremendously stretched.

One can easily see that Pope Paul VI's eager enthusiasm for ecumenism is rooted in this document that presupposes that false religions can and do lift the soul to "perfect liberation," "supreme illumination," and "submission to His inscrutable decrees." Pope Leo XIII and Pope Saint Pius X would not have agreed with these theological assertions, but Freemasons would agree wholeheartedly that any and all religions suffice to illuminate humanity. Whether Pope Paul VI was indeed a Freemason has never been substantiated, but his thinking conformed to Freemasonic goals so much that even the venerable Padre Pio once quipped after the election of Paul VI: "Courage, courage, courage! For the Church is already invaded by Freemasonry," adding also, "Freemasonry has already arrived at the slippers of the Pope."[96] No doubt the Freemasons rejoiced when, during

[95] Ibid., no. 3.

[96] Original Italian: "Coraggio, coraggio, coraggio! perché la Chiesa è già invasa dalla Massoneria, aggiungendo: La Massoneria è già arrivata alle pantofole del Papa." Franco Adessa, *Chi è don Luigi Villa?* (Oconomowoc, WI: Apostolate of Our Lady of Good Success, 2011), 6. Padre Pio said this regarding Paul VI toward

Vatican II, Pope Paul VI ascended to the altar of Saint Peter's, removed his papal tiara and laid it on the altar to signify that he renounced the glory and power of the world and sought only to accompany the world as one without a crown. The days of Pope Pius X were definitively over.

Pope Paul VI promulgated *Dignitatis humanae* on 7 December 1965, and the next day he closed the Second Vatican Council and stated: "The magisterium of the Church did not wish to pronounce itself under the form of extraordinary dogmatic pronouncements."[97] This effectively hamstrung the Council. It's true that theological statements are made throughout the Conciliar documents. *Yet the Council made no extraordinary dogmatic pronouncements*. Nothing binding came from Vatican II. Paul VI clarified this a little over one month later when he explained: "In view of the pastoral nature of the Council, it has avoided proclaiming in an extraordinary manner any dogma carrying the mark of infallibility."[98] By a divine miracle, the pope of Vatican II taught that Vatican II contained no extraordinary dogma and did not carry the mark of infallibility—meaning the documents of Vatican II are fallible and may contain error. Unlike the previous twenty ecumenical councils, the pope placed an asterisk next to Vatican II.

In the years following the Council, the crypto-Modernist theologians created a theological journal by which they could continue and promote the so-called spirit of Vatican II and the *aggiornamento* of the Catholic Church. The founders of this new

---

the end of 1963. The Italian word used by Padre Pio, *pantofole*, is the term usually used to refer to the slippers worn by the pope.

[97] Pope Paul VI, Discourse closing Vatican II, 7 December 1965.

[98] Pope Paul VI, Audience of 12 January 1966.

journal were the victorious theologians of the *nouvelle théologie* who had drafted and composed the documents of Vatican II:

- Karl Rahner
- Hans Küng
- Edward Schillebeeckx
- Joseph Ratzinger
- Henri de Lubac
- Anton van den Boogaard
- Paul Brand
- Yves Congar
- Johann Baptist Metz

The journal was aptly named *Concilium* and was created in order to disseminate the spirit of the recently completed Council. For the crypto-Modernist theologians, the previous twenty councils remained in the attic. As Karl Rahner had emphasized, only the existential present moment was required to apply theology pastorally to the needs of modern humanity. To disseminate their bolder theology to colleges and seminaries, *Concilium* was published five times annually in six languages: Croatian, English, German, Italian, Portuguese, and Spanish. Father Schillebeeckx had admitted, "We used ambiguous phrases during the [Second Vatican] Council and we know how we will interpret them afterwards."[99] The journal *Concilium* would be the means by which they would "interpret them afterwards."

Concilium went off the rails. Hans Küng and Edward Schillebeeckx especially led the guard into open heterodoxy as they challenged the historicity of the Immaculate Conception, the virgin birth of Christ, the Resurrection of Christ, the miracle

[99] Cited in Marcel Lefebvre, *Open Letter to Confused Catholics* (Kansas City: Angelus Press, 1992), 106.

of transubstantiation, the assumption of Mary, and other de fide dogmas of the Catholic Church. *Concilium* theologians also advocated more extreme liturgical reforms for the sake of enculturation and pastoralism.

Concerned over the increasingly radical direction of *Concilium*, several theologians associated with *aggiornamento* hit the brakes and determined to create a new journal that sought to remain within the boundaries of Catholic orthodoxy; they named it *Communio*. The founders of *Communio* in 1972 were Joseph Ratzinger, Henri de Lubac, Hans Urs von Balthasar, Walter Kasper, Marc Ouellet, and Louis Bouyer. The years following the implementation of the Novus Ordo Mass in 1970 were turbulent in the Catholic Church, and factions arose. Traditionalists held to Thomism and the moral theology of Saint Alphonsus Liguori and begged for the traditional Latin Mass. They were led by Cardinal Ottaviani and Archbishop Lefebvre. Rahner, Küng, and Schillebeeckx continued in their giddy enthusiasm for Modernism under Paul VI, but Ratzinger, de Lubac, and Balthasar retreated to a more conservative interpretation of Vatican II. This latter group, while embracing *nouvelle théologie*, would develop the theology and language of the "Reform of the Reform" and the "Hermeneutic of Continuity." Pope John Paul II certainly embraced this "Reform of the Reform" persuasion. He enthusiastically tapped Ratzinger in 1981 to serve as his chief theological adviser as prefect of the Congregation for the Doctrine of the Faith.

The Ratzingerian epic from 1981 to his resignation from the papacy in 2013 is a thirty-two-year project to restrain the "spirit of Vatican II" released by Rahner, Küng, Schillebeeckx, and even by Ratzinger himself in the 1960s. The legacy of the "John Paul conservatives" or "Ratzingerians" lived on through *Communio* but also through the books of Ignatius Press, which widely published the works of John Paul II, Ratzinger (Benedict XVI), Balthasar, de Lubac, Ouellet, Schönborn, and Bouyer and created the Ratzingerian legacy for theologians of the 1980s through the 2000s. Magazines such as *First Things*, the programming of EWTN, the advent of Catholic radio, and the writings of George Weigel and Father Richard John Neuhaus further popularized what it meant to be a "JP2 Catholic" or a "JP2 priest." And yet the Catholic Church still leaned toward Hans Küng-liberalism in nearly every diocese, chancery, and seminary.

While John Paul II had little patience for the traditionalists, the later years of Ratzinger (Benedict XVI) show growing sympathy for the traditionalist position and the possibility of a smaller, more faithful Church. In fact, it seems that Ratzinger eventually became one of the "prophets of doom" that John XXIII warned us about in his spirit of optimism.

20

Infiltration of the Liturgy

I hear around me reformers who want to dismantle the Holy Sanctuary, destroy the universal flame of the Church, discard all her adornments, and smite her with remorse for her historic past."

—Cardinal Eugenio Pacelli (future Pope Pius XII) to Count Enrico P. Galeazzi

Pope Paul VI's opening address to the resumed Second Vatican Council indicated that the Council would focus not on dogma but on the role of the bishop, ecumenism and unity with non-Catholics, and dialogue with the contemporary world. On 4 December 1963, the Council approved its first constitution—the Constitution on the Sacred Liturgy titled *Sacrosanctum concilium*. It passed with a vote of 2,147 to 4. The goal of the document was to reform the Catholic liturgy so that the laity would more actively participate in the worship of God.

Pope Pius X had previously urged that all Catholics learn to participate in the Holy Sacrifice of the Mass in his 1903 motu proprio on music, titled in Italian *Tra le sollecitudini*:

> Filled as We are with a most ardent desire to see the true Christian spirit flourish in every respect and be preserved by all the faithful, We deem it necessary to provide before

> anything else for the sanctity and dignity of the temple, in which the faithful assemble for no other object than that of acquiring this spirit from its foremost and indispensable font, which is the *active participation* in the most holy mysteries and in the public and solemn prayer of the Church.[100]

Liturgical scholars note that this is the first historical exhortation to "active participation" of the laity in the liturgy. The text, however, has been exaggerated in the Italian translation, which reads "*partecipazione attiva*," and also in the English version, which reads "active participation." In the original Latin version of the text, the qualifier "active" is nowhere present: "*quae est participatio divinorum mysteriorum*,"[101] or "which is the participation in the divine mysteries." The idea of "active participation" is not the official Latin version of the text. It has been added. Even if "active participation" is included, the context of the document is music and Gregorian chant and, indeed, Pope Pius X did desire the congregation to know the sung responses and participate in Gregorian chant.

The Second Vatican Council, however, meant something quite different by "active participation" when it stated:

> The rite of the Mass is to be revised in such a way that the intrinsic nature and purpose of its several parts, as also the connection between them, may be more clearly manifested, and that devout and *active participation* by the faithful may be more easily achieved.

100 Pope Pius X, *Tra le sollecitudini* (22 November 1903).
101 Pope Pius X, Motu Proprio *SS.MI D. N. PII PP. X de musica sacra. Acta Sanctae Sedis*, 388.

> For this purpose the rites are to be simplified, due care being taken to preserve their substance; elements which, with the passage of time, came to be duplicated, or were added with but little advantage, are now to be discarded; other elements which have suffered injury through accidents of history are now to be restored to the vigor which they had in the days of the holy Fathers, as may seem useful or necessary.[102]

Here the baptismal "royal priesthood" of the laity is confused and conflated with the ordained ministerial priesthood. The document explains that the need for "active participation" requires "rites to be simplified." Why? Because laypeople need to be able to perform them to fulfill "active participation." This is a dangerous approach to "simplifying" the Roman Rite. The text and rubrics of the Holy Mass and liturgy are not subject to simplifying rites. Note also that *Sacrosanctum* refers to the traditional Roman Rite with terms such as "duplicated," "added with but little advantage," "discarded," "suffered injury," and "accidents of history." The liturgy is reduced to utility, since the rites will be henceforth changed "as may seem useful or necessary." This is Bugnini's approach to liturgy—and it was also the approach used by Martin Luther for Lutherans and by Thomas Cranmer and Martin Bucer for the Anglican liturgy.

Lex orandi, lex credendi: the law of prayer is the law of belief. If you change the liturgy and prayers, you will necessarily change the Faith. *Sacrosanctum concilium* also called for the vernacular, and by 1965, modifications to the liturgy of the Holy Sacrifice

[102] Second Vatican Council, Constitution on the Sacred Liturgy *Sacrosanctum concilium* (4 December 1963), no. 50.

of the Mass were made *ad experimentum*, as Bugnini had successfully achieved ten years previously in 1955 with the Holy Week Reform. Pope Paul VI immediately began making modifications to the liturgy to conform it to the new "active participation" of *Sacrosanctum concilium*:

- 1964: Pope Paul VI appoints Bugnini secretary of the Council for the Implementation of the Constitution on the Liturgy.
- 1964: Pope Paul VI reduces the Eucharistic fast to one hour before reception of Holy Communion.
- 1965: Pope Paul VI allows an experimental missal. The changes include the following:

    Use of the vernacular is permitted.

    Freestanding table altars are encouraged.

    The psalm *Judica* is omitted at the beginning of Mass.

    The Last Gospel is omitted at the end of Mass.

    The Leonine Prayers after Low Mass (including the Saint Michael Prayer), ratified by Pope Leo XIII, are suppressed.
- 1966: National episcopal conferences are ratified by Pope Paul VI's motu proprio *Ecclesiae sanctae*.
- 1967: The document *Tres abhinc annos* simplifies the rubrics and vestments of the priest. Concelebration of priests at the altar is made standard. Holy Communion under both species is now permitted to the laity.
- 1967: Married deacons are allowed by Pope Paul VI in *Sacrum diaconatus ordinem*.
- 1968: Pope Paul VI changes the *Rite of Ordination for Bishops, Priests, and Deacons*.

- 1969: Pope Paul VI grants the indult for Holy Communion in the hand to nations where it is "already the custom" (Holland, Belgium, France, and Germany).
- 1969: Pope Paul VI promulgates the *Novus Ordo Missae* with his Apostolic Constitution *Missale Romanum* of 3 April.
- 1969: Pope Paul VI appoints Bugnini secretary of the Congregation for Divine Worship in May.
- 1970: *Novus Ordo Missale* of Pope Paul VI is published on 26 March.

All these changes were drafted and implemented by Bugnini, who finished his work by being appointed secretary of the Congregation for Divine Worship. Most notably, the Freemasonic Bugnini arranged for the abolishing of the powerful Leonine Prayers after Low Mass going back to Pope Leo XIII (three Hail Marys, the Salve Regina, the prayer to Saint Michael, and prayer for defense of the Church). The naive optimism of Vatican II wrongly led Pope Paul VI to remove the protection of Our Lady and Saint Michael over the liturgy and the universal Catholic Church.

Before Bugnini's Mass was formally published to the world in 1970, a group of holy cardinals and bishops joined together in one last-ditch effort to block the Pauline-Bugnini reforms over concerns that the Bugnini Mass promoted theological error. This was the Ottaviani Intervention of 1969.

21

Ottaviani Intervention against Pope Paul VI

When the 1969 *Novus Ordo Missae* of Bugnini was unveiled, the stalwart French missionary Archbishop Marcel Lefebvre gathered twelve theologians to study the liturgy thoroughly. Led by the eminent Thomist theologian Michel-Louis Guérard des Lauriers, O.P., they produced an academic presentation for Pope Paul VI titled *A Short Critical Study of the Novus Ordo Missae*. Cardinal Ottaviani and Antonio Cardinal Bacci wrote an introduction to this document and presented the study to Pope Paul VI on 25 September 1969. For this reason, *A Short Critical Study of the Novus Ordo Missae* is most often referred to as the "Ottaviani Intervention." The cover letter by Cardinal Ottaviani and Cardinal Bacci explains that the Novus Ordo departs from the theology of the Council of Trent in text and in theology and will cause confusion among priests and laity alike.

They argued that the Novus Ordo Mass undercut the oblationary, sacrificial, and sacerdotal doctrines of the Council of Trent. In other words, the new Mass leaned toward Protestantism. This was not a baseless accusation. Six Protestant scholars had been invited to Vatican II to participate in discussions regarding ecumenism and liturgy: A. Raymond George (Methodist), Ronald Jaspar (Anglican), Massey Shepherd (Anglican), Friedrich Künneth (Lutheran), Eugene Brand (Lutheran), and Max Thurian (Reformed Community of Taizé). Max Thurian, as a Protestant liturgist, had the most influence on the outcomes leading to the Novus Ordo Mass. At supper once with Hans Küng, Max Thurian and another Protestant scholar, Roger Schutz, asked him what they should do at this historical moment of the Council, to which Küng replied: "It is best for you to remain Protestants."[103]

The theological group behind Lefebvre pleaded that they at least be allowed to use the previous rite. The goal was that this presentation would gain support and lead Pope Paul VI to delay or scrap the new Bugnini rites. And if the promulgation did move forward, perhaps a universal indult might be offered to those priests who did not want to celebrate the Novus Ordo.

Pope Paul VI received the so-called Ottaviani Intervention coolly. The Holy See issued a response on 12 November 1969, replying that the "critical study" contained claims that were "superficial, exaggerated, inexact, emotional, and false."[104] Pope Paul VI moved forward and published the *Novus Ordo Missale* on 26 March 1970. Cardinal Ottaviani backed down and accepted the reform. Cardinal Bacci and Archbishop Lefebvre, however, did not accept the *Novus Ordo Missae*.

[103] De Mattei, *Second Vatican Council*, 202.

[104] Christophe Geffroy and Philippe Maxence, *Enquête sur la messe traditionnelle* (Montfort l'Amaury, France: La Nef, 1988), 21.

22

Archbishop Lefebvre and the Traditionalist Resistance

Archbishop Marcel Lefebvre, founding father of the *Coetus Internationalis Patrum* (CIP) or "International Group of Fathers," had been one of the leading anti-Modernist bishops who participated at the Second Vatican Council. He vocally rejected what he called "false ecumenism" that sought ecclesial union in any way other than conversion to the Catholic Faith. He opposed the Council's decree on religious liberty. He opposed episcopal collegiality in favor of papal supremacy. As a French Catholic, he vehemently opposed Freemasonry and the spirit of the French Revolution. But Archbishop Lefebvre would become known chiefly for his rejection of the Novus Ordo Mass of Paul VI. The liturgy was the line in the sand that set him apart from the rest.

Archbishop Lefebvre, as superior of the Holy Ghost Fathers, was greatly disappointed by the outcomes of Vatican II and even more concerned about the liturgies being crafted by Bugnini under Pope Paul VI. To seek consolation in his vocation, he traveled to Pietrelcina, Italy, in April 1967 to meet and seek the prayers and blessing of Padre Pio for the forthcoming general chapter of the Holy Ghost Fathers, fearing that the Vatican II spirit of *aggiornamento* would infect his religious order. Padre Pio instead asked for Lefebvre's blessing, kissed his episcopal ring, and headed to the confessional.

Unfortunately, most of the Holy Ghost Fathers were eager to implement the new reforms of Vatican II. Already an old man, Lefebvre decided it best to tender his resignation as superior in 1968.

During the dustup of the Ottaviani Intervention of 1969 (which was actually the project of Lefebvre and not Ottaviani), Lefebvre received permission from the local bishop of Fribourg to establish a seminary in Fribourg with nine seminarians. In November 1970, the bishop established for Archbishop Lefebvre the International Priestly Society of Saint Pius X (SSPX) as a pious union on a provisional basis for six years. This was the only seminary in the world that did *not* celebrate the Novus Ordo Mass of Pope Paul VI. Archbishop Lefebvre celebrated only the liturgies of 1962, using the missal last issued by Pope John XXIII before he called Vatican II. The seminary formation also included traditional theological training in Saint Thomas Aquinas and moral theology following Saint Alphonsus Liguori.

23

Resistance to the *Novus Ordo Missae*

Cardinal Ottaviani and Archbishop Lefebvre were not the only intellectuals displeased with the Novus Ordo Mass. A petition was circulated among prominent laymen who asked for permission to continue attending the traditional or Tridentine Latin Mass. Signers included Graham Greene, Romano Amerio, Malcolm Muggeridge, Jorge Luis Borges, Marcel Brion, Agatha Christie, Vladimir Ashkenazy, Kenneth Clark, Robert Graves, F. R. Leavis, Cecil Day-Lewis, Nancy Mitford, Iris Murdoch, Yehudi Menuhin, and Joan Sutherland.[105] Fantasy author J. R. R. Tolkien was also opposed to the Novus Ordo Mass. Simon Tolkien recalls his grandfather's protest to the Novus Ordo:

> I vividly remember going to church with him in Bournemouth. He was a devout Roman Catholic and it was soon after the Church had changed the liturgy from Latin to English. My grandfather obviously didn't agree with this and made all the responses very loudly in Latin while the rest of the congregation answered in English. I found the whole experience quite excruciating, but my

[105] For the list of more than one hundred signers, see *Una Voce* 7 (1971): 1–10.

grandfather was oblivious. He simply had to do what he believed to be right.[106]

Eminent philosopher Dietrich von Hildebrand also objected to the Novus Ordo Mass as "pedestrian":

> My concern is not with the legal status of the changes. And I emphatically do not wish to be understood as regretting that the Constitution has permitted the vernacular to complement the Latin. What I deplore is that the new mass is replacing the Latin Mass, that the old liturgy is being recklessly scrapped, and denied to most of the People of God....
>
> The basic error of most of the innovations is to imagine that the new liturgy brings the holy sacrifice of the Mass nearer to the faithful, that shorn of its old rituals the mass now enters into the substance of our lives. For the question is whether we better meet Christ in the mass by soaring up to Him, or by dragging Him down into our own pedestrian, workaday world. The innovators would replace holy intimacy with Christ by an unbecoming familiarity. The new liturgy actually threatens to frustrate the confrontation with Christ, for it discourages reverence in the face of mystery, precludes awe, and all but extinguishes a sense of sacredness. What really matters, surely, is not whether the faithful feel at home at mass, but whether they are drawn out of their ordinary lives into the world of Christ—whether their attitude is the

[106] Simon Tolkien, "My Grandfather JRR Tolkien" Simon Tolkien, http://www.simontolkien.com/mygrandfather.html.

> response of ultimate reverence: whether they are imbued with the reality of Christ.[107]

On behalf of those longing for the traditional Latin Mass, John Cardinal Heenan of Westminster asked Pope Paul VI for an indult for the Tridentine Mass. Pope Paul VI read the letter in sober silence and then exclaimed, "Ah, Agatha Christie" and then signed the indult. Although she was not a Catholic, the novelist Agatha Christie was opposed to the Novus Ordo Mass for cultural and literary reasons. And thanks to her name catching the eye of Pope Paul VI, the indult has been known ever since as the "Agatha Christie indult."[108]

Except for the Agatha Christie indult, the Novus Ordo Mass was issued in 1970, and Pope Paul VI issued a series of canonical and liturgical changes that magnified what became known as the "spirit of Vatican II":

- 1971: Paul VI excludes cardinals over eighty years from voting in papal elections.
- 1972: Clerical tonsure, minor orders of porter, exorcist, acolyte, and subdeacon are abolished by Pope Paul VI in *Ministeria quaedam*.
- 1973: Extraordinary Lay Ministers of Holy Communion are allowed.

[107] Dietrich von Hildebrand, "Case for the Latin Mass," *Triumph* (October 1966).

[108] The so-called Agatha Christie indult was actually a preservation not of the 1962 missal, which traditionalists observe, but the 1965 missal with 1967 modifications: "The edition of the Missal to be used on these occasions should be that published again by the Decree of the Sacred Congregation of Rites (27 January 1965), and with the modifications indicated in the *Instructio altera* (4 May 1967)."

- 1977: The indult to receive Communion in the hand is granted to the United States.

The suppression of clerical tonsure, minor orders (porter, lector, exorcist, acolyte), and subdeacon went against the clear teaching of the Council of Trent that stated:

> From the very beginning of the church, the names of the following orders, and the ministrations proper to each one of them, are known to have been in use; to wit, those of subdeacon, acolyte, exorcist, lector, and porter; though these were not of equal rank: for the subdiaconate is classed amongst the greater orders by the Fathers and sacred Councils, wherein also we very often read of the other inferior orders.[109]

And, their rejection carried an anathema:

> Can. 2. If anyone says that besides the priesthood there are in the Catholic Church no other orders, both major and minor, by which as by certain grades, there is an advance to the priesthood: let him be anathema.[110]

Pope Paul VI's decision to authorize laymen as Extraordinary Ministers of Holy Communion broke with Western and Eastern tradition, which absolutely forbade anyone but a priest from administering Holy Communion. In the Roman Rite, only a deacon or a subdeacon could touch the sacred Eucharistic vessels. The Church Fathers confirm this tradition. Paul VI set it aside.

[109] Council of Trent. Session XXIII, ch. 2.
[110] Council of Trent, Session XXIII, canon 2.

Paul VI also extended to the laity the permission to receive Holy Communion in the hand. These changes had two negative consequences. One was that they reduced belief in transubstantiation. The Protestant Reformers Martin Luther, John Calvin, Martin Bucer, and Thomas Cranmer had each insisted that people receive Communion in the hand because it signified that the Eucharist was ordinary bread and not Christ Himself. The other negative consequence of Communion in the hand is that it allowed for Hosts to be dropped on the floor more easily or, worse, for people to steal Hosts for desecration and occult potions. It is difficult to understand how Pope Paul VI would lament the demonic infiltration of the Church while he promoted reforms that encouraged it: "We would say that, through some mysterious crack—no, it's not mysterious; through some crack, the smoke of Satan has entered the Church of God. There is doubt, uncertainty, problems, unrest, dissatisfaction, confrontation."[111]

The liturgical, theological, and philosophical changes of Vatican II and Pope Paul VI were detrimental to the laity. In 2003, Kenneth C. Jones published his *Index of Leading Catholic Indicators: The Church Since Vatican II*, documenting the collapse of Catholic practice since the close of the Council in 1965 (these numbers are limited to America):[112]

Sunday Mass Attendance

1958: 74 percent of Catholics went to Sunday Mass.
2000: 25 percent of Catholics went to Sunday Mass.

[111] Pope Paul VI, Homily, 29 June 1972.

[112] Kenneth C. Jones, *Index of Leading Catholic Indicators: The Church Since Vatican II* (St. Louis: Oriens Publishing, 2003).

Infant Baptisms

1965: There were 1.3 million infant baptisms.

2002: There were 1 million infant baptisms, despite the population rise.

Adult Baptisms (Converts)

1965: There were 126,000 adult baptisms.

2002: There were 80,000 adult baptisms.

Catholic Marriages

1965: There were 352,000 Catholic marriages.

2002: There were 256,000 Catholic marriages, despite the population rise.

Annulments

1965: There were 338 annulments.

2002: There were about 50,000 annulments!

Priests

1965: 58,000 priests.

2002: 45,000 priests.

Ordinations

1965: There were 1,575 ordinations to the priesthood.

2002: There were 450 ordinations to the priesthood.

Priestless Parishes

1965: 1 percent of parishes were priestless. There were 549 parishes without a resident priest.

2002: 15 percent of parishes were priestless. There were 2,928 parishes without a resident priest.

Seminarians

1965: 49,000 seminarians enrolled.
2002: 4,700 seminarians enrolled.

Nuns and Religious Sisters

1965: 180,000 religious sisters.
2002: 75,000 religious sisters (with an average age of 68).

Nonordained Religious Brothers

1965: 12,000 religious brothers.
2002: 5,700 religious brothers.

Jesuits

1965: There were 5,277 Jesuit priests and 3,559 seminarians.
2000: There were 3,172 Jesuit priests and 38 seminarians.

Franciscans

1965: There were 2,534 OFM Franciscan priests and 2,251 seminarians.
2000: There were 1,492 priests and 60 seminarians.

Christian Brothers

1965: There were 2,434 Christian brothers and 912 seminarians.
2000: There were 959 Christian brothers and 7 seminarians!

Redemptorists

1965: There were 1,148 Redemptorist priests and 1,128 seminarians.
2000: There were 349 priests and 24 seminarians.

Catholic High Schools

1965: 1,566 Catholic high schools.
2002: 786 Catholic high schools.

Parochial Grade Schools

1965: 10,503 parochial grade schools.
2002: 6,623 parochial grade schools.

Catholic Parochial Students

1965: 4.5 million students
2002: 1.9 million students

The numbers do not lie. The Catholic Church has been in a tailspin since Vatican II. Any business, club, or corporation with evidence of such declining numbers would fire management and return to their once-winning strategy. When Coca-Cola issued New Coke in 1985, it was met with consumer outcry and dismal sales numbers. Their leadership corrected course after only seventy-eight days of failure. After fifty years, the Catholic numbers for Mass attendance, priestly and religious vocations, baptisms, and marriages has declined, decade after decade. The updated numbers for 2015 are even worse. Yet the popes and the hierarchy keep telling the laity that this is the new Advent and the new springtime and that Vatican II brought about great renewal in the Church. The novus ordo Church is just as unpopular as New Coke: even though nobody wants to drink it, the bishops keep telling us how much better it is than Catholicism Classic.

24

Infiltration of the Vatican Bank under Paul VI

Infiltration was not limited to thinking or to liturgy. The post-conciliar Church was also plagued by the infiltration of her finances. The Vatican Bank is officially known as the Institute for the Works of Religion, which in Italian is the Istituto per le Opere di Religione (IOR). It was founded by papal decree of Pope Pius XII on 27 June 1942. It reorganized the Administration of the Works of Religion, or Amministrazione per le Opere di Religione (AOR), dating back to the pontificate of Pope Leo XIII in 1887 (the year after Leo composed the prayer to Saint Michael).

Many ask, "Why does the Catholic Church have its own bank?" After the Catholic Church lost her temporal sovereignty in 1870, she also lost her wealth in the form of land holdings. Prior to modern banking and checking accounts, wealth was maintained and protected by land holdings. Without her sovereignty, any wealth she owned would be overseen and restricted by a temporal sovereign, such as the secular state of Italy. This was completely unacceptable, so the Church sought a way to guard her funds for the "administration of the works of religion."

The reformulation of the IOR in 1942 seems to have allowed it to be manipulated. By the 1960s and 1970s, there were serious concerns that the IOR was being used illicitly by organized crime for the purpose of money laundering. The contemporary or current IOR is still shrouded in mystery. It is *not* the property of the Holy See. Rather, it remains *outside* the jurisdiction of the Prefecture for the Economic Affairs of the Holy See. The IOR is currently governed by a commission of five cardinals and a lay board of superintendence.

The written mission of the IOR is "to provide for the safekeeping and administration of movable and immovable property transferred or entrusted to it by physical or juridical persons and intended for works of religion or charity."[113] It is a charitable organization instituted to fund charitable work. Since 2013, the IOR claims that it does not use its deposits for purposes of money lending, and it does not issue securities.[114] Currently, the IOR is estimated to hold billions of dollars on deposit.

In 1968, after a six-year battle between Italy and Vatican City, Italy revoked the tax-exempt status on investment income received by the Holy See—the same year that Paul VI issued his final encyclical, *Humanae vitae*, condemning abortion and artificial contraception. To handle this new arrangement and diversify the Vatican's assets, Pope Paul VI hired financial adviser Michele "the Shark" Sindona, who would be murdered by poisoning in 1986 while serving a prison sentence. Sindona was a notorious member of the Italian Freemasonic organization Propaganda Due (P2). He was also likely a member of the Sicilian Mafia. Why Pope Paul VI hired this monster remains a mystery, but it points

[113] *Annuario Pontificio* 2012, 1908.

[114] "Vatican Bank Launches Website in Effort to Increase Transparency," *Catholic Herald*, 1 August 2013.

Michele "the Shark" Sindona

to deep Freemasonic infiltration in the corridors of the Vatican by 1968, three years after Vatican II.

Until his election as Pope Paul VI, Cardinal Montini had served as the archbishop of Milan since 1954. As archbishop, he became friends with Sindona who was also based in Milan—although some claim that Montini and Sindona were friends before Montini became archbishop of Milan.[115] Sometime around 1957, the Mafioso Gambino family tasked Sindona with laundering their illegal profits from heroin sales. To accomplish this, Sindona

[115] The details regarding the workings of Sindona and the Vatican Bank derive from "Sindona's World" in *New York Magazine*, 24 September 1979. Montini allegedly met Sindona while he was still a monsignor.

purchased his first bank in Milan—at age thirty-eight. The Mafia continually seeks ways to appear legitimate in the eyes of the world and especially in the eyes of law enforcement. Sindona continued to acquire more banks in Milan and created a legitimate banking front for the Sicilian Mafia. As a young and successful "legitimate" banker, his relationship with Montini blossomed.

Montini was elected pope in 1963 because he was well connected within the reforming arms of the Church during the illness of Pius XII, but perhaps also because of his deep connection to European banking. So, when Paul VI ran afoul of the Italian government because of the Church's tax status, he turned to his banking friend Michele "the Shark" Sindona, who was more than eager to help with the Vatican Bank.

By 1969, Sindona was allegedly moving money through the Vatican Bank to Swiss bank accounts and speculating against major currencies. Under Paul VI, the Vatican provided the perfect invisible tool by which to move money internationally. He was credited with saving the Italian currency in 1974 and had established himself as respected. Having major influence in Europe, Sindona cast his eyes across the Atlantic to the United States. In early 1974, he purchased a controlling interest in Long Island's Franklin National Bank, but he had overpaid. Due to a dip in the stock market, he lost forty million dollars in his leveraged position. This triggered a cascade, and Sindona began to lose his European banks and holdings. This put him in a tight place because his wealth and portfolio were due not to brilliant banking but to bloating his banks with Mafia money derived chiefly from the drug trade. As the money disappeared, the Mafia wanted their money back as soon as possible. Back in Milan, a warrant was issued for Sindona's arrest. He disappeared and then resurfaced hiding in Switzerland.

The Mafia families weren't the only ones left holding the bag. The 1974 failure of Sindona's papier-mâché banking system deeply injured the Vatican. Under Paul VI, the Vatican lost 35 billion Italian lire (or 53 million in 1974 U.S. dollars). That number amounts to a loss of 288 million in 2019 American dollars.[116] Financial historians unanimously agree that Sindona was mixing Vatican funds with heroin profits from Mafia families. There is no escaping it—except that Pope Paul VI died on 6 August 1978 and left the scene of the crime. The aftermath would be left to John Paul I, John Paul II, and eventually Benedict XVI.

After the death of Paul VI, the drama continued. The Milanese lawyer responsible for liquidating Sindona's assets, Giorgio Ambrosoli, was murdered on 11 July 1979. The crime was traced back to a hit ordered by Sindona. The Sicilian Mafia also murdered the police chief Boris Giuliano, who was investigating the Mafia's heroin sales and connecting it to Sindona's operation. Sindona was kidnapped by the Sicilian Mafia and brought to Sicily. The Mafia sought to blackmail politicians to reacquire their lost assets through Milan and New York. Their plot failed, and Sindona surrendered himself to the FBI. In 1980, he was convicted on sixty-five counts of money laundering, fraud, perjury, and misappropriation of funds. The Italian government then extradited Sindona back to Italy to stand trial for the murder of Giorgio Ambrosoli. He was convicted and given a life sentence. In prison, he was poisoned with cyanide in his coffee and died on 18 March 1986.[117] The Freemason Milanese Mafia banker was sixty-five on the day of his murder.

[116] "Sindona's World."

[117] "Michele Sindona, Jailed Italian Financier, Dies of Cyanide Poisoning at 65," *New York Times*, 23 March 1986.

25

Infiltration and the Mysterious Death of John Paul I

Before his death, Pope Paul VI openly denounced accusations of sodomy. The controversy surfaced when the Congregation for the Doctrine of the Faith issued a document entitled *Persona humana*, which addressed the immorality of adultery, homosexuality, and masturbation.[118] This provoked the author Roger Peyrefitte, who had written two books in which he claimed that Montini/Paul VI had maintained a long homosexual relationship with an Italian actor.[119] The rumor of Paul VI's secret homosexual relationship was spread in French and Italian print. The alleged homosexual partner of Paul VI was the Italian actor Paolo Carlini, who appeared in forty-five films between 1940 and 1979. Americans would recognize him as Audrey Hepburn's hairdresser in the 1954 film *Roman Holiday*. In a public address to approximately twenty thousand people in Saint Peter's Piazza on 18 April 1976, Paul VI denied the allegation of sodomy. He referred to the allegations as "horrible and slanderous

[118] *Persona Humana: Declaration on Certain Questions concerning Sexual Ethic* (29 December 1975).

[119] Roger Peyrefitte, "Mea culpa? Ma fatemi il santo piacere," *Tempo*, 4 April 1976.

insinuations."[120] The following year, Pope Paul VI fell ill with an enlarged prostate. His health continued to fail, and he died of heart failure on 6 August 1978 at Castel Gandolfo.

Not only had Pope Paul VI revoked the voting rights of cardinals over the age of eighty in 1970;[121] he had also created an innovation in 1975 by expanding the number of cardinal electors from 70 (like the 70 elders of Moses and the 70 disciples of Christ) to 120. The revocation of the voting rights of cardinals over eighty is one of the greatest coups in Catholic history. Pope Paul VI essentially banned all older cardinals appointed by Pius XII from voting in future papal elections. By this maneuver, Paul VI ensured that his cardinals, and his alone, would choose his successor. The math worked. In the August 1978 papal conclave, of the 111 cardinal electors, 100 had been personally appointed by Pope Paul VI; 8 had been appointed by John XXIII, and only 3 by Pius XII. Eliminating the voting rights of cardinals over eighty nearly erased the legacy of the former generation of cardinals.

Since Paul VI had radically revamped the College of Cardinals, the conclave of August 1978 had no conservative candidate. Nearly every cardinal elector to the man was fully supportive of Pope Paul VI and the reforms of Vatican II. The reforms of Vatican II were assured, and the next pope would be tasked with issuing a new catechism and a new Code of Canon Law to conform with Vatican II.

The pressing need, however, was the financial scandal at the Vatican Bank, of which the world knew little. Nevertheless,

[120] Jose Torress, "Paul VI Denies He Is Homosexual," *Observer Reporter*, Associated Press, 5 April 1976, 27.

[121] Pope Paul VI, *Ingravescentem aetatem* (21 November 1970).

the inside circle of curial cardinals deeply understood that the Sindona scandal could reach and expose them.

The short conclave lasted from 25 to 26 August 1978. Cardinal Albino Lúciani was favored to win and he knew it, as he told his secretary that he would decline if elected pope.[122] The College of Cardinals, stacked by Paul VI, elected Cardinal Lúciani on the first day of voting after four ballots. When Jean-Marie Cardinal Villot asked Lúciani for his acceptance, he replied, "May God forgive you for what you have done." He then became the first pope to take a double papal name "John Paul" in honor of the two popes of Vatican II: John XXIII and Paul VI. Notable also is the fact that his two papal successors, Karol Wojtyła and Joseph Ratzinger were among the cardinals present to elect him as Pope John Paul I.

John Paul I was in line with the modernizing and liberalizing tendencies in doctrine, politics, and liturgy of Vatican II. Prior to 1968, he had openly supported the position of Giovanni Cardinal Urbani of Venice that artificial birth control could be used responsibly by married Catholics in good conscience.[123] After Pope Paul VI issued *Humanae vitae* in 1968, Cardinal Lúciani conformed to the teaching against artificial contraception, but quietly.

Pope John Paul I reigned for only thirty-three days, dying on 28 September 1978. This was during the financial scandal surrounding the enormous loss of funds from the Vatican Bank through the machinations of the Freemasonic Michele "the

[122] John Allen Jr., "Debunking four myths about John Paul I, the 'Smiling Pope,'" National Catholic Reporter. 2 November 2012. Retrieved 28 February 2019.

[123] John Julius Norwich, *The Popes* (London, 2011), 445.

Shark" Sindona. There was pressure by voices in the Vatican to join with the Sicilian Mafia in restoring their lost funds. The modern equivalent of a loss of $288 million dollars in Vatican funds is nothing to sneeze it.

Three Vatican officials were working on the Vatican Bank scandal: Jean-Marie Cardinal Villot, secretary of state; John Cardinal Cody of Chicago; and Archbishop Paul "the Gorilla" Marcinkus, head of the Vatican Bank, or IOR. All three were big players. Archbishop Marcinkus, an ex-rugby player who stood at six foot four, would later be indicted in Italy in 1982 as an accessory in the $3.5 billion collapse of Banco Ambrosiano. Marcinkus is famous for telling Pope John Paul II, "You cannot run a Church on Hail Marys." Conspiracy theories link these men together in a plot to murder John Paul I, with Cardinal Villot as the one who would organize it and later destroy all evidence.

All three were working in 1978 with Roberto Calvi, the chairman of the Banco Ambrosiano. Calvi was a Freemasonic member of P2 and nicknamed "God's Banker." In 1982, the same year as Archbishop Marcinkus's indictment, the body of Calvi was found hanging from Blackfriars Bridge in London. This was thought to be a sign, since the Italian P2 Lodge refers to themselves as "black friars." The death was ruled a suicide, but this has been contested ever since.

The five players in the story are Cardinal Villot, Cardinal Cody, Archbishop Marcinkus, and the two prominent bankers Sindona and Calvi. Three of these five, Marcinkus, Sindona, and Calvi were indicted—and the latter two died untimely deaths. Something deeply evil was at work in 1978. Villot died in 1979. Cody died in 1982. Within a few years, everyone involved was either dead from natural causes, had committed suicide, or was in prison.

The reconstructed theory is that Villot, Cody, and Marcinkus were working together with the Freemasons and the Sicilian Mafia to hide the Vatican Bank involvement in the heroin profits laundered through the Vatican Bank to Banco Ambrosiano and Sindona's banks. Beyond hiding the crime, they may also have been working with Calvi and Sindona's people to reacquire the Vatican Bank's loss of funds of $288 million, adjusted for inflation today. Paul VI, who was a friend of Sindona and himself complicit in the loss, was willing to play along until his death. Pope John Paul I was not willing to comply, and so, the theory holds, he was murdered after thirty-three days as pope.

David Yallop published *In God's Name* in 1984. He recreates the timeline of the death of John Paul I and pins it on Cardinal Villot as the person with the most to gain and the most to lose. Yallop claims that John Paul I received a list of Freemasonic cardinals during his short papacy. On 12 September 1978, Mino Pecorelli released his list of prominent Italian Freemasons, which named several cardinals and archbishops.[124] Pecorelli himself was a member of the Freemasonic Propaganda Due (P2) Lodge, and six months after publishing this list, he was found murdered (20 March 1979). Featured on "Pecorelli's List" were:

- Jean Cardinal Villot (Pope Paul VI's secretary of state, whose family is believed to have historic ties to the Rosicrucian Lodge)
- Agostino Cardinal Casaroli (future secretary of state for Pope John Paul II)
- Ugo Cardinal Poletti (president of Pontifical Works and of the Liturgical Academy)

[124] The principal "list" appeared in *Osservatorio Politica Internazionale Magazine* on 12 September 1978.

- Sebastiano Cardinal Baggio (camerlengo and president of the Pontifical Commission of the Vatican State)
- Monsignor Pasquale Macchi (Pope Paul VI's personal secretary from 1954 to 1978)
- Joseph Cardinal Suenens (one of the four moderators at Vatican II)
- Archbishop Annibale Bugnini (creator of the Novus Ordo liturgies for Pope Paul VI)
- Archbishop Paul Marcinkus (president of the Vatican Bank from 1971 to 1989)

When Cardinal Villot realized that Pope John Paul I had taken interest in Pecorelli's List, Villot began to plot against him. Pecorelli's List was published on 12 September 1978 and the pope was found dead on 28 September 1978.

At 4:45 a.m. of that day, Sister Vincenza Taffarel entered the papal apartment and saw Pope John Paul I sitting in bed, holding papers in hand, with an expression of agony.[125] After checking his pulse, she confirmed he was dead. At 5:00 a.m. Cardinal Villot arrived from across town. He gathered the pope's prescription of Effortil on the bedside table, took up the papers in the pope's hands, and removed the pope's glasses and slippers, probably because they had vomit on them. He also took the pope's will. All these items were never seen again. Villot asked Sister Vincenza to take a vow of silence over everything she had just seen.

Cardinal Villot called the morticians and sent a Vatican car to fetch them. Allegedly the embalmers had already gone to work on the dead pope before a doctor was called to issue a death certificate. When the doctor did arrive, the death was attributed

[125] All details about the death of John Paul I here are derived from David Yallop, *In God's Name* (New York: Basic Books, 1984).

to acute myocardial infarction that likely occurred at 11:00 p.m. the previous night.

Villot began to notify the cardinals beginning at 6:30 a.m. Sergeant Roggan of the Swiss Guard, who was on duty, saw Paul Marcinkus on the premises at 6:45 a.m. The Vatican officially announced the pope's death to the world at 7:30 a.m. The morticians returned at 11 a.m. allegedly to restructure the pope's gruesome face. Villot instructed them to embalm the pope by the end of the day. The nuns were asked to clean and polish the room (removing vomit, fingerprints, and evidence), and the pope's clothes, books, and notes were taken away in boxes. By 6 p.m. of the day of his death, every belonging of Pope John Paul I had been removed from the papal apartments

The morticians began embalming the body with formalin that night but were instructed by Villot *not* to drain the pope's blood, as was custom. The allegation here is that Villot did not want any of the blood to be tested during an autopsy, since it likely contained poison that was introduced into the pope's veins through a falsified dose of his nightly prescription of Effortil—which is why Villot took the bottle of Effortil when he first arrived.

26

Infiltration of John Paul II's Pontificate

The second papal conclave of 1978 was held from 14 to 16 October. Cardinal Villot oversaw the conclave as camerlengo. The early death of Pope John Paul I and the rumors of the Vatican Bank scandal made the way forward more complicated than the conclave held less than two months before. Once again, 111 cardinals participated in the voting, but this time a non-cardinal would be admitted. A young (future cardinal) Donald Wuerl was admitted to the conclave to assist the frail John Cardinal Wright.

Cardinal Siri of Genoa, who had been the conservative candidate twenty years earlier in 1958, was favored again as a dependable father figure in a time of uncertainty. The liberals had rallied to Giovanni Cardinal Benelli of Florence, who had been a dear friend of John Paul I. Surprisingly, the liberal Benelli could not attain the two-thirds majority initially. Attention turned to a moderate candidate in the person of Giovanni Cardinal Colombo, who explicitly stated that it was a waste to vote for him—he would decline the papacy if elected.

The arch-liberal Franz Cardinal König, who had publicly dissented from Paul VI's 1968 condemnation of artificial contraception in *Humanae vitae*, suggested that the perfect compromise candidate would be the Polish cardinal Karol Wojtyła. Oddly, Cardinal Cody had traveled to Kraków, Poland, just before the death of John Paul I to meet with Cardinal Wojtyła. Why this happened we do not know, but Wojtyła was perhaps asked whether he were willing to ascend to the papacy. Wojtyła was relatively unknown, but he was an ideal compromise candidate. He was non-Italian, signaling a universal pontificate. This would make him the first non-Italian pope since Adrian VI, who died in 1523. Moreover, Wojtyła was young at age fifty-eight. The American cardinals, wanting to see a non-Italian pope, rallied to him. Best of all, the conservative Cardinal Siri agreed to support Wojtyła.

On the third day, Cardinal Wojtyła won by a landslide with 99 of the 111 votes. He captured 89 percent of the conclave's votes when papal election only required 67 percent. He accepted by saying, "With obedience in faith to Christ, my Lord, and with trust in the Mother of Christ and the Church, in spite of great difficulties, I accept." It's rumored that he initially suggested taking Stanislaus as his papal name but was encouraged to take something more Roman.[126] To honor the recently deceased John Paul I and his predecessors John XXIII and Paul VI, he chose the papal name John Paul II.

Thousands of books have been written on the long and celebrated pontificate of Pope John Paul II. The young Wojtyła grew up in Poland under pious parents; he attributes his vocation to the faithful witness of his father. He played soccer as a goalie and enjoyed theater. He learned twelve languages, including Polish, Ukrainian, Serbo-Croatian, Slovak, French, Italian, Spanish, Portuguese, German, English, and Latin. He discerned the priesthood and studied covertly during the Nazi occupation of Poland. He was smart, affable, masculine, and inspiring. He

[126] "A Foreign Pope," *Time*, 30 October 1978, 1.

had been consecrated bishop in 1958 and had partaken in the Second Vatican Council. He was an enthusiastic supporter of Vatican II, but his Eastern European patrimony disposed him to political conservatism—especially against Communism.

As Pope John Paul II, he returned to Poland in June 1979 and inspired the Solidarity movement that would exert soft pressure against Soviet Communism and its eventual demise in Eastern Europe. Theologically, however, John Paul II advocated the *ressourcement* or *nouvelle théologie* authors. He was influenced by Balthasar, de Lubac, and even Rahner. He appointed Rahner's theological protégé Cardinal Ratzinger as his doctrinal chief and prefect of the Congregation for the Doctrine of the Faith in 1981. Throughout his pontificate, John Paul II innovated by making Ratzinger his number two and not the cardinal secretary of state, as was the centuries-long tradition for popes.

A few months prior to appointing Cardinal Ratzinger, John Paul II was shot *on the feast day of Our Lady of Fatima*—13 May 1981. The Turkish gunman Mehmet Ali Ağca fired two shots from his Browning 9mm pistol into the pope's colon and small intestine. Both bullets missed his mesenteric artery and abdominal aorta, but he lost three-fourths of his blood during the ride to Gemelli Hospital. Piously, John Paul II asked the doctors not to remove his Brown Scapular before surgery. The gunman claimed that he received his mission from the Turkish mafioso Bekir Çelenk of Bulgaria. In 2010, he changed his story and said that the cardinal secretary of state under John Paul II, Agostino Casaroli, had arranged the assassination. In 2013, he changed his story again. This time he claimed that the Iranian government and Ayatollah Khomeini ordered the assassination. We may never know the reason or forces behind the assassination plot.

Also in 1981, John Paul II made the mistake of appointing Archbishop Marcinkus as head banker and pro-president of Vatican City—even though John Paul II knew that Marcinkus was implicated in the Sindona scandal. A year later, Marcinkus himself would be indicted and imprisoned; Marcinkus, however, is credited with saving the pope's life. In 1982, he was present with John Paul II in Fatima, Portugal, when Father Juan Maria Fernández y Krohn, a deranged priest, attacked the pope with a bayonet. Interestingly enough, Marcinkus had also saved the life of Pope Paul VI when a blaspheming Bolivian painter thrust a knife at the pope's neck during a visit to the Philippines in 1970. There's a reason Marcinkus was known as "the Gorilla."

In 1983, John Paul II changed the Code of Canon Law. The new Code conformed to Vatican II and was laxer. One crucial example is the change in specificity and penalties for sexually immoral priests—a problem that would haunt his papacy later. Compare the 1917 Code with the 1983 Code regarding sexually immoral priests. Here is the canon law punishing clergy from 1917:

> All clerics found to have committed any delict against the Sixth Commandment with a minor below the age of sixteen, or engaged in adultery, debauchery, bestiality, sodomy, pandering, or incest, they are suspended, publicly declared as having committed sexual misconduct, and deprived of any office, pension, dignity, and function if they have any, and in graver cases, dismissed from the clerical state. (Canon 2359 § 2, 1917 Code)

Notice that the sexual sins are clearly described and distinguished. Moreover, the penalties are clear: loss of office, pension (money), dignity, and function, and, in some cases dismissal, from the clerical state.

Now compare the canon from 1917 with the abysmally weak revision made by Pope John Paul II in the Code of Canon Law of 1983:

> Can. 1395 §1. A cleric who lives in concubinage, other than the case mentioned in can. 1394, and a cleric who persists with scandal in another external sin against the sixth commandment of the Decalogue is to be punished by a suspension. If he persists in the delict after a warning, other penalties can gradually be added, including dismissal from the clerical state.
>
> §2. A cleric who in another way has committed an offense against the sixth commandment of the Decalogue, if the delict was committed by force or threats or publicly or with a minor below the age of sixteen years, is to be punished with just penalties, not excluding dismissal from the clerical state if the case so warrants.

The revised version by John Paul II states that clergy in "external sin" against the sixth commandment are to be suspended. If they persist after warning, "penalties can gradually be added, including dismissal from the clerical state," but these penalties are not prescribed. This means that a bishop could have a harsh talk with them or send them to a sex rehab center. He can transfer them to a different assignment. Contrast this with 1917, which states explicitly and clearly that they are to be "suspended, publicly declared as having committed sexual misconduct, and deprived of any office, pension, dignity."

The canon of 1983 also does not identify specific sexual sins —only one against a minor below the age of sixteen. The 1917 Code is far superior in that it explicitly lists the sins worthy of punishment committed by clergy:

- sex with a minor below the age of sixteen
- adultery
- debauchery
- bestiality
- sodomy
- pandering
- incest

Why did the Code of Canon Law under John Paul II remove the language of "adultery," bestiality," and "sodomy" from clerical punishment? Under the 1917 Code, Theodore McCarrick would have been censured for homosexual sodomy. But under the 1983 Code, there is no longer a specified crime of homosexual sodomy. Canonically, sexually immoral clerics such as McCarrick get a free pass on that sin.

The scandalous Judas priest Father Marcial Maciel abused the same canonical loophole. Father Maciel was a Mexican priest and founder of the celebrated Legion of Christ and the Regnum Christi movement. Like McCarrick, he was an extraordinary fund-raiser and recruiter of handsome seminarians.

His life and movement were built of straw. It became public that Father Maciel had sexually abused countless seminarians, young men, and boys. He had secret residences and maintained sexual relations with at least two women, one of whom was a minor. He fathered as many as six children and allegedly abused two of these children as well.[127] He was a morphine addict, and his written works contained overt plagiarism. Maciel was also able to walk between the raindrops through bribes given to Monsignor Stanisław Dziwisz, beloved friend and counselor of John Paul II.

[127] Emilio Godoy, "Pope Rewrites Epitaph for Legion of Christ Founder," IPS News: 3 May 2010.

Yet even after Maciel was internally exposed, the nondescript canon law of 1983 prevented him from being censured for the precise crime of sodomy as indicated in the 1917 Code.

This is a glaring deficiency in the updated Code of John Paul II. Why make the law less specific and laxer? This is a rhetorical question, because there is no possible reason to relax the law of the Church and make it less precise. Is there any doubt that the Catholic Church largely ceased disciplining her sexually aberrant priests and bishops in the 1980s and 1990s?

The 1983 Code of Canon Law introduced the rule that Catholic clergy may administer Penance, Anointing of the Sick, and Holy Communion to Christians in danger of death but not in full communion with the Catholic Church, "provided that they manifest Catholic faith in respect to these sacraments and are properly disposed" (Canon 844 §4). The new Code also reversed the two ends of matrimony: (1) the procreation and education of children and (2) the mutual good of the spouses (Canon 1055).

The 1983 Code introduced the canonical authority of the "conference of bishops" over a nation with quasi-jurisdiction over the dioceses therein:

> A conference of bishops, a permanent institution, is a group of bishops of some nation or certain territory who jointly exercise certain pastoral functions for the Christian faithful of their territory in order to promote the greater good which the Church offers to humanity, especially through forms and programs of the apostolate fittingly adapted to the circumstances of time and place, according to the norm of law. (Canon 447)

Also in 1983, John Paul II changed the process for canonizing saints. Previously, a Catholic being considered for sainthood had to display heroic virtue that was examined and contested by a "devil's advocate," who was tasked with finding all the dirt on the person in question. John Paul II abolished the devil's advocate. The entire process was transformed from a legal investigation into a theological study, in which the candidate's writings were examined. So, the emphasis for sainthood was shifted from the person's historical acts to his personal beliefs.

The years 1983 to 1986 marked the beginning of John Paul II's advanced ecumenism. By the end of 1983, John Paul II had become the first pope to preach inside a Lutheran church in Rome. In February 1984, he oversaw the new revision of the Lateran Treaty, which abolished the condition that "the Roman and Apostolic Catholic religion is the only religion of the State." In May 1984, John Paul II sent "particular greetings to the members of the Buddhist tradition who are preparing to celebrate the feast of the coming of the Lord Buddha."[128] Days later, he visited a Buddhist temple in Thailand, removed his papal shoes, and sat down before an altar on which stood a large idol of Buddha. In June of that year, the pope visited Geneva, where he participated in an ecumenical "liturgy of the word" with Protestants and affirmed that "the Catholic Church's involvement in the ecumenical movement is irreversible."[129] In 1985, he participated in an animist rite in Togo. In February 1986, he received the sacred ashes of the Hindu religion. In August of that year, he would be received by a synagogue in Rome.

[128] *L'Osservatore Romano*, 7–8 May 1984, *Documentation Catholique*, 1878: 619, 4.

[129] *L'Osservatore Romano*, 12 June 1984, *Documentation Catholique*, 1878: 704.

On 28 October 1986, John Paul II invoked and hosted the Assisi World Day of Prayer for Peace. In 1895, Pope Leo XIII had condemned a "Congress of Religions" held in Chicago. But less than a century later, the pope of Rome was organizing and celebrating such an event. Pope John Paul II and his cardinals invited representatives from thirty-two world religions, including Muslim imams, Jewish rabbis, Buddhists, Sikhs, Bahais, Hindus, Jains, Zoroastrians, Native American chiefs, and African shamans, to pray with them for peace. This was the first time a pope prayed with members of other religions and sat with them on equal standing. Most scandalous of all was that the Tibetan Buddhist delegation led by the Dali Lama were allowed to place an idol of Buddha *on top of a Catholic tabernacle* in the Chapel of San Pietro, as reported by the *New York Times*.[130] To this idol they burned incense within a Catholic church *with permission from the pope.*

By an act of Christ Our Lord on 26 September 1997, the ceiling of that very chapel collapsed and destroyed the altar and the chapel where this sacrilege had occurred eleven years before.

At the meeting, Pope John Paul II appealed to their *deeper level of humanity*: "If there are many and important differences among us, is it not true to say that at the deeper level of humanity, there is a common ground whence to operate together in a solution of this dramatic challenge of our age: true peace or catastrophic war?" In the closing ceremony, two American Indians of the Crow tribe, John and Burton Pretty on Top, stood before the pope in their plumed headdresses and lit up their peace

[130] Roberto Suro, "12 Faiths Join Pope to Pray for Peace," *New York Times*, 28 October 1986.

pipe, and "the crowd responded with a great clicking of pocket cameras and then applause."[131]

Two bishops violently objected to Pope John Paul II's participation in the 1986 Assisi meeting. Archbishop Marcel Lefebvre and Bishop de Castro Mayer publicly protested:

> Public sin against the unicity of God, the Word Incarnate, and His Church makes one shudder with horror: John Paul has encouraged false religions to pray to their false gods: it is unprecedented and immeasurable scandal,... an inconceivably impious and intolerable humiliation to those who remain Catholic, loyally professing the same Faith for twenty centuries.[132]

For Archbishop Lefebvre and his priests in the Society of Saint Pius X, the Assisi 1986 meeting was a bridge too far. Lefebvre was now eighty-one years old and growing frail. Concerned over apostasy in the Church and even committed by the pope, Lefebvre began to make plans to appoint his successors. Despite his disappointment over John Paul II's participating in and encouraging pagan idolatry in a Catholic basilica, he did not fall into sedevacantism. He fully recognized the authority of John Paul II as pope, but he doubted the orthodoxy and leadership of the pope.

Pope John Paul II and Archbishop Lefebvre reached an agreement in May 1988 that would allow Lefebvre to consecrate one bishop for the continuation of the Society of Saint Pius X (SSPX). The agreement was brokered between Joseph Cardinal Ratzinger

[131] Ibid.

[132] Bernard Tissier de Mallerais, *The Biography of Marcel Lefebvre* (Kansas City, MO: Angelus Press, 2002), 537.

and Archbishop Lefebvre and approved by Pope John Paul II with the following terms:

- All censures against Lefebvre and the clergy and laity within SSPX would be removed.
- The SSPX would be recognized as a clerical society of apostolic life of pontifical right.
- The Holy See had agreed to consecrate a bishop recommended by Lefebvre for the SSPX as soon as 15 August 1988.

On 24 May, Lefebvre asked Cardinal Ratzinger for three bishops, instead of just one, and asked that a majority of traditionalists be represented on the commission overseeing the society, rather than two of the five, as outlined in the agreement.[133] Through Ratzinger, Pope John Paul II declined the revision to the proposal. The following morning, Lefebvre called together some clergy and explained, "I am inclined to consecrate four bishops anyway on June 30. My age and my failing health urge me, before the good Lord calls me to Him, to assure the safeguarding, not of 'my work,' but of this modest venture to restore the priesthood and preserve the Catholic Faith. I can do this giving the episcopacy to bishops who are free to make the Faith live in a setting that is entirely cut off from modern errors."[134]

That same day Lefebvre learned that Ratzinger rejected all the candidates that Lefebvre had put forward for consideration as bishops for the SSPX. In a letter to Pope John Paul II, dated 2 June 1988, the feast of Corpus Christi, Lefebvre explained that he would move forward and consecrate bishops even though they

[133] Ibid., 556.

[134] Ibid., 557–558.

had not been pre-approved by Pope John Paul II.[135] One week later, John Paul II wrote Lefebvre, warning him that this would be a schismatic act.

Archbishop Lefebvre and his priests and religious appealed to a state of ecclesial emergency in light of scandals from 1970 to 1988: the papally sanctioned idolatry at Assisi in 1986, the new Code of Canon Law of 1983, the new process of 1983 for canonizing saints, the apparent abrogation of the Tridentine Latin Mass, the new liturgies for all seven sacraments, the new ecumenism, and the heretical formation in most seminaries. Lefebvre invoked the Code of Canon Law stating, "the salvation of souls must always be the supreme law in the Church."[136] Convinced that he was operating for the salvation of souls, Archbishop Lefebvre consecrated four of his priests as bishops at the SSPX seminary at Écône, Switzerland, on 30 June 1988. The next day, Bernardin Cardinal Gantin of the Congregation of Bishops affirmed Lefebvre's automatic excommunication:

> Monsignor Marcel Lefebvre, Archbishop-Bishop Emeritus of Tulle, notwithstanding the formal canonical warning of 17 June last and the repeated appeals to desist from his intention, has performed a schismatic act by the episcopal consecration of four priests, without pontifical mandate and contrary to the will of the Supreme Pontiff, and has therefore incurred the penalty envisaged by Canon 1364, paragraph 1, and canon 1382 of the Code of Canon

[135] Ibid., 560.

[136] Canon (1983) 1752: "In cases of transfer the prescripts of can. 1747 are to be applied, canonical equity is to be observed, and the salvation of souls, which must always be the supreme law in the Church, is to be kept before one's eyes."

> Law. . . . Having taken account of all the juridical effects, I declare that the above-mentioned Archbishop Lefebvre, and Bernard Fellay, Bernard Tissier de Mallerais, Richard Williamson, and Alfonso de Galarreta have incurred ipso facto excommunication *latae sententiae* reserved to the Apostolic See.

In the papal motu proprio *Ecclesia Dei*, dated 2 July 1988, Pope John Paul II confirmed Lefebvre's excommunication for having consecrated bishops despite the pope's admonition not to do so. Lefebvre would die three years later on the feast of the Annunciation, 25 March 1991, at age eighty-five in Martigny, Switzerland. Archbishop Lefebvre's excommunication was the only excommunication of a bishop that Pope John Paul II recognized formally during his pontificate.

The pontificate of John Paul II continued into the 1990s with his apostolic constitution *Fidei depositum*, which ordered the publication of a new catechism that would include the reforms of Vatican II. Originally published in French in 1992, the *Catechism of the Catholic Church* became available in English in 1994. The official Latin edition was not published until 1997. It was enthusiastically received by conservatives who desperately sought a flotation device for orthodoxy after the turbulent 1970s and 1980s. In 1993, John Paul II issued his controversial encyclical *Veritatis splendor*, which upheld the intrinsic evil of acts such as abortion and contraception.

Leading up to the Jubilee Year 2000, John Paul II began issuing apologies—numbering more than one hundred—to the world on behalf of the Catholic Church. These included apologies for the persecution of Galileo, the African slave trade, burning heretics at the stake, the religious wars following the Protestant

Reformation, the denigration of women and their rights, and the silence of Catholics during the Holocaust. These apologies were controversial because they implicated guilt on the part of the Catholic Church and not merely on the misled sinful Catholics who had committed these misdeeds.

Prior to the Jubilee Year, Pope John Paul II scandalized the world when a photo surfaced of him kissing the Koran on 14 May 1999. He was visited by a delegation composed of the Shiite imams of Khadum mosque and the Sunni president of the council of administration of the Iraqi Islamic Bank and a representative of the Iraqi ministry of religion. The Catholic patriarch of Babylon Raphael Bidawid was present for the meeting and told the Vatican's own FIDES News Service what had transpired at this photographed meeting: "At the end of the audience the Pope bowed to the Muslim holy book the Koran, which was presented to him by the delegation and he kissed it as a sign of respect."[137] The Koran explicitly states that Jesus Christ is *not* the Son of God and that the Trinity is a false doctrine. How a pope of the Catholic Church could kiss the scriptures of Islam is unimaginable.

Flanked by representatives of Eastern Orthodoxy and Protestantism, Pope John Paul II opened the Jubilee Year 2000. One year later, he would be diagnosed with Parkinson's disease and begin his slow, painful descent in health.

Whether one admires John Paul II or not, he was certainly not an infiltrator of the Church. His pontificate is clearly conflicted, and he seems to be the first pope truly formed by the Second Vatican Council. Recall that the *Alta Vendita* never mandated placing an open Freemasonic atheist in the Chair of Peter. Rather,

[137] FIDES News Service, 14 May 1999.

the Freemasons sought to create (beginning in the mid-1800s) a climate among youth, seminarians, and young priests who grew up breathing the air of ecumenism, indifference to religious disagreements, and a mission for world brotherhood.

John Paul II is the first pope who moved freely in these ideals while still maintaining his old-world Polish devotions for Eucharistic Adoration, the Rosary, Confession, and processions. As a theologian and a youthful bishop, he drank deeply of Vatican II, but he still retained the piety of a Catholic. To ensure that the next pope would not possess these impediments to progress, certain liberal cardinals began to assemble and plan for the next pope.

27

Sankt Gallen Mafia: Homosexuality, Communism, and Freemasonry

As early as 1995, prominent cardinals began to assemble regularly in Sankt Gallen, Switzerland, to politick for the successor of John Paul II. These were all Modernists who favored the spirit of Vatican II. What bound them together was their allegiance to the Jesuit cardinal Carlo Maria Martini, archbishop of Milan. Cardinal Martini was the most prominent and outspoken opponent of Pope John Paul II and his prefect for doctrine, Cardinal Ratzinger.

The young John Paul II naively appointed Martini archbishop of Milan in 1979 and named him cardinal in 1983. Martini held considerable sway over the European bishops and served as the president of the European Bishops' Conference from 1987 until 1993. He openly and repeatedly rejected *Humanae vitae* and the Church's condemnation of artificial contraception, and her understanding of the beginning of human life. He was lax on euthanasia and advocated for the ordination of female deacons. He supported homosexuality and even civil marriage for homosexuals, saying, "It is not bad, instead of casual sex between men, that two people have a certain stability" and that the "state could recognize them."[138] On his deathbed, Martini said that the Catholic Church was "200 years out of date."[139]

In 1995, Martini called like-minded prelates to Sankt Gallen, Switzerland, to discuss reforming the Church. This first meeting may have been called in response to the 1994 decree *Ordinatio sacerdotalis* by John Paul II, which affirms that women can never be ordained to Holy Orders.[140] The topics popular with this group of bishops were collegiality, grooming future bishops, women as deacons, Communion for Protestants, Communion for the divorced and civilly remarried, and relaxing restrictions on sexual morality. These bishops were united in their deep concern that Cardinal Ratzinger would be voted in as papal heir apparent to John Paul II. Consequently, they needed time to cultivate a papal candidate who could defeat Cardinal Ratzinger at the next papal conclave.

Even though their leader, Cardinal Martini, was their most obvious choice for pope, he was Italian and did not have the support of the global bishops. So, the Sankt Gallen group examined the College of Cardinals and chose Jorge Cardinal Bergoglio of Argentina as their chief candidate, knowing that he would pursue the theological and moral agenda that they advocated.

The members of this Sankt Gallen Mafia changed over time, but the names reveal the usual suspects of crypto-Modernist Catholic prelates:

[138] Terence Weldon, "Cardinal Martini on Gay Partnerships," Queering the Church, 29 March 2012.

[139] L'Addio a Martini, "Chiesa indietro di 200 anni, L'ultima intervista: 'Perché non si scuote, perché abbiamo paura?'": Corriere della Sera, 1 September 2012.

[140] John Paul II, Apostolic Letter on Reserving Priestly Ordination to Men Alone *Ordinatio sacerdotalis* (22 May 1994).

- Swiss bishop Ivo Fürer, bishop of Sankt Gallen from 1995 to 2005
- Italian cardinal Carlo Martini, archbishop of Milan from 1980 to 2002 (died 31 August 2012 at age eighty-five)
- Belgian cardinal Godfried Danneels, metropolitan archbishop of Brussels from 1979 to 2010 (died 14 March 2019 at age eighty-five)
- German cardinal Walter Kasper, president of the Pontifical Council for Promoting Christian Unity from 2001 to 2010
- Dutch bishop Ad van Luyn, bishop of Rotterdam from 1994 to 2011
- German cardinal Karl Lehmann, bishop of Mainz from 1983 to 2016 (died 11 March 2018 at age eighty-one)
- Italian cardinal Achille Silvestrini (administrative secretary to Vatican secretary of state Jean-Marie Villot)
- British cardinal Basil Hume, archbishop of Westminster from 1976 to 1999 (died 17 June 1999 at age seventy-six)
- British cardinal Cormac Murphy-O'Connor, archbishop of Westminster from 2000-2009 (died 1 September 2017 at age eighty-five)
- Portuguese cardinal José Policarpo, patriarch of Lisbon, Portugal, from 1998 to 2013 (died 12 March 2014 at age seventy-eight)
- Ukrainian cardinal Lubomyr Husar, Ukrainian Catholic archbishop of Kiev from 2005 to 2011 (died 31 May 2017 at age eighty-four)

We know of the existence of these Sankt Gallen meetings thanks to Godfried Cardinal Danneels of Belgium, who has publicly supported same-sex marriage and the legalization of abortion in Belgium. In 2010, a clerical friend of Danneels, Bishop Roger

Vangheluwe (whom Danneels consecrated as bishop), was found to have molested his own nephew. (Danneels was caught on tape recordings, made secretly, telling the young man not to pursue the matter until after the bishop retired "honorably," and he unpassionately told the victim, "You can also acknowledge your own guilt," rather than accuse his uncle the bishop.)[141] Danneels described the Sankt Gallen meetings as a circle of friends hosted by Bishop Ivo Fürer, bishop of Sankt Gallen.

The official biographers of Danneels explained that "the election of Bergoglio was prepared in St. Gallen" because the "election of Bergoglio corresponded with the aims of St. Gallen, on that there is no doubt. And the outline of its program was that of Danneels and his confreres, who had been discussing it for ten years."[142] Danneels himself referred to the group as the Sankt Gallen "mafia."[143]

Why Sankt Gallen, Switzerland? Sankt Gallen has historical roots in European Communism. Originally the town grew around the missionary base of an Irish missionary monk named Saint Gallus along the River Steinach in A.D. 612. Saint Othmar established a monastery on the site in 720. The dairy-farming town grew up around the abbey. By the beginning of the 1900s,

[141] The typed transcript of the conversation between Danneels and the young man can be read in "Belgium Cardinal Tried to Keep Abuse Victim Quiet," *National Catholic Reporter*, 30 August 2010.

[142] The biographers of Danneels are Karim Schelkens and Jürgen Mettepenningen, and their comments can be found with clarification in Walter Pauli, "Godfried Danneels a oeuvré pendant des années à l'élection du pape François," *Le Vif*, 23 September 2015.

[143] "Cardinal Danneels Admits to Being Part of 'Mafia' Club Opposed to Benedict XVI," *National Catholic Register*, 24 September 2015.

however, the region became associated with ritual Satanism and Communism, as shall be demonstrated below.

Vladimir Lenin used Switzerland as his headquarters and place of exile on and off between 1903 and 1917. During the 1917 February Revolution in Russia, in which Tsar Nicholas II abdicated the throne, Lenin remained in exile in Switzerland. He inspired his revolution by having his writings and articles printed in Switzerland and smuggled into Russia. Encouraged by the February Revolution, he decided to return to Russia.

Fritz Platten organized Lenin's return to Russia. Platten was a native of Sankt Gallen—a Freemason and a Communist. He arranged to have Lenin sneaked out of Switzerland and through Germany in a sealed train car and then to find a ferry to Sweden and through Finland, where he would arrive back in Russia as leader apparent.

Our Lady of Fatima predicted these horrors in July 1917, when she warned the children that "Russia will spread her errors throughout the world, causing wars and persecutions of the Church. The good will be martyred, the Holy Father will have much to suffer, various nations will be annihilated." Led by Vladimir Lenin, the Bolsheviks violently seized power in November 1917 (one month after the Miracle of the Sun in Fatima) and murdered Tsar Nicholas II and his family on 17 July 1918.

Fritz Platten not only smuggled Lenin out of Switzerland back to Moscow; he also saved his life. Platten was in the backseat of Lenin's car when it was attacked in Petrograd on 14 January 1918. When gunfire rang out, Platten grabbed Lenin by the head and pushed him down. His hand was grazed by a bullet and covered in blood.[144] Without this intervention by this native of Sankt

[144] Dmitri Volkogonov, *Lenin: A New Biography* (New York: Free Press, 1994), 229.

Gallen, the world may not have known the horrors of Marxist-Leninism. Platten also founded the Communist International in 1919 as a means for encouraging world Communism. As a representative of the Swiss Communist Party, he spent much of his life in the Soviet Union. It seems that Platten is the link between Leninism and the origin of Sankt Gallen as a hotbed for Communism and dissent.

The infamous occultist Aleister Crowley (1875–1947) and his adherents also possess a ritualistic connection to Sankt Gallen. Crowley was a pioneer in recreational drug experimentation, a bisexual, an esoteric occultist, poet, painter, and outdoorsman. He was derided as the "wickedest man in the world" and labeled a Satanist. He was not formally a Satanist but was a self-proclaimed prophet and founder of the religion of Thelema. As an enthusiastic mountaineer, Crowley spent much of his time in Switzerland.

His religion centered on "sex-magick" of the Order of Templars of the Orient (OTO), of which Crowley was a member. Originally OTO was European Freemasonry, but under the leadership of Crowley, OTO was reorganized around the Law of Thelema: "Do what thou wilt shall be the whole of the Law."[145] Unlike explicit Freemasonry, the OTO includes an ecclesiastical and liturgical "church": the Ecclesia Gnostica Catholica (EGC) or Gnostic Catholic Church. The purpose of this church is to restore Christianity to its original status as a "solar-phallic religion." The OTO is a phallic cult, and its oldest lodge is in Switzerland.

[145] Aleister Crowley, *Liber AL vel Legis*, I:40. See also Leo Lyon Zagami, "Evidence of the Collaboration between the St. Gallen Mafia and the Ordo Templi Orientis," leozagami.com, 7 December 2017.

The OTO also celebrates the rite of Liber XV or the Gnostic Mass, which Crowley wrote in Moscow in 1913. The liturgy calls for five officers: a priest, a priestess, a deacon, and two acolytes, called "children" and culminates in the consummation of a faux Eucharistic rite and the consumption of wine and a cake of light (made of menstrual fluid) after which the recipient recites: "There is no part of me that is not of the gods!" It seems that the Diocese of Sankt Gallen allegedly assisted the OTO in celebrating this false Mass.

The Swiss-born Hermann Joseph Metzger became the patriarch of the Gnostic Catholic Church in 1960.[146] He dressed in a white cassock and zucchetto just like the Catholic pope. He also served as head of his Order of the Illuminati, head of his Fraternitas Rosicruciana Antiqua. Allegedly, "Patriarch" Metzger and the Swiss OTO acquired three thousand hosts from 1963 to 1967 from a Catholic convent. Whether these hosts were consecrated is not stated. Moreover, they claim that they received incense from the chief sacristan at the Sankt Gallen Cathedral and wine directly from Joseph Hasler, bishop of Sankt Gallen and Council father at the Second Vatican Council from 1963 to 1965.[147]

In 1954, the headquarters of OTO moved to Appenzell, Switzerland, which is thirty-one miles from the township of Sankt Gallen proper. The name Appenzell derives from the Latin *Abbatis cella*, or "abbot's cell." Although geographically within the canton of Sankt Gallen, Appenzell maintains its independence, having rebelled against the abbot of Sankt Gallen in 1403.

[146] "Metzger, Herman Joseph (1919–1990)," Encyclopedia.com.

[147] Aleister Crowley's Sexmagical System described in Zagami, "Evidence of the Collaboration between the St. Gallen Mafia and the Ordo Templi Orientis."

Going back to the 1360s, the lay inhabitants of the town of Sankt Gallen and the town of Appenzell had been in conflict with the prince abbot of Sankt Gallen over grazing rights and tithes due to the abbey. To counter their resistance, Abbot Kuno von Stoffeln acquired the direct support and patronage of the Austrian House of Habsburg against these towns under his ancient jurisdiction. In response, the township of Sankt Gallen submitted to the abbot, but Appenzell sought the support of the Old Swiss Confederation and staged a rebellion against the abbot in 1403. Appenzell retained its independence, and although it was sympathetic to Lutheran and Anabaptist preachers in the 1500s, it retained a Catholic majority. Oddly, Appenzell still civilly follows the Julian calendar and marks New Year's Day accordingly on our 14 January.

Appenzell, surrounded by the canton of Sankt Gallen, thus became the headquarters and capital of the OTO and Crowley's religion of Thelema in 1954. It also operates the largest lodge of World Federation of Illuminati.[148] Within this religion, the sex-magick techniques were taught by degree to initiates; for example the eighth degree of masturbation magic, the ninth degree of heterosexual magic, and the eleventh degree of anal sex magic.[149]

The year 1954 corresponds to the activities of the young Theodore McCarrick in Sankt Gallen, Switzerland, as revealed in an interview between McCarrick's child victim James Grein and me on 5 December 2018. Theodore McCarrick is the most notorious child molester and homosexual predator of the Catholic

[148] Zagami, "Evidence of the Collaboration."

[149] Aleister Crowley, *Magical Diaries of Aleister Crowley* (York Beach, ME: Weiser Books, 1979), 241.

Church, having been removed from the College of Cardinals in 2018 and from the clerical state in 2019.

Theodore McCarrick's father was a ship captain who died from tuberculosis when McCarrick was three years old. His mother raised him alone. He stayed at home while his mother worked at an automobile factory in the Bronx. As a teenager, he was expelled from Xavier High School in 1946. According to McCarrick it was for lack of attendance: "I think I felt the obligation of going daily to school was too strict an obligation.... They said, 'You've had it, you're out' more days than 'we'd like you to be here.'"[150] After being expelled, he missed one full academic year (1946–1947), and his whereabouts are unknown. A friend of the family was able to get him into the Jesuit Fordham Preparatory School in the Bronx, where he began his junior year in September 1947. McCarrick excelled at Fordham Prep. Before graduating in 1949, he was elected president of the Student Council and voted "Most Likely to Succeed, Best Speaker, Most Diplomatic, and Did the Most for Prep." Explaining his change of character, he recounted, "I guess I realized how unhappy I had made my mother and my family."[151]

While at Fordham Prep, McCarrick became friends with Werner Edelmann, the maternal uncle of James Grein, one of McCarrick's child victims. McCarrick graduated from Fordham Prep in May of 1949, just months before his nineteenth birthday. After his graduation, McCarrick said that he "spent a year with

[150] Chuck Conconi, "The Man in the Red Hat: With a Controversial Catholic in the Presidential Race, the Cardinal Is Seen by Many as the Vatican's Man in Washington and He May Play a Big Role in the Selection of the Next Pope," *Washingtonian*, 1 October 2004.

[151] Ibid.

a friend in Switzerland working on his language skills."[152] James Grein identifies that friend as his uncle Werner Edelmann.

We can place this year by examining the words of McCarrick, who said that he took "a religious retreat in a monastery in the Alps on his 20th birthday [where] he made the decision to become a priest."[153] In a separate interview, McCarrick identified the monastery as a Carthusian one.[154] McCarrick was born on 7 July 1930, so this places the retreat on 7 July 1950. This means that he spent a year in Switzerland, from about May 1949 until after 7 July 1950.

According to Grein, McCarrick traveled to Sankt Gallen, Switzerland, with his friend Werner Edelmann for a yearlong trip to visit Werner's father, Otto Edelmann. Otto Edelmann was a wealthy business owner who had invented a style and means to manufacture bras and girdles. To confirm this fact, one can consult the US patent #US2145075A issued on 1 August 1938 to "Otto Edelmann" for "Garment and method of making the same" under the patent category of "A41C1/00 Corsets or Girdles."[155] McCarrick spent his year in Sankt Gallen studying languages at the prestigious and expensive Institut auf dem Rosenberg, a private boarding school in Sankt Gallen, under the patronage of Otto Edelmann. According to Grein, it was at this time that his grandfather Otto Edelmann told McCarrick that he would financially sponsor him for any vocational path that he desired. Otto Edelmann thus became the patron of Theodore McCarrick.

[152] Ibid. He is fluent in Spanish, German, French, and Italian.

[153] Ibid.

[154] Kerry Kennedy, *Being Catholic Now: Prominent Americans Talk about Change in the Church and the Quest for Meaning*, (New York: Crown Publishers, 2008), 196.

[155] Otto Edelmann apparently sold his company around 1971.

Theodore McCarrick and James Grein, 1974

Grein relates that his uncle Werner rarely saw his friend Theodore during this time. Supposedly, he spent his nights at an unnamed monastery. Theodore discerned during this year at Sankt Gallen that he was called to be a priest. The devoutly Catholic Otto Edelmann was eager to assist him. With the financial support of the Edelmann family, McCarrick returned to New York by September 1950 to study at Fordham University and St. Joseph's Seminary in Yonkers. He was ordained to the priesthood by the reputed homosexual Cardinal Francis "Nellie" Spellman, archbishop of New York, on 31 May 1958. Otto Edelmann purchased a new automobile for Father Theodore McCarrick on the occasion of his ordination.

Father McCarrick became the de facto chaplain of the Edelmann and Grein families. The first baby that Father McCarrick baptized was the grandson of Otto Edelmann, James Grein, who would be molested by McCarrick at the age of eleven, and repeatedly for years, even within the context of sacramental confession.

The Grein family went to Sankt Gallen every Christmas from 1955 to 1963. Grein claims that Father McCarrick also traveled to Sankt Gallen annually for ten to fifteen years. He was deeply connected to this small town in Switzerland.

It is remarkable that this notorious pedophile and homosexual predator overlapped his time in Sankt Gallen with the establishment of Crowley's OTO religion and the headquarters of the Gnostic Catholic Church's being moved to Appenzell, thirty-one miles from the town of Sankt Gallen. Sankt Gallen provides a convergence of false Catholic religion focused on phallic worship, sex magick, and homosexuality with the visits of the young Theodore McCarrick. Decades later, Sankt Gallen became ground zero for a "mafia" of Modernist clergy that supported homosexuality, covered up sexual abuse, openly worked against Ratzinger/Benedict XVI, and lobbied to have Jorge Bergoglio elected as pope. The small town of Sankt Gallen served (and still serves) as the headquarters of the Council of European Bishops' Conferences (Consilium Conferentiarum Episcoporum Europae, or CCEE). Notably, two Sankt Gallen Mafia members served as presidents of the CCEE: Basil Cardinal Hume of Westminster (1979–1986) and Carlo Maria Cardinal Martini of Milan (1986–1993).[156]

One cannot help but wonder if Sankt Gallen served as an infiltration center for recruiting young men to infiltrate the priesthood in a way similarly described by Bella Dodd. Perhaps the arrival of the fatherless Theodore McCarrick to Sankt Gallen in 1949 provided them a perfect agent to infiltrate the American Catholic Church with pedophilia, sex magick, and Communism. The gross sex magick of Aleister Crowley's Gnostic Catholic Church is symbolically connected

[156] "The Presidency," Consilium Conferentiarum Episcoporum Europae.

with Theodore McCarrick since Crowley's cremated ashes are buried in Hampton, New Jersey—within McCarrick's first diocese of Metuchen, New Jersey, where he served as bishop from 1980 to 1986.[157] McCarrick magically ascended to priest (1958), monsignor (1965), bishop (1977), archbishop (1986), and cardinal (2001) without ever having served as a pastor of a parish. His ascent through the hierarchy happened impressively after his initial visit to Sankt Gallen in 1949 and at least ten other visits subsequently.

[157] The ashes of Aleister Crowley are buried in an urn next to a tree on the property of Crowley's successor or "caliph" Karl Germer in Hampton, New Jersey. Theodore McCarrick was the first bishop of Metuchen, New Jersey.

28

Ratzinger versus Bergoglio in the Papal Conclave of 2005

Pope John Paul II died on 2 April 2005. His death signaled global mourning for the man who was truly the first televised pope. Joseph Cardinal Ratzinger, as dean of the College of Cardinals, preached at the pope's funeral and was considered as a likely candidate for pope in the following conclave. The papal conclave met from 18 to 19 April 2005. John Paul II had relaxed the rules for the conclave so that the cardinal electors could move freely, dine, and sleep in the air-conditioned individual rooms of Casa Santa Marta, the five-story hotel built in 1996 for visiting clergy.

There were at the time 183 cardinals, but only 117 cardinal-electors under the age of eighty. Two were absent on account of bad health—Jaime Cardinal Sin of the Philippines and Adolfo Antonio Cardinal Suárez Rivera of Mexico—bringing the number of electors to 115. Of these, only two electors (Cardinal Ratzinger and Cardinal Baum) had not been appointed cardinals by John Paul II due to the rule change made by Paul VI that only cardinals under eighty may vote. With 115 cardinal electors, the two-thirds majority required would be 77 votes.

One ballot was counted in the afternoon of the first day of conclave and then three more ballots on the next day. An anonymous cardinal provided his diary to an Italian journalist in September 2005. If it can be trusted, it gave the following votes for the first ballot:[158]

Joseph Ratzinger—47 votes
Jorge Bergoglio—10 votes
Carlo Maria Martini—9 votes
Camillo Ruini—6 votes
Angelo Sodano—4 votes
Oscar Maradiaga—3 votes
Dionigi Tettamanzi—2 votes
Giacomo Biffi—1 vote
Others—33 votes

Notice Jorge Bergoglio in second place. These ten votes are undoubtedly the Sankt Gallen Mafia members.

The second ballot on the following morning:

Ratzinger—65 votes
Bergoglio—35 votes
Sodano—4 votes
Tettamanzi—2 votes
Biffi—1 vote
Others—8 votes

Twenty-four new votes appear for Bergoglio in this second ballot. Note well that all the votes for Cardinal Martini (9 votes), Cardinal Ruini (6 votes), and Cardinal Maradiaga (3 votes), tallying up to 18 votes, have been withdrawn and given to Cardinal Bergoglio. This shows that at this point, these three men had instructed their followers to rally to Bergoglio.

The third ballot, also in the morning, counted as follows:

[158] Andrea Tornielli, "Il diario segreto dell'ultimo conclave," *La Stampa*, 27 July 2011.

Ratzinger—72 votes
Bergoglio—40 votes
Darío Castrillón Hoyos—1 vote
Others—2 votes

Bergoglio managed to gain another 5 votes, but the great majority rallied to Ratzinger to block Bergoglio. After this third ballot, it became clear that Ratzinger would need only 5 more votes, or a compromise candidate would need to emerge to break the gridlock (there were only 3 votes still up for grabs) between Bergoglio and Ratzinger. As the votes moved toward Cardinal Ratzinger, he recalled, "I prayed to God 'Please don't do this to me.' Evidently, this time He didn't listen to me."[159]

That afternoon, the fourth and final ballot counted as follows:

Ratzinger—84 votes
Bergoglio—26 votes
Biffi—1 vote
Bernard Law—1 vote
Christoph Schönborn—1 vote
Others—2 votes

Surprisingly, at least 14 cardinals retreated from Bergoglio in this fourth ballot when it became clear that Ratzinger had the most support. Ratzinger won easily with 84 votes, 7 more than he needed to capture the two-thirds majority. The Sankt Gallen Mafia failed in their goal to elect Cardinal Bergoglio.

[159] Allen Pizzey, "Benedict: I Prayed Not to Be Pope" CBS News, 11 February 2009.

29

Infiltration and the Plot against Benedict XVI

It is the role of the dean of the College of Cardinals to ask the elected candidate if he accepts the papacy. Since Cardinal Ratzinger was the dean of the College, that task fell to the vice dean, Angelo Cardinal Sodano. The cardinal protodeacon, Jorge Medina emerged on the balcony of Saint Peter's Basilica and announced the election of Cardinal Ratzinger and that he had chosen the name Benedict XVI, in honor of both Pope Benedict XV and Saint Benedict of Nursia.

Pope Benedict XVI's reputation as a scholar endured when he wrote three encyclicals *Deus caritas est*, *Spe salvi*, and *Caritas in veritate*, rooted in the theological virtues. He ruffled liberals by returning to the papal dress and ceremonies not seen since the days of Pope Pius XII, such as the red shoes, the camauro, and the red cappello romano.

Two years into his pontificate, Benedict XVI issued his controversial motu proprio *Summorum pontificum*, which stated that the traditional pre–Vatican II Latin Mass (commonly known as the Tridentine Mass) had never been abrogated or forbidden. He clarified that all Catholic priests can and may celebrate the traditional Latin Mass according to the Missal of 1962. He explained that the 1969 Novus Ordo Mass of Paul VI remained the "ordinary form" of the Roman Rite and that the 1962 Mass would be the "extraordinary form" of the Roman Rite—and that these two "forms" should mutually enrich each another. This document was met with relief and praise from traditionalists who had avoided the gaze of non-accommodating bishops for forty years.

In a way, *Summorum pontificum* exonerated the now deceased Archbishop Lefebvre, who had insisted that the Missal of 1962 was never formally abrogated when Paul VI issued the *Novus Ordo Missae* in 1962.

To substantiate this further, Pope Benedict XVI formally remitted the excommunications of the four bishops of Lefebvre's Society of Saint Pius X (SSPX) on 21 January 2009. This remission was made without the four bishops repenting of their consecrations in 1988 at the hands of Archbishop Lefebvre without papal mandate from John Paul II. It seemed that Ratzinger was now untying a knot that had been tied in May 1988, when communications between Lefebvre and him broke down.

Most bishops of the world did not favor Benedict's remission of the SSPX excommunications. Six months later, Pope Benedict XVI issued his motu proprio *Ecclesiae unitatem*, in which he explained his reason for lifting the excommunications and clarified the status of the SSPX:

> The remission of the excommunication was a measure taken in the context of ecclesiastical discipline to free the individuals from the burden of conscience constituted by the most serious of ecclesiastical penalties. However, the doctrinal questions obviously remain and until they

are clarified the Society has no canonical status in the Church and its ministers cannot legitimately exercise any ministry.[160]

Benedict XVI seemed intent on bringing the spiritual children of Lefebvre into regular canonical status. He handwrote a note to their superior, Bishop Bernard Fellay, in June 2012, assuring him of the canonical structure of a personal prelature (such as Opus Dei) if he and the Society of Saint Pius X would recognize the documents of Vatican II. Bishop Fellay responded that it was impossible for them to affirm the Council's doctrine on religious freedom. Communications between the SSPX and Benedict XVI seemed to have completely broken down by the end of the year.

[160] The final line in Latin reads: "*et eius ministri nullum ministerium legitime agere possunt*." Some critics of the SSPX have wrongly translated this as "and its ministers have no legitimate ministry." But the Latin *legitime* is an adverb, so it means: "and its ministers cannot *legitimately* perform any ministry." This means that the SSPX still lacks canonical status licitly, not that its ministry is invalid or illegitimate, in the English sense of the term.

30

Infiltration of the Vatican Bank and the Butler of Pope Benedict XVI

Meanwhile a plot had been hatched against Pope Benedict to pressure him to resign the papacy. All this would climax by the end of 2012 with money laundering at the Vatican Bank, the revelation of homosexual predators among the cardinals and Vatican staff, and the freezing of funds. But the story begins in 2007, when Paolo Gabriele was hired as the personal butler of Pope Benedict XVI. For reasons unknown, he would leak important confidential documents to the public, creating the scandal known as Vatileaks. Paolo Gabriele's mysterious action publicized a plot to humiliate, frame, and remove Pope Benedict XVI from the Chair the Peter.

Pope Benedict XVI soon began to be aware of financial discrepancies in the Governorate of Vatican City State—the executive authority over the Vatican City State. Giovanni Cardinal Lajolo was the president of the Governorate at this time. The president serves as head of Vatican City and answers to the cardinal secretary of state and then the pope. He is second in line, administratively, under the pope.

On 16 July 2009, Pope Benedict appointed Archbishop Carlo Maria Viganò as secretary-general of the Vatican City

Governorate. This placed Viganò as third in line administratively under the pope. Archbishop Viganò immediately insisted on a centralized accounting procedure and full financial accountability. His new policies turned a negative U.S. $10.5 million deficit for Vatican City into a surplus of U.S. $44 million in just one year.[161] Viganò was not a savvy stockbroker. Instead, his new accounting policies uncovered millions of dollars in hidden accounts. The accounting books had shown a deficit of $10.5 million in the primary checking account, but by revealing the many accounts off the books, Viganò flushed out $55 million in only twelve months. No doubt, Pope Benedict was delighted to have financial clarity (and funds) but was disappointed in his leadership at the Vatican City Governorate.

In January 2012, a leaked document emerged regarding homosexual and financial scandals within the Vatican. Among them were two letters from Viganò to Pope Benedict XVI and to the cardinal secretary of state, Bertone, complaining of continued corruption in the Vatican finances. The very next month, Viganò's direct superior, the president, Cardinal Giovanni Lajolo, along with Giuseppe Bertello, Giuseppe Sciacca, and Giorgio Corbellini retaliated against Viganò and issued a joint statement on behalf of the Governorate of the Vatican:

> The unauthorized publication of two letters of Archbishop Carlo Maria Viganò, the first addressed to the Holy Father on March 27, 2011, the second to the Cardinal Secretary of State on May 8, for the Governorate of Vatican City is a source of great bitterness.... The allegations contained

[161] John L. Allen Jr., "Vatican Denies Corruption Charges attributed to U.S. Nuncio," *National Catholic Reporter*, 26 January 2012.

> in them cannot but lead to the impression that the Governorate of Vatican City, instead of being an instrument of responsible government, is an unreliable entity, at the mercy of dark forces. After careful examination of the contents of the two letters, the President of the Governorate sees it as his duty to publicly declare that those assertions are the result of erroneous assessments, or fears based on unsubstantiated evidence, even openly contradicted by the main characters invoked as witnesses."[162]

Secretary of State Cardinal Bertone was Viganò's superior and was also unhappy with the leaked letters to him and the pope.

Months before the accusations had been made public, Cardinal Bertone told Viganò that he would be transferred away from the Governorate of Vatican City. Viganò is rumored to have resisted this change in assignment. On 19 October 2011, Pope Benedict reassigned Viganò as apostolic nuncio to Washington, D.C., the pope's ambassador to the United States. Many saw this as a demotion, but it is more likely that Pope Benedict wanted an honest man in Washington whom he could trust to investigate. Of particular importance was the fact, later made public, that Pope Benedict had learned of the homosexual predatory deeds of Cardinal McCarrick in Washington and wanted Viganò to maintain restrictions against the public ministry of Cardinal McCarrick that had been in place since 2006.

As mentioned above, the Vatileaks scandal spilled out beginning in January 2012, revealing financial corruption, international money laundering, and schemes of blackmail against homosexual

[162] "*Dichiarazione della Presidenza del Governatorato dello Stato della Città del Vaticano*," 4 February 2012.

clergy. Italian journalist Gianluigi Nuzzi published the two letters of Archbishop Viganò describing corrupt practices that cost the Holy See millions of dollars. One leaked letter revealed a potential death threat against Pope Benedict XVI, wherein Cardinal Romeo of Palermo of Sicily predicted that the pope would be dead within twelve months.[163] In May 2012, Nuzzi published a book entitled *His Holiness: The Secret Papers of Benedict XVI* consisting of confidential letters and memos between Pope Benedict and his personal secretary. The book documented a subculture of Vatican jealousy, discord, and party infighting. Nuzzi revealed details of Pope Benedict XVI's personal finances and showed how bribery gained a special audience with the pope.

Vatican police arrested the pope's personal butler, Paolo Gabriele, on 23 May 2012 after confidential letters and documents addressed to the pope and other Vatican officials were discovered in his apartment. He was accused of being the mole that leaked copies of the documents to Nuzzi, since the documents found in Gabriele's apartment matched the documents that had been leaked over the previous five months. One week later, the pope publicly acknowledged the scandal: "The events of recent days about the Curia and my collaborators have brought sadness in my heart.... I want to renew my trust in and encouragement of my closest collaborators and all those who every day, with loyalty and a spirit of sacrifice and in silence, help me fulfill my ministry."[164]

At his trial, Gabriele pleaded guilty to stealing the papal documents but claimed he had done so in order to expose and fight the

[163] Michael Day, "Vatileaks: Hunt is on to find Vatican Moles," *Independent*, 28 May 2012.

[164] Associated Press, "Pope Breaks Silence over Vatileaks Scandal," 30 May 2012.

corruption within the Church. On 6 October, Gabriele was found guilty of theft and received a sentence of eight years in prison, which was then commuted to eighteen months along with fines.

In the midst of the Vatlileaks scandal, the embarrassed Pope Benedict secretly commissioned three of his trusted cardinals to investigate the Vatileaks and report back to him on financial irregularities, rumors of blackmail, and sexually immoral cardinals and curial staff. The three-man commission was led by Julián Cardinal Herranz Casado of Opus Dei and included Jozef Cardinal Tomko and Salvatore Cardinal De Giorgi. On 17 December 2012 (the birthday of Cardinal Bergoglio), the three cardinals presented a three-hundred-page dossier to Pope Benedict XVI in strict secrecy. This detailed dossier (allegedly contained in one or two red binders) described Vatican hierarchs dressed in drag with lewd details about them by Italian male prostitutes. It also confirmed rampant financial irregularities throughout the Vatican. Pope Benedict has cited 17 December 2012 as the day on which he formally decided to resign. The contents of the red binder were just too much for the aging pontiff. Pope Benedict personally visited his butler, Paolo Gabriele, and pardoned him on 22 December 2012. Did Pope Benedict XVI now see that the Vatileaks scandal via Gabriele was a blessing in disguise?

On 1 January 2013, ATM machines in Vatican City ceased working, as Deutsche Bank had closed its accounts with the Vatican Bank on 31 December 2012. The Sistine Chapel could only process cash for ticket receipts.[165] On 11 February 2013,

[165] Rachel Sanderson. "The Scandal at the Vatican Bank: An 11-Month FT Investigation Reveals the Extent of Mismanagement at the €5bn-Asset Bank," *Financial Times*, 6 December 2013.

Pope Benedict XVI announced that he would formally resign the papacy. That night, an omen appeared when lighting struck the dome of Saint Peter's Basilica.

The next morning, 12 February 2013, the Swiss Aduno Group took over operation of Vatican cash machines, avoiding Italian and EU regulation. The timing of the pope's announcement and the new role of Aduno cannot be coincidental, given the scandal and intrigue of the preceding months. Something happened between 17 December 2012, when the pope received the red-binder dossier, and 1 January 2013, when the Vatican cash machines ceased working.

On 28 February 2013, the unimaginable happened: Pope Benedict XVI resigned the papacy and flew off in a helicopter as the world watched, baffled. Benedict was the first pope to resign since Pope Gregory XII in 1415, almost 598 years before. Unlike Pope Gregory XII, this pope indicated that he would be called Papa Emeritus, and he would continue to wear the white cassock and red shoes and ring of a pope.

31

Infiltration and the Election of Pope Francis

I saw also the relationship between two Popes. I saw how baleful the consequences of this false church would be. I saw it increase in size; heretics of every kind came into the city of Rome. The local clergy grew lukewarm, and I saw a great darkness. Then the vision seemed to extend on every side. Whole Catholic communities were being oppressed, harassed, confined, and deprived of their freedom. I saw many churches closed, great miseries everywhere, wars and bloodshed. A wild and ignorant mob took violent action. But it did not last long. . . . Once more I saw that the Church of Peter was undermined by a plan evolved by the secret sect [Freemasons], while storms were damaging it. But I saw also that help was coming when distress had reached its peak. I saw again the Blessed Virgin ascend on the Church and spread her mantle"

—Blessed Anne Catherine Emmerich, Allocution of 13 May 1820

As instructed, the cardinals gathered in the Eternal City for the election of the next pope during a conclave lasting from 12 to 13 March 2013. To the wonderment of the cardinals, a valid pope left the See of Peter *vacante*, and while still living, called them to elect another. There were 207 cardinals during the *sede vacante*, with 117 being under the age of eighty and eligible to vote. Only 115 participated because Julius Cardinal Darmaatmadja of Indonesia was prevented by the deterioration of his eyesight and Keith Cardinal O'Brien of Scotland because of his admitted sexual misconduct with priests.

On the first ballot of 12 March, the unsubstantiated and alleged leaders were subsequently reported by *La Repubblica* as:

Angelo Scola—35 votes

Bergoglio—20 votes

Ouellet—15 votes

Cardinal Scola was seen as a safe conservative to follow in the way of Benedict XVI. After two ballots the following morning, no progress was made, and Cardinal Ouellet allegedly asked for his supporters to transfer their votes to Cardinal Bergoglio in succeeding ballots. Theoretically, this would hold Scola at 35 votes and Bergoglio at 35 votes. That afternoon, on the fourth ballot, Bergoglio had the majority (more than 58 votes) but not yet the 77 votes required to capture a two-thirds majority.

On the fifth and final ballot, the cardinals coalesced around the clear leader. Bergoglio received 90 votes (13 more than necessary). According to Seán Cardinal Brady of Ireland, applause broke out during the tallying of votes when Bergoglio's count reached the 77 votes.[166]

At 7:06 p.m. Italian time, white smoke plumed from the Sistine Chapel, and the sounding of the bells indicated that the cardinals had successfully elected a pope. Bergoglio appeared unceremoniously on the balcony of Saint Peter's as Pope Francis, and in a reversal of roles, he asked the people below to pray for

[166] John Allen Jr., "Path to the Papacy: 'Not Him, Not Him, Therefore Him,'" *National Catholic Reporter*, 17 March 2013.

him. Standing next to him was Cardinal Danneels, the man who had admitted to the existence of a "mafia" to elect Bergoglio. Cardinal Murphy-O'Connor, also a member of the Sankt Gallen Mafia, told *La Stampa* and the *Independent* that, "Four years of Bergoglio would be enough to change things."[167] Subsequently, even Cardinal McCarrick confessed that an "influential Italian gentleman ... a very brilliant man, very influential man in Rome" visited him at the seminary where McCarrick was staying in Rome and said, "What about Bergoglio? ... He could do it, you know, reform the church." And so McCarrick promoted the cause of Bergoglio among the cardinals prior to the election.[168]

Mission accomplished for the Sankt Gallen Mafia: at last they delivered to the world a "Revolution in Tiara and Cope" as had been prophesied by the Freemasonic document *Alta Vendita* more than 150 years before. After a slow, patient revolution, they had secured "a Pope according to our heart; it is a task first of all to form for this Pope a generation worthy of the kingdom that we desire."

The Problematic Teachings of Pope Francis

After Pope Francis was elected on 13 March 2013, things moved rapidly. On 15 June 2013, Pope Francis appointed Monsignor Battista Mario Salvatore Ricca—who allegedly carried on a homosexual affair with the captain of the Swiss Guard—as prelate of the Vatican Bank (IOR). In July 2013, the money laundering

[167] Paul Vallely, "Pope Francis Puts People First and Dogma Second. Is This Really the New Face of Catholicism?" *The Independent*. 31 July 2013.

[168] Elizabeth Yore, "Was Predator Cardinal McCarrick a Key U.S. Lobbyist for Pope Francis' Election?" LifeSite News, 27 June 2018.

case against former Vatican Bank chief Gotti Tedeschi was suddenly dropped. The pontificate of Pope Francis has been documented in detail by others and represents a strong shift toward ecumenism, globalism, immigration, and socialism. His encyclicals and teaching stress environmentalism (*Laudato si'*), the redistribution of wealth by governments, a relaxation of sexual morality, and a supreme emphasis on following one's conscience over and above Catholic dogma.

Pope Francis's *Amoris laetitia* sparked considerable criticism for stating "No one can be condemned forever, because that is not the logic of the Gospel! Here I am not speaking only of the divorced and remarried, but of everyone, in whatever situation they find themselves."[169] The statement entails that hell is not eternal—a doctrine taught by Giordano Bruno, whose statue had been erected in Rome just a century before. The pope's *Amoris laetitia* also opened the way for civilly divorced and remarried Catholics to receive absolution and Holy Communion while remaining sexually active.[170] On 19 September 2016, four cardinals, the Italian Carlo Caffarra, the American Raymond Burke, and the Germans Walter Brandmüller and Joachim Meisner, formally sought clarification from the pope regarding what appeared to be heretical teaching. The pope did not respond to their *dubia*.

Pope Francis has explicitly stated that God wills for some to break the moral law when they cannot reach the ideal.[171] Pope

[169] Pope Francis, Post-Synodal Apostolic Exhortation on Love in the Family *Amoris laetitia*, (19 March 2016), no. 297.

[170] Pope Francis, *Amoris laetitia*, nos. 301, 303, 305 and footnotes at 329 and 351.

[171] In *Amoris Laetitia*, no. 303, Pope Francis states that a sinful act as a "most generous response which can be given to God ... is what God himself is asking." This suggests that God is asking for

Francis also has taught that God divinely and wisely wills the "diversity and plurality of religions" with the same will "by which he created human beings."[172] Pope Francis also endorsed the 2030 Plan of the United Nations regarding environmentalism, reproductive rights, and population control.[173] His worldview

---

an objectively sinful act that "does not correspond objectively to the overall demands of the Gospel." Some have sought to justify this language by appealing to Saint Thomas Aquinas in the *Summa theologiae* I-II q. 19, art. 5, which reads: "but when erring reason proposes something as being commanded by God, then to scorn the dictate of reason is to scorn the commandment of God." In *Amoris* 303, however, Francis does not speak of conscience wrongly thinking that "something is commanded by God"; he speaks of something "that does not correspond objectively to the overall demands of the Gospel."

So, according to Saint Thomas, if a man truly thinks that having two wives is what God commands, and he marries two wives, he is not culpable. If he knows, however, that God commands monogamy and nonetheless chooses to have two wives, he cannot (as Francis suggests) justify this as "the most generous response" possible at the moment, claim that this is what God asks at the moment," and keep two wives.

[172] "The pluralism and the diversity of religions, colour, sex, race and language are willed by God in His wisdom, through which He created human beings. [El pluralismo y la diversidad de religión, color, sexo, raza y lengua son expresión de una sabia voluntad divina, con la que Dios creó a los seres humanos.] This divine wisdom is the source from which the right to freedom of belief and the freedom to be different derives. Therefore, the fact that people are forced to adhere to a certain religion or culture must be rejected, as too the imposition of a cultural way of life that others do not accept." Pope Francis, "Document on Human Fraternity for World Peace and Living Together" (5 February 2019).

[173] Pope Francis's remarks to the participants in the International Conference "Religions and the Sustainable Development Goals

and the philosophy is essentially that of a nineteenth-century member of the Freemasonic Carbonari.

Saint Pius X would have placed Pope Francis under the ban of Modernism. How can we have two popes in theological contradiction?

(SDGs): Listening to the Cry of the Earth and of the Poor," organized by the Dicastery for Promoting Integral Human Development and by the Pontifical Council for Interreligious Dialogue, Vatican's New Synod Hall, 8 March 2019. Lydia O'Kane, "Pope: Sustainable Development Rooted in Ethical Values," *Vatican News*, 8 March 2019.

32

Solving the Current Crisis

Where does the scheming of the Sankt Gallen Mafia and the election and teaching of Pope Francis leave us?

There are several options for Catholics attempting to make sense of this.

Become a Modernist Catholic

The most popular and widespread solution is simply to grant that Pope Francis and the Modernist tendency since the late 1950s is the true and correct path desired by Almighty God. Prior popes rejected ecumenism and burned heretics at the stake; Pope Francis, however, teaches that God wills the plurality and diversity of religions. Since the Catechism of Trent, Pope Pius XI, Pope Leo XIII, and Pope Pius XII affirmed and defended the death penalty, why not admit that Pope Francis has rightly contradicted previous popes by teaching that the death penalty is inadmissible?

Pope Francis teaches that divorced and civilly remarried people may remain Catholic and receive the Holy Eucharist and the other sacraments. Yet Pope Clement VII vigorously opposed King Henry VIII's attempt at remarriage and endured the friction that would create the Church of England and the loss of the entire European nation to Protestantism. Pope Pius V further resisted the Church of England and created a strong animosity that led to wars and a string of martyrdoms.

The Modernist Catholic says Pope Francis is right and Pope Clement VII and Pope Pius V were dead wrong. And when Pope Leo X and his successors condemned Martin Luther, they did so wrongly, as Pope Francis has publicly commended Luther and even issued a Vatican City stamp in his honor. All this requires that we recognize that Pope Francis formally disagrees with previous popes and previous Councils and that he is correct. In other words, why not confess that the spirit of Vatican II is none other than the Holy Spirit? The Modernist truly believes that the new liturgy, the new code of canon law, the new theology, and the new popes are superior to those of the previous nineteen hundred years. Why not rejoice to live in the age of the New Pentecost?

Most serious and informed Catholics cannot swallow this pill.

Catholicism is a perennial religion, and by its nature it cannot change or contradict itself. Certain cardinals and bishops may act as if Catholicism after the Council is a "new advent" in the history of the Church, but to be deep in history is to cease to be Modernist. So, if one refuses to accept the Modernist version of Catholicism as intellectually dishonest, he must find a new narrative.

I present the following solutions to the current ecclesial crisis.

Become an Atheist

Since there is an apparent rupture between recent papacies and previous papacies and councils, one may simply relent and confess that Catholicism and Christianity as a whole were merely accidents of Western history and the most successful world religion to date. Catholicism was able to endure and envelop the globe by running off the fumes of the fallen Roman Empire. Recent advances in science and sociology reveal that concepts such as creation, original sin, healings, demonic possession, resurrection, and life after death are premodern man's attempt to understand his mysterious prescientific world. Instead of trying to foist our modern scientific view on a medieval system such as Catholicism, why not simply reject it altogether? Atheism easily and swiftly accounts for the disjunction experienced by contemporary Catholics.

For myself, I cannot accept atheism because I have personally encountered Christ, His Blessed Mother, and the saints in my life. I also remain fully convinced of the existence of God and His full revelation of Himself in the incarnate Person of our Lord Jesus Christ. So, the remaining options are the following.

Accept the Protestant Position

The next possibility is to accept the ancient biblical testimony about Jesus Christ found in Sacred Scripture but to reject the historical apparatus that we identify with the institution of the Catholic Church. As Martin Luther taught, we can enjoy a direct encounter with Jesus Christ through *faith alone*, without the mediation of popes, priests, or sacraments. The teaching authority for the Christian is found not in ancient councils, papal bulls, or encyclicals but only in the pure Word of God.

For reasons explained in my books *The Crucified Rabbi* and *The Catholic Perspective on Paul*, I converted from Protestantism to Catholicism because of the patent testimony of Sacred Scripture for the mediated redemption of Christ through the sacraments He instituted and through the clergy in apostolic succession ordained by Him. Moreover, Christ clearly instituted a Church prior to the composition and canonization of the Holy Bible. For this reason, Protestantism is not a valid option.

Accept the Eastern Orthodox Position

Another tempting option before us is to accept that the Eastern Orthodox are correct about the papacy—that the papacy has erred in the past and continues to err. The papacy never was infallible and never possessed universal supreme jurisdiction. The First Vatican Council was gravely wrong on this subject. Instead, magisterial authority in the Orthodox Church is established only by ecumenical councils including the pope as patriarch of Rome in union with the ancient patriarchal sees of the East. In this way, biblical ecclesiology and sacraments are retained, but the bishop of Rome is knocked down from his ultramontane pedestal.

This position is untenable for the reasons I set out in my book *The Eternal City*. The supremacy and universal role of the city of Rome is not an accident of history. Rather, the Roman origin and structure of the Catholic Church is explicitly prophesied in the Old Testament by the prophet Daniel regarding the Son of Man and his saints receiving the Fourth Kingdom of Rome as His own kingdom for the Church. As demonstrated in *The Eternal City*, the Church of Rome assumed universal jurisdiction from the second century, even presuming to excommunicate dozens of sees in Anatolia over the Quartodeciman Controversy. Eastern Orthodoxy, while attractive in our contemporary situation, does not account for Scripture or history. Moreover, the Orthodox have already ecclesiastically approved divorce and remarriage and contraception. It seems apparent to me that Pope Francis actually holds the Eastern Orthodox position on the papacy, collegiality, divorce, and the "pastoral" notion of *economia* revamped as being true to conscience.

Accept the Sedevacantist Position

One position with growing and enthusiastic support is that of sedevacantism. The sedevacantists hold that the papal conclave of 1958 was irregular, since the white smoke and ringing bells indicated a papal election, but no pope appeared on that occasion. They point to this oddity and suspect that Cardinal Siri was validly elected but falsely pressured to resign. No one knows exactly what happened within the conclave of 1958, but sedevacantists resolutely affirm that Cardinal Roncalli was not validly elected as Pope John XXIII—either because he was a Freemason and a heretic or because the election itself was invalid. They also note that the Third Secret of Fatima was to be revealed in 1960 and that John XXIII refused to reveal it because it indicated that he was an antipope or warned the Church of an impending false and heretical council.

Sedevacantism is attractive because, in one swoop, all the problems of infiltration, Modernism, Vatican II, Paul VI's new liturgies, and a pope kissing a Koran disappear. When the Catholic asks "How could Pope [insert a pope's name since 1958] do or say such a thing?" the sedevacantist coolly replies, "Because he is not and never was a true pope. The answer is that a true pope would never do or say such a thing."[174] I have noticed an increasing number of young men, weary of the effeminacy of the post-conciliar liturgy and doctrine, rallying to sedevacantism as a logical, calm, and stoic solution to ecclesial chaos.

Sedevacantism originated chiefly in the late 1970s, when the Thomistic theologian Father Michel-Louis Guérard des Lauriers

[174] For a thorough explanation and refutation of the sedevacantist position, see John Salza and Robert Siscoe, *True or False Pope: Refuting Sedevacantism and Other Modern Errors* (Dillwyn, VA: Saint Thomas Aquinas Seminary, 2016).

proposed the "Cassiciacum Thesis," otherwise known as sedeprivationism. Guérard des Lauriers had served as a theological consulter to Pope Pius XII on the dogma of the Assumption of Mary in 1950. He was the sacramental confessor of Pope Pius XII before being replaced by Cardinal Bea. He was a contributing author to the Ottaviani Intervention, and he was an early collaborator with Archbishop Lefebvre. His hypothesis suggested that Paul VI was, in fact, the pope materially and functionally, but due to heresy, he lacked the formal charism of the papacy. The pope was *deprived* of something, and hence his position became known as sedeprivationism.

By 1980, many were enthusiastic about this Cassiciacum Thesis, but not Archbishop Lefebvre. By 1981, Guérard des Lauriers parted from Lefebvre and received episcopal consecration. By 1984, nine SSPX priests in the United States had broken with Lefebvre and were espousing not just sedeprivationism (the belief that the current pope lacks the formal papacy) but full-blown sedevacantism (the belief that the current pope is not valid at all).

My objection to sedevacantism is twofold: sedevacantists do not present a consistent theological narrative for the origin of a crisis (without a pope), and they also lack a consistent solution for the formal restoration of the papacy on earth. Sedevacantism teaches that, from 1958 until around 1980, 100 percent of the cardinals who were present in the 1958 conclave, 100 percent of the bishops, and 100 percent of the laity were duped into submitting to antipopes and their doctrine without a true pope on earth as a valid rival. According to the sedevacantist, every Catholic bishop, including Cardinal Ottaviani, Archbishop Lefebvre, and their own Archbishop Thuc followed and submitted to an antipope for their entire lives or at least for several years.

Around 1980, a handful of priests and some laity began to wake up to the fact that the Catholic Church had existed in an interregnum without a real pope for twenty years! Moreover, this sudden ecclesial crisis was not signaled by a proximate Marian apparition, miracles, prophesies by holy priests, or signs and wonders. Even Padre Pio of Pietrelcina, who spoke regularly with Jesus, Mary, the saints, and the holy souls, failed to learn that John XXIII and Paul VI were antipopes! So much for the sedevacantist narrative of origin.

The second problem with sedevacantism is that it lacks a means for restoring the papacy on earth. If there has not been a valid pope since 1958, then there are no valid cardinals walking the earth. Hence, the canonical process that elected Pope Pius XII in 1939 and his successors previously is no longer an option. Any future papal conclave in accord with canon law is now an impossibility.

When you press sedevacantists on how the current ecclesial crisis will be resolved with a new pope, they present a variety of speculations. Some say that it is the end times and there shall never again be a valid pope. Others say angels or the Holy Ghost shall descend on a man, and this will indicate to the Church that he is the true pope. Some appeal to private revelations that claim that Saint Peter and Saint Paul shall appear from heaven and personally delegate a man as pope. Yet none of these resolutions are found in Scripture or the Tradition of the Catholic Church. The clergy of Rome have always elected the pope, and the cardinals are the electing titular clergy of Rome. Some sedevacantists resort to teaching that the clergy of Rome will one day elect a future pope and yet they teach that the entirety of the clergy of Rome are Modernists with invalid ordinations. Consequently, since sedevacantists cannot produce a consistent origin narrative and cannot provide a means by which the current crisis will be resolved with a future valid and orthodox pope, it is an untenable theological position. It is broken at both ends. One might wish it to be true, but that does not make it so.

Accept the Resignationist Position: Is Benedict Still Pope?

Since Ratzinger chose to retain the title of pope and continues to dress and bless as pope, many faithful have concluded that Pope Benedict remains pope and that Pope Francis is an antipope without the charism and protection of the papacy. This is why the pontificate of Francis is so far off the rails.

This resignationist theory finds adherents going back to the election of Pope Francis in 2013. This position is much more palatable and socially acceptable than the raw sedevacantist position extending back to 1958. Moreover, the position is not sedevacantist at all, since it holds that Pope Benedict is still currently the true reigning pope on earth.

Two versions of the resignationist hypothesis exist. The most popular version is that Pope Benedict XVI was placed under duress or blackmail in 2012 in the context of the Vatileaks controversy, which I described previously. Canon 332, paragraph 2, states a pope must resign freely: "If it should happen that the Roman Pontiff resigns his office, it is required for validity that he makes the resignation freely and that it be duly manifested but not that it be accepted by anyone." Also, Canon 188 states: "A resignation made out of grave fear that is inflicted unjustly or out of malice, substantial error, or simony is invalid by the law itself." Here again we have an explanation that a resignation made from grave fear is invalid. Hence, if it could be shown that Pope Benedict did not resign freely, but under duress or grave fear, his resignation would be invalid.

A second version of resignationism cites Canon 188 with respect to the fact that "substantial error" alone renders a resignation invalid. This version claims that Ratzinger, prior to his papacy, falsely believed that the papacy could be expanded or shared by more than one occupant, and that the *ministerium* (ministry) of the papacy is divisible from the *munus* (office) of the papacy. Despite formally resigning, they cite the pope's words that he sought to retain a portion of the papacy:

> My decision to resign the active exercise of the ministry does not revoke this. I do not return to private life, to a life of travel, meetings, receptions, conferences, and so on. I am not abandoning the cross but remaining in a new way at the side of the crucified Lord. I no longer bear the power of office for the governance of the Church, but in the service of prayer I remain, so to speak, in the enclosure of Saint Peter.[175]

The resignationist argues that Benedict resigned from the *ministerium* of the papacy but wrongly believed that he still retained the *munus* of the papacy. He remained inside "the enclosure of Saint Peter." Since he held "substantial error" about his resignation regarding *ministerium* and *munus*, Canon 188 kicks in and renders his resignation invalid. He remains pope whether or not he realizes it. Many resignationists claim that Benedict only pretends not to know it, but that he craftily wears the papal white cassock to affirm his continued status as pope and bishop of Rome.

My response to both versions of resignationism is that we do not know whether Benedict resigned under duress or fear. He claims that he did not and without knowing anything more, we cannot claim it be so. The second version that looks to Canon 188 and "substantial error" is more compelling. This hypothesis, however, wrongly assumes from the beginning that the false division of *ministerium* and *munus* in the mind of Ratzinger is a real

[175] Benedict XVI, General Audience, 27 February 2013.

ontological division. It is not. The *ministerium* of the papacy is one and the same with the *munus* of the papacy. Even if Benedict subjectively maintained at the moment of his resignation a false doctrine that holds a division between *munus* and *ministerium*, we cannot prove it. We can only allege it.

Yet even if Benedict did hold this false dichotomy of papal *munus* and *ministerium* at the moment of his resignation, it still would not invalidate the resignation. Canon 188 does refer to interior mental substantial error, *but to substantial error in the actual resignation itself*. One may read Benedict's resignation, and he clearly resigned the *ministerium*, and, in Catholic theology, the Petrine *ministerium* and the *munus* are one and the same office. He may have subjectively thought otherwise, but objectively on paper, he presented a valid resignation from the ministry of the papacy. He receives an A+ for clearly describing that office from which he resigns. There is no subjective error in the objective resignation document of Benedict:

> For this reason, and well aware of the seriousness of this act, with full freedom I declare that I renounce (*renuntiare*) the ministry (*ministerio*) of Bishop of Rome, Successor of Saint Peter, entrusted to me by the Cardinals on 19 April 2005, in such a way, that as from 28 February 2013, at 20:00 hours, the See of Rome, the See of Saint Peter, will be vacant (*vacet*) and a Conclave to elect the new Supreme Pontiff will have to be convoked by those whose competence it is.

Here Benedict renounces the ministry of "Bishop of Rome, Successor of Saint Peter entrusted to him by the Cardinals" that he received on the date of his election. He is precise about what he is giving up: the office he received on 19 April 2005. He also explicitly states that "the See of Rome, the See of Saint Peter will be vacant." If he believed himself still to be pope somehow, then the See of Saint Peter would not be vacant but filled. Within his resignation document, Benedict uses the term *munus* twice and *ministerium* thrice. It is obvious in the document that the words refer to one and the same reality—that office he held from the date of his election as pope. The resignationist hypothesis does not correspond to the objective text.

Resignationism also creates two more ecclesial problems that cannot be resolved. First, Pope Francis has stacked the college of cardinals with his own appointments. When Benedict and Francis die, how will a valid conclave elect a new pope if Francis, as antipope, has invalidly appointed a majority of the cardinals? Resignationism renders all those Francis cardinals as invalid cardinals. A conclave including invalid cardinals would itself be invalid.

Secondly, Catholics are obliged to attend only those Masses that commemorate the true pope and their local bishop. Any Mass that does not commemorate the true pope and the local bishop is de facto schismatic. Resignationism wrongly places on the conscience of the faithful the arduous task of discovering Masses in which Francis is either not named or in which Benedict is named. This is a practical impossibility, and it forces Catholics to unite themselves to a Mass in union with a false antipope, which is repulsive to Catholic piety and tradition. Pope Benedict presented a clear and valid resignation, and without evidence that he was forced to resign under duress, we must conclude (with all the living cardinals) that Pope Benedict is no longer a true pope.

Accept the Recognize and Resist Position

The "recognize and resist" position goes back to the 1960s in the persons of Cardinal Ottaviani and Archbishop Lefebvre.

They and others recognized that the pope and bishops of their time were valid, but that they had fallen into error on several topics. Since no pope since 1950 has exercised his extraordinary magisterium by declaring anything infallibly ex cathedra, the Catholic may in good faith and conscience resist errors spoken by a pope on Twitter, on an airplane, or even in a papal document.

This position of "recognize and resist" applies to Vatican II as well. As explained previously, Pope Paul VI, at the closing of Vatican II, explicitly stated regarding the Council: "The magisterium of the Church did not wish to pronounce itself under the form of extraordinary dogmatic pronouncements."[176] Months later Paul VI taught, "In view of the pastoral nature of the Council, it has avoided proclaiming in an extraordinary manner any dogma carrying the mark of infallibility."[177] Since Vatican II did not bear the mark of infallibility or the extraordinary magisterium, a Catholic can claim without impiety that the Council may have contained mistakes.

The terminology of resistance derives from the Latin Vulgate version of Saint Paul's language in his Epistle to the Galatians 2:11: *Cum autem venisset Cephas Antiochiam, in faciem ei restiti, quia reprehensibilis erat*. "When however Cephas came to Antioch, I resisted (*restiti*) him to his face because he was to be blamed." Here Saint Paul *recognizes* the authority of Cephas (Saint Peter) as a valid and true pope but still *resists* him in defense of the Gospel.

The "recognize and resist" position comes in a variety of shades. One observes conservative diocesan bishops who celebrate

[176] Pope Paul VI, Discourse closing Vatican II, 7 December 1965.

[177] Pope Paul VI, Audience of 12 January 1966.

the Novus Ordo Mass and sometimes praise Vatican II, but who also resist certain statements and actions of the pope. Prelates such as Cardinal Burke, Cardinal Sarah, Cardinal Brandmüller, and Bishop Athanasius Schneider represent this moderate "recognize and resist" position with reverence for the pope and the Chair of Peter.

Perhaps more strictly, there are traditional priests and laity who subscribe to the "recognize and resist" position by attending the 1962 Latin Mass at diocesan parishes or at parishes served by the Priestly Fraternity of Saint Peter, the Institute of Christ the King, or other canonically approved bodies. In these circles, there are frank discussions and debates about problems with certain phrases or documents of the Second Vatican Council and subsequent papal statements. These traditionalists are usually supportive and enthusiastic about the witness of men such as Cardinal Burke and Bishop Schneider and seek to cooperate with them. The most strident example of "recognize and resist" is that of Archbishop Marcel Lefebvre, who pioneered the position into a global movement after Vatican II. Controversially, Lefebvre resisted as far as papal censure and excommunication—denying his status as excommunicate on canonical grounds until the day of his death. Pope Benedict XVI did much to rehabilitate the legacy of Lefebvre and regularize his Society of Saint Pius X, but without success. To the surprise of many, Pope Francis has granted privileges and faculties to the SSPX well beyond those of Pope Benedict in order that they might be fully and canonically regular.

I trace out each of these positions in charity with the firm belief that this final "recognize and resist" position is the *only* solution that conforms to Scripture, Tradition, and our contemporary crisis. The Catholic Church has been infiltrated all the way to the top. We have a valid pope and valid cardinals, but we have received the mantle of Saint Athanasius and Saint Catherine of Siena to call, respectfully and reverently, certain spiritual fathers back to Christ and the unadulterated Apostolic Faith.

33

Spiritual Weapons against Demonic Enemies

Holding to a reverent "recognize and resist" position is not enough. This is the diagnosis, not the medicine. Our vocation is to fight spiritually and rebuild that which has been destroyed. Pope Saint Pius X observed: "In our time more than ever before, the chief strength of the wicked lies in the cowardice and weakness of good men."[178] Good men must throw off cowardice and weakness and stand under the banner of Christ with their hands readied for battle. We are reminded of the story in Nehemiah of the warriors who both built the city and bore arms while doing so.

> When our enemies heard that it was known to us and that God had frustrated their plan, we all returned to the wall, each to his work. From that day on, half of my servants worked on construction, and half held the spears, shields, bows, and coats of mail; and the leaders stood behind all the house of Judah, who were building on the wall. Those who carried burdens were laden in such a way that each with one hand labored on the work and with the other

[178] Pope Pius X, *Discourse at the Beatification of Saint Joan of Arc*, *Acta Apostolicae Sedis* 1 (1908): 142.

> held his weapon. And each of the builders had his sword girded at his side while he built. The man who sounded the trumpet was beside me. And I said to the nobles and to the officials and to the rest of the people, "The work is great and widely spread, and we are separated on the wall, far from one another. In the place where you hear the sound of the trumpet, rally to us there. Our God will fight for us." (Neh. 4:15–20)

Our enemies are not chiefly Freemasons, Communists, Modernists, Küng, Schillebeeckx, or the Sankt Gallen Mafia. Our enemies are Satan and his demons, who do not die. As in Nehemiah, "when our enemies hear that it was known to us"—when our enemy realizes that we know his plan of attack—we will need to protect ourselves. Pope Francis may say that "building walls is not Christian," but Nehemiah disagrees. The City of God requires a wall because we are daily under attack.

"Half of my servants worked on construction, and half held the spears, shields, bows, and coats of mail." The servants of God—our bishops and priests—are building (on the foundation of Christ) this defensive visible wall, brick by brick, through the breviary, the Holy Sacrifice of the Mass, preaching, and the sacraments. The laity must provide them cover to accomplish their work, and we do this by taking up the humble weapons for spiritual battle: the Rosary, the Scapular, prayer, fasting, abstinence from meat, novenas, almsgiving, Advent and Lent, ember days, vigils, First Fridays, First Saturdays, sexual chastity, modesty, regular catechesis of children, and rigorous study of the theological sources of our Catholic Faith. We must also attack with sound Catholic doctrine and be on guard against all heresy and schism within our ranks. Saint Francis de Sales once affirmed:

> The declared enemies of God and His Church, heretics and schismatics, must be criticized as much as possible, as long as truth is not denied. It is a work of charity to shout: "Here is the wolf!" when it enters the flock or anywhere else.[179]

"And each of the builders had his sword girded at his side while he built." The Rosary, then known as Our Lady's Psalter consisting of one hundred fifty Hail Mary's, is the weapon that the Blessed Mother gave to Saint Dominic, and along with the Holy Sacrifice of the Mass, it is our most powerful weapon against the "wickedness and snares of the devil." When Pope Leo XIII saw demons gather on Rome, he did not institute new congregations or policies. He instituted more prayer to the Mother of God and to Saint Michael, the Prince of the Heavenly Host—*daily*. Demons scoff at policies. They tremble before the Mother of God and Saint Michael.

Last of all, Nehemiah laments "The work is great and widely spread, and we ... are far from one another." Our participation in building and protecting the Catholic Church is widely spread, but Nehemiah reveals the solution: "In the place where you hear the sound of the trumpet, rally to us there. Our God will fight for us." This fight is not ours. The trumpet call is the sanctus bell that gently rings out. In that silent moment we rally to our Lord Jesus Christ, who is now present and hidden in the holy and venerable hands of the priest. Although widely spread, in that precious and spotless Host we are called together both to fight and to find peace.

[179] Saint Francis de Sales, *Introduction to the Devout Life*, pt. 3, chap. 29.

Saint Joseph, terror of demons, patron of the Church, pray for us.

This book is consecrated to Christ through Mary *ad majorem Dei gloriam*.

If you benefited from this book, please share it with family and friends, and review it on Amazon.

Please pray a Hail Mary for the author of this book.

Appendices

Who's Who in This Book

Angeli, Rinaldo. Monsignor. Private secretary of Pope Leo XIII. It is reported that Leo XIII received a mysterious vision of demonic spirits assembling in Rome. It is said that this vision inspired the pontiff to write the prayer to Saint Michael.

Balthasar, Hans Urs von. 1905–1988. Cardinal elect, theologian, writer. Swiss. He is considered one of the greatest theologians and writers of the twentieth century. He was influenced in his early years by theologians, such as Heni de Lubac, who turned away from neo-Scholaticism in favor of the teachings of the Church Fathers. He made the controversial assertion that Christ descended into hell, not as a victor over Satan, but to experience the suffering of separation from God the Father.

Bea, Augustin. 1881–1968. Cardinal. German. Jesuit. First president of the Secretariat for Promoting Christian Unity. He was highly influential in the drafting of the Second Vatican Council's declaration *Nostra aetate*, concerning non-Christian religions, and was an advocate for Catholic-Jewish relations.

Bergoglio, Jorge Mario. 1936–present. Argentinian. Jesuit. He was elected to the papacy in 2013, taking the name Francis. Has been subject to open criticism within the Church for the ambiguity of his moral teachings and his stance on Church doctrine and, especially, for possible complicity in the cover-up of clergy sexual abuse. A letter published in August 2018 by former papal nuncio Carlo Maria Viganò accused the pontiff of having had knowledge of Theodore Cardinal McCarrick's decades of sexual misconduct. The letter called for Pope Francis to resign. The pontiff has refused to comment on Viganò's accusations.

Bugnini, Annibale. 1912–1982. Prelate and archbishop. Following the Second Vatican Council, he served as secretary of the Congregation for Divine Worship, which was charged with the implementation of the Council's Constitution on the Liturgy. In 1976, Italian writer Tito Casini published a report from an anonymous source who claimed that incriminating documents had been discovered in Bugnini's briefcase, indicating the archbishop's intimate involvement in Freemasonry.

Calvi, Roberto. 1920–1982. Financier. Italian. Chairman of the Italian bank Banco Ambrosiano. When the bank collapsed in 1982 amid charges of fraud, the president of the Vatican Bank, Paul Marcinkus, was accused of sharing in Banco Ambrosiano's illegal activity. Calvi, who was a member of Propaganda Due (P2), an illegal Masonic lodge, was found hanged by the neck from a bridge over the River Thames in a ritualized killing just days after the scandals broke.

Casaroli, Agostino. 1914–1998. Cardinal secretary of state. Italian. Appointed secretary of state by Pope John Paul II in 1979. He was the key architect of the Vatican's efforts to end Communist aggression against the Church.

Congar, Yves. 1904–1995. Cardinal and theologian. French. Dominican. He is recognized as one of the most important theologians of the twentieth century, specifically in the realm of ecclesiology. He is considered possibly the most influential contributor to the declarations of the Second Vatican Council.

Danneels, Godfried. 1933–2019. Cardinal. Belgian. Advocate for the "modernization" of the Church. He was accused in 2010 of covering up the sexual-abuse case of Bishop Roger Vangheluwe. Having learned of Vangheluwe's guilt, Danneels concealed the information and urged the bishop's victim not to make the case public. Danneels was also a known member of the Sankt Gallen "Mafia," a secret group of high-ranking, liberal clergy who actively attempted to prevent the election of Pope Benedict XVI in 2005 and are believed to have influenced the conclave in 2013 to ensure the election of Pope Francis.

de Chardin, Pierre Teilhard. 1881–1955. Priest, philosopher, paleontologist. French. Jesuit. His writings on evolution and the destiny of man earned him disapproval from the Church. The Vatican banned several of his works, requiring that Catholic bookstores remove them and any books supporting de Chardin's ideas, and he was forbidden to teach. Henri de Lubac wrote three books in support of de Chardin's ideas in the 1960s, and de Chardin was later praised by both Pope Benedict XVI and Pope John Paul II.

de Lubac, Henri. 1896–1991. Cardinal, theologian, and writer. French. Jesuit. In 1950, controversy regarding several of his books arose due to the Vatican's judgement that they contained dogmatic errors. In the following years, he continued to write and publish under the censorship of the Vatican and became one of the Second Vatican Council's theological experts. Later, along with Joseph Cardinal Ratzinger and Hans Urs Von Balthasar, he founded the conservative theological journal *Communio.*

Dziwisz, Stanisław. 1939–present. Prelate and cardinal. Polish. Private secretary of Pope John Paul II. He served as Archbishop of Kraków from 2005 to 2016. He supported Legion of Christ founder Father Marcial Maciel, who was revealed to have abused minors and fathered several illegitimate children. Dziwisz is alleged to have blocked an investigation into the sexual misconduct of Hans Hermann Cardinal Groër, who was credibly accused of abusing multiple young boys and monks. Dziwisz is also reported to have been involved in the appointment of Theodore Cardinal McCarrick as archbishop of Washington, D.C., and to have regularly accepted cash donations from McCarrick.

Guérard des Lauriers, Michel-Louis. 1898–1988. Priest and theologian. French. Dominican. Confessor of Pope Pius XII. He was the theologian for Pope Pius XII's *Munificentissimus Deus*, which dogmatized the Assumption of Mary and the chief ghostwriter of the Ottaviani Intervention. He was a strong proponent of the sedevacantist movement, believing Pope Paul VI to have been guilty of heresy. In 1981, he was consecrated bishop without the Vatican's approval by the sedevacantist former archbishop Pierre Martin Ngô Đình Thuc. Guérard des Lauriers was subsequently excommunicated.

König, Franz. 1905–2004. Cardinal. Austrian. He served as Archbishop of Vienna from 1956 to 1985. He emphasized ecumenism and made significant contributions to the Second Vatican Council's declaration on relations with non-Christian religions, *Nostra aetate*. He served as a Vatican diplomat to Communist countries.

Köenig was instrumental in securing the pontifical election of Pope John Paul II in 1978, but he later criticized the pontiff for rejecting the progressive spirit of the Second Vatican Council.

Küng, Hans. 1928–present. Priest, theologian, writer. Swiss. In 1960, he was appointed by Pope John XXIII as a theological expert for the Second Vatican Council. In 1979, his public rejection of the doctrine of papal infallibility caused him to be officially stripped of his license to teach Catholic theology. He is known also for his work toward creating a common "global ethic" among world religions and for his controversial liberal opinions on euthanasia and assisted suicide.

Lefebvre, Marcel. 1905–1991. Archbishop. French. Founder of the Society of Saint Pius X and superior general of the Holy Ghost Fathers. Lefebvre was a member of the conservative Coetus Internationalis Patrum during the Second Vatican Council. He was a critic of the *Novus Ordo Missae* of Paul VI, promulgated in 1969 and a promoter of the traditional Latin Mass of 1962. He also remained critical of Vatican II on matters of religious liberty and ecumenism. Lefebvre was notified of *latae sententiae* excommunication in 1988 for consecrating four bishops without papal mandate.

Luciani, Albino. 1912–1978. Italian. He served as head of the Catholic Church with the name Pope John Paul I from August 1978 until his death, thirty-three days later. Contradictory reports at that time regarding the cause of the pontiff's death have given rise to suspicions of foul play. David Yallop's 1984 book, *A Thief in the Night: Life and Death in the Vatican*, asserts that Archbishop Paul Marcinkus and Jean-Marie Cardinal Villot, along with Italian financiers Roberto Calvi, Michele Sindona, and Licio Gelli, conspired in the murder of the pontiff.

Maffi, Pietro. 1858–1931. Cardinal. Italian. He served as archbishop of Pisa from 1903 until his death. He was a leading candidate in the papal conclave of 1914, which elected Pope Benedict XV. He also participated in the conclave of 1922 and was instrumental in securing the election of Pope Pius XI.

Marcinkus, Paul. 1922–2006. Archbishop. American. He served as president of the Vatican Bank from 1971 to 1989. He was implicated in major financial scandals in 1982, when the Italian bank Banco Ambrosiano, of which the Vatican Bank was a main shareholder, collapsed amid charges of fraud. The bank's chairman, Roberto Calvi, was a member of an illegal Masonic lodge and was murdered days after the scandals broke. Marcinkus was revealed to have been involved in illegal transactions carried out by Banco Ambrosiano. He had also been implicated in earlier scandals surrounding Italian financier Michele Sindona, a Freemason with connections to the Mafia.

Martin, Malachi. 1921–1999. Priest, exorcist, and writer. Irish. Jesuit. He served as secretary to Augustin Cardinal Bea during the Second Vatican Council. He was released from his Jesuit vows in 1965 at his own request. There remains controversy over whether he was officially laicized or remained bound to his vow of chastity. His works of fiction gave insider accounts of several pontificates. Notably, his novel *Windswept House* tells the story of high-ranking members of the Church hierarchy making blood oaths to corrupt the orthodoxy of the Faith and to destroy the Church from within.

Martini, Carlo Maria. 1927–2012. Cardinal. Italian. Jesuit. He was known as a liberal member of the Church's hierarchy. He held progressive views on matters concerning same-sex unions, the ordination of women to the diaconate, and some bioethical issues, including contraception. In his final interview, published just hours after his death, he notoriously called the Church "200 years out of date."

McCarrick, Theodore. 1930–present. Defrocked bishop. American. Former prelate and cardinal. From 2001 to 2006, he served as archbishop of Washington, D.C., where he was connected to several prominent politicians. After retiring in 2006, he continued to serve as a diplomat on behalf of the Vatican and the U.S. State Department. He was removed from public ministry by the Vatican in July 2018 due to credible allegations of sexual misconduct with adult male seminarians over the course of decades, as well as sexual abuse against male minors.

Merry del Val, Rafael. 1865–1930. Cardinal secretary of state. Spanish. He served as the secretary of the papal conclave of 1903, in which Austria vetoed the election of Mariano Cardinal Rampolla del Tinarda, and which, in four days, elected Pope Pius X. He was appointed secretary of state by Pius X at only thirty-eight years old, aiding the pontiff in his efforts to remove the Church from political affairs and to combat the rise of Modernism among clergy.

Montini, Giovanni Battista Enrico Antonio Maria. 1897–1978. Italian. He served as head of the Catholic Church with the name Pope Paul VI from 1963 to 1978. He continued the Second Vatican Council (which had begun with his predecessor, Pope John XXIII) until its close in 1965. With the conclusion of the council, the pontiff took charge of the implementation of its reforms. He published his most widely known encyclical, *Humane vitae*, in

1968, reinforcing the Church's teachings on the marital union and condemning artificial birth control. In 1970, he promulgated the *Novus Ordo Missae*, a revised order of the liturgy according to the mandates of Vatican II which was to be celebrated in vernacular languages. He was canonized in October 2018.

Pacelli, Eugenio Maria Giuseppe Giovanni. 1876–1958. Italian. He served as head of the Catholic Church with the name Pope Pius XII from 1939 to 1958. Contrary to accusations concerning public silence and even cooperation with Nazi Germany during the Holocaust, the pontiff is known to have rescued thousands of persecuted Jews during the Second World War. He also strongly opposed Communism, approving the Church's 1949 Decree against Communism, which declared that Catholics professing Communist ideology are to be excommunicated.

Rahner, Karl. 1904–1984. Priest and theologian. German. Jesuit. He is recognized as one of the foremost Catholic theologians of the twentieth century. He worked alongside Henri de Lubac and Yves Congar. In 1962, he was appointed by Pope John XXIII as a theological expert for the Second Vatican Council, and he had a major impact on the work of the Council, especially the development of the declaration *Lumen gentium.*

Rampolla, Mariano. 1843–1913. Cardinal. Italian. He was a chief candidate during the 1903 papal conclave. His candidacy, however, was opposed by the Austrian emperor, who imposed a veto against him. Giuseppe Melchiorre Cardinal Sarto was subsequently elected, becoming Pope Pius X. One of Pius's first acts as pope was to abolish the emperor's veto right, making Rampolla the last man in a papal conclave to be vetoed by an emperor.

Roncalli, Angelo Giuseppe. 1881–1963. Italian. He served as head of the Catholic Church with the name Pope John XXIII from 1958 to 1963. He called the Second Vatican Council to session in 1962, opening the Church up to dramatic changes, but the pontiff remained conservative in terms of doctrine. As pope, he emphasized the pastoral role of the Church and her involvement in political affairs. He was canonized in April 2014.

Ratzinger, Joseph. 1927–present. Pope emeritus. Theologian. German. He served as head of the Catholic Church with the name Pope Benedict XVI from 2005 to 2013, when he resigned from the office due to his advanced age and declining physical condition. As pope, he defended orthodoxy and Church doctrine on topics such as birth control and homosexuality, he reaffirmed Christianity as a religion in accord with reason, and he spoke pointedly against the evil of relativism. As pope emeritus, he now resides at a monastery in the Vatican Gardens, where he continues to study and write.

Schillebeeckx, Edward. 1914–2009. Priest and theologian. Belgian. Dominican. He was one of the most active theological advisers to clergy participating in the Second Vatican Council. He argued that Catholic ecclesiology placed too much emphasis on hierarchy and papal authority. Along with Yves Congar, Karl Rahner, Hans Küng, and others, Schillebeeckx founded the progressive theological journal *Concilium*.

Schweigl, Joseph. Died in 1964. Priest. Jesuit. In 1952, he was charged by Pope Pius XII to interrogate Sister Lúcia de Jesus Rosa dos Santos (one of the three child visionaries at Fátima) about the details of the Third Secret of Fátima.

Sindona, Michele. 1920–1986. Financier. Italian. He was a known Freemason and was connected to the Sicilian Mafia. He became associated with the Vatican Bank in 1969, dealing with large amounts of the bank's money. In 1974, his banking empire collapsed amid revelations of fraud, bribery, and murder. The president of the Vatican Bank at the time was accused of sharing involvement in these crimes. Sindona was poisoned with cyanide while serving his prison sentence.

Sodano, Angelo. 1927–present. Dean of the College of Cardinals. Italian. He served as secretary of state from 1991 to 2006. Multiple reports accuse him of having blocked investigations into sexual abuse by both Hans Hermann Cardinal Groër and Legion of Christ founder Father Marcial Maciel, from whom Sodano regularly accepted large monetary donations.

Viganò, Carlo Maria. 1941–present. Archbishop. Former apostolic nuncio to the United States. Italian. On 25 August 2018, he released an eleven-page letter describing multiple warnings to the Vatican over several years regarding the sexual misconduct of Theodore Cardinal McCarrick that were ignored until Pope Benedict XVI finally placed severe restrictions on McCarrick's public ministry. The letter also accused Pope Francis of later removing these restrictions and making McCarrick a trusted adviser, having full knowledge of the cardinal's decades of grave sexual misconduct. Several other high-ranking Church officials were also implicated.

Villot, Jean-Marie. 1905–1979. Prelate and cardinal. French. He served as cardinal secretary of state from 1969 to 1979. He was the subject of claims that Pope John Paul I's death was a homicide. David Yallop's 1984 book, *A Thief in the Night: Life and*

Death in the Vatican, named Villot as a leading suspect in the alleged murder, which Yallop claims may have been motivated by personnel changes within the Vatican that the pontiff was on the verge of making.

Wojtyła, Karol. 1920–2005. Polish. Served as head of the Catholic Church with the name Pope John Paul II from 1978 to 2005. He was elected to the papacy immediately after Pope John Paul I, who reigned only thirty-three days before his death. Wojtyła is recognized for the critical role he played, as pope, in bringing an end to Communist rule in Europe. While he supported the reforms of the Second Vatican Council, he was generally seen as doctrinally conservative, and he upheld the Church's traditional teachings. He was canonized in April 2014.

Timeline of Popes in This Book

Gregory XVI (1831–1846)
Blessed Pius IX (1846–1878)
Leo XIII (1878–1903)
Saint Pius X (1903–1914)
Benedict XV (1914–1922)
Pius XI (1922–1939)
Pius XII (1939–1958)
Saint John XXIII (1958–1963)
Saint Paul VI (1963–1978)
John Paul I (1978)
Saint John Paul II (1978–2005)
Benedict XVI (2005–2013)
Francis (2013–)

Vatican Secretaries of State by Papacy and Dates

Under Pope Pius IX

Giacomo Antonelli (29 November 1848–6 November 1876) (second time)

Giovanni Simeoni (18 December 1876–7 February 1878)

Alessandro Franchi (5 March–31 July 1878)

Under Pope Leo XIII

Lorenzo Nina (9 August 1878–16 December 1880)

Luigi Jacobini (16 December 1880–28 February 1887)

Mariano Rampolla (2 June 1887–20 July 1903)

Under Pope Pius X

Rafael Merry del Val (12 November 1903–20 August 1914)

Under Pope Benedict XV

Domenico Ferrata (4 September–10 October 1914)

Pietro Gasparri (13 October 1914–7 February 1930)

Under Pope Pius XI

Pietro Gasparri (13 October 1914–7 February 1930)

Eugenio Pacelli (9 February 1930–10 February 1939) then elected Pope Pius XII

Under Pope Pius XII

Luigi Maglione (10 March 1939–22 August 1944)
Domenico Tardini (15 December 1958–30 July 1961)

Under Popes John XXIII and Paul VI

Amleto Giovanni Cicognani (12 August 1961–30 April 1969)

Under Pope Paul VI, John Paul I, and John Paul II

Jean-Marie Villot (2 May 1969–9 March 1979)

Under Pope John Paul II

Agostino Casaroli (1 July 1979–1 December 1990)

Under Popes John Paul II, Benedict XVI and Francis

Angelo Sodano (29 June 1991–22 June 2006)
Tarcisio Bertone (15 September 2006–15 October 2013)

Under Pope Francis

Pietro Parolin (15 October 2013–)

Permanent Instruction of the *Alta Vendita*

by Piccolo Tigre

Reproduced in English translation in the lecture by Right Rev. Msgr. George Dillon, D.D., at Edinburgh in October 1884, about six months after the appearance of Pope Leo XIII's famous Encyclical Letter, *Humanum Genus, On Freemasonry*. A few changes were made by Dr. Taylor Marshall to update the language and spelling to modern standards.

Ever since we have established ourselves as a body of action, and that order has commenced to reign in the bosom of the most distant lodge, as in that one nearest the center of action, there is one thought which has profoundly occupied the men who aspire to universal regeneration. That is the thought of the enfranchisement of Italy, from which must one day come the enfranchisement of the entire world, the fraternal republic, and the harmony of humanity. That thought has not yet been seized upon by our brethren beyond the Alps. They believe that revolutionary Italy can only conspire in the shade, deal some stabs to cops or traitors, and tranquilly undergo the yoke of events which take place beyond the Alps for Italy, but without Italy.

This error has been fatal to us on many occasions. It is not necessary to combat it with phrases, which would only propagate it. It is necessary to kill it by facts. Thus, amidst the cares which have the privilege of agitating the minds of the most vigorous of our lodges, there is one which we ought never to forget.

The papacy has always exercised a decisive action upon the affairs of Italy. By the hands, by the voices, by the pens, by the hearts of its innumerable bishops, priests, monks, nuns and people in all latitudes, the papacy finds devotedness without end ready for martyrdom, and that to enthusiasm. Everywhere, whenever it pleases to call upon them, it has friends ready to die or lose all for its cause. This is an immense leverage which the popes alone have been able to appreciate to its full power, and as yet they have used it only to a certain extent.

Today there is no question of reconstituting for ourselves that power, the prestige of which is for the moment weakened. Our final end is that of Voltaire and of the French Revolution, the destruction forever of Catholicism and even of the Christian idea which, if left standing on the ruins of Rome, would be the resuscitation of Christianity later. But to attain more certainly that result, and not prepare ourselves with gaiety of heart for reverses which adjourn indefinitely, or compromise for ages, the success of a good cause, we must not pay attention to those braggarts of Frenchmen, those cloudy Germans, those melancholy Englishmen, all of whom imagine they can kill Catholicism, now with an impure song, then with an illogical deduction; at another time, with a sarcasm smuggled in like the cottons of Great Britain. Catholicism has a life much more tenacious than that. It has seen the most implacable, the most terrible adversaries, and it has often had the malignant pleasure of throwing holy water on the tombs of the most enraged. Let us permit, then, our brethren of these countries to give themselves up to the sterile intemperance of their anti-Catholic zeal. Let them even mock at our Madonnas and our apparent devotion. With this passport we can conspire at our ease and arrive little by little at the end we have in view.

Now the Papacy has been for seventeen centuries inherent to the history of Italy. Italy cannot breathe or move without the permission of the Supreme Pastor. With him she has the hundred arms of Briareus; without him she is condemned to a pitiable impotence. She has nothing but divisions to foment, hatreds to break out, and hostilities to manifest themselves from the highest chain of the Alps to the lowest of the Apennines. We cannot desire such a state of things. It is necessary, then, to seek a remedy for that situation. The remedy is found.

The Pope, whoever he may be, will never come to the secret societies. It is for the secret societies to come first to the Church, with the aim of winning them both. The work which we have undertaken is not the work of a day, nor of a month, nor of a year. It may last many years, a century perhaps, but in our ranks the soldier dies, and the fight continues.

We do not mean to win the Popes to our cause, to make them neophytes of our principles, and propagators of our ideas. That would be a ridiculous dream, no matter in what manner events may turn. Should cardinals or prelates, for example, enter, willingly or by surprise, in some manner, into a part of our secrets, it would be by no means a motive to desire their elevation to the See of Peter. That elevation would destroy us. Ambition alone would bring them to apostasy from us. The needs of power would force them to immolate us. That which we ought to demand, that which we should seek and expect, as the Jews expected the Messiah, is a Pope according to our wants.

Pope Alexander VI, with all his private crimes, would not suit us, for he never erred in religious matters. Pope Clement

XIV, on the contrary, would suit us from head to foot. Borgia was a libertine, a true sensualist of the eighteenth century strayed into the fifteenth. He has been anathematized, notwithstanding his vices, by all the voices of philosophy and incredulity, and he owes that anathema to the vigor with which he defended the Church. Ganganelli gave himself over, bound hand and foot, to the ministers of the Bourbons, who made him afraid, and to the incredulous who celebrated his tolerance, and Ganganelli is become a very great Pope.

He is almost in the same condition that it is necessary for us to find another, if that be yet possible. With that we should march more surely to the attack upon the Church than with the pamphlets of our brethren in France, or even with the gold of England. Do you wish to know the reason? It is because by that we should have no more need of the vinegar of Hannibal, no more need of the powder of cannon, no more need even of our arms. We have the little finger of the successor of St. Peter engaged in the plot, and that little finger is of more value for our crusade than all the Innocents, the Urbans, and the Saint Bernards of Christianity.

We do not doubt that we shall arrive at that supreme term of all our efforts; but when? but how? The unknown does not yet manifest itself. Nevertheless, as nothing should separate us from the plan traced out; as, on the contrary, all things should tend to it—as if success were to crown the work scarcely sketched out tomorrow—we wish in this instruction which must rest a secret for the simple initiated, to give to those of the Supreme Lodge, counsels with which they should enlighten the universality of the brethren, under the form of an instruction or memorandum. It is of special importance, and because of discretion, the motives of which are transparent, never to permit it to be felt that these counsels are orders emanating from the *Alta Vendita*. The clergy is put too much in peril by it, that one can at the present hour permit oneself to play with it, as with one of these small affairs or of these little princes upon which one need but blow to cause them to disappear.

Little can be done with those old cardinals or with those prelates, whose character is very decided. It is necessary to leave them as we find them, incorrigible, in the school of Consalvi, and draw from our magazines of popularity or unpopularity the arms which will render useful or ridiculous the power in their hands. A word which one can ably invent, and which one has the art to spread amongst certain honorable chosen families by whose means it descends into the *cafés* and from the *cafés* into the streets; a word can sometimes kill a man. If a prelate comes to Rome to exercise some public function from the depths of the provinces, know presently his character, his antecedents, his qualities, his defects above all things. If he is in advance a declared enemy, an Albani, a Pallotta, a Bernetti, a Della Genga, a Riverola, envelop him in all the snares which you can place beneath his feet; create for him one of those reputations which will frighten little children and old women; paint him cruel and sanguinary; recount, regarding him, some traits of cruelty which can be easily engraved in the minds of people. When foreign journals shall gather for us these recitals, which they will embellish in their turn (inevitably because of their respect for truth), show, or rather cause to be shown, by some respectable fool those papers where the names and the excesses of the personages implicated are related. As France and England, so Italy will never be wanting in facile pens which know how to employ themselves in these lies so useful to the good cause. With a newspaper, the language of which they do not understand, but in which they will see the name of their delegate or judge, the people have no need of other proofs. They are in the infancy of liberalism; they believe in liberals, as, later, they will believe in us, not knowing very well why.

Crush the enemy whoever he may be; crush the powerful by means of lies and calumnies; but especially crush him in the egg. It is to the youth we must go. It is them we must seduce; it is them we must bring under the banner of the secret societies. In order to advance by steps, calculated but sure, in that perilous way, two things are of the first necessity. You ought to have the air of being simple as doves, but you must be prudent as the serpent. Your fathers, your children, your wives themselves, ought always to be ignorant of the secret which you carry in your bosoms. If it pleases you, in order the better to deceive the inquisitorial eye, to go often to confession, you are as by right authorized to preserve the most absolute silence regarding these things. You know that the least revelation, that the slightest indication escaped from you in the tribunal of penance, or elsewhere, can bring on great calamities and that the sentence of death is already pronounced upon the revealer, whether voluntary or involuntary.

Now then, in order to secure to us a Pope according to our own heart, it is necessary to fashion for that Pope a generation worthy of the kingdom of which we dream. Leave on one side old age and middle life, go to the youth, and, if possible, even to children. Never speak in their presence a word of impiety or impurity. *Maxima debetur puero reverentia.* Never forget these words of the poet for they will safeguard you from every license which it is absolutely essential to guard against for the good of the cause. In order to reap profit at the home of each family, in order to give yourself the right of asylum at the domestic hearth, you ought to present yourself with all the appearance of a man grave and moral. Once your reputation is established in the colleges, in the gymnasiums, in the universities, and in the seminaries—once you shall have captivated the confidence of professors and students, so act that those who are principally engaged in the ecclesiastical state should love to seek your conversation. Nourish their souls with the splendors of ancient Papal Rome. There is always at the bottom of the Italian heart a regret for Republican Rome. Excite, enkindle those natures so full of warmth and of patriotic fire. Offer them at first, but always in secret, inoffensive books, poetry resplendent with national emphasis; then little by little you will bring your disciples to the degree of cooking desired. When upon all the points of the ecclesiastical state at once, this daily work shall have spread our ideas as the light, then you will be able to appreciate the wisdom of the counsel in which we take the initiative.

Events that in our opinion precipitate themselves too rapidly, go necessarily in a few months' time to bring on an intervention of Austria. There are fools who in the lightness of their hearts please themselves in casting others into the midst of perils, and, meanwhile, there are fools who at a given hour drag on even wise men. The revolution which they meditate in Italy will only end in misfortunes and persecutions. Nothing is ripe, neither the men nor the things, and nothing shall be for a long time yet; but from these evils you can easily draw one new chord and cause it to vibrate in the hearts of the young clergy. That is the hatred of the stranger. Cause the German to become ridiculous and odious even before his foreseen entry. With the idea of the Pontifical supremacy, mix always the old memories of the wars of the priesthood and the Empire. Awaken the shouldering passions of the Guelphs and the Ghibellines, and thus you will obtain for yourselves the reputation of good Catholics and pure patriots.

The reputation of a good Catholic and good patriot will open the way for our doctrines to pass into the hearts of the young clergy and go even to the depths of convents. In a few years the young clergy will have, by the force of events, invaded all offices. They will govern, administer, and judge. They will form the Council of the Sovereign. They will be called upon to choose the Pontiff who will reign; and that Pontiff, like the greater part of his contemporaries, will be necessarily imbued with the Italian and humanitarian principles which we are about to put in circulation. It is a little grain of mustard which we place in the earth, but the sun of Justice will develop it even to be a great power, and you will see one day what a rich harvest that little seed will produce.

In the way which we trace for our brethren there are found great obstacles to conquer, difficulties of more than one kind to surmount. They will be overcome by experience and by wisdom. The goal is so beautiful that we must put all sails to the wind in order to attain it. If you want to revolutionize Italy, look for the Pope whose portrait we have just drawn. Do you want to establish the reign of the chosen ones on the throne of the Whore of Babylon? Let the clergy march under your banner, while they naively believe they are marching under the banner of the Apostolic Keys.

Do you want to wipe out the last vestige of the tyrants and oppressors? Cast out your nets like Simon Bar Jona! Cast them deep into the sacristy, the seminaries and monasteries, rather than to the bottom of the sea. And if you do not rush things, we promise you a catch more miraculous than this!

The fisherman of fish became a fisherman of men. You too will fish some friends and lead them to the feet of the Apostolic See. You will have preached revolution in tiara and cope, preceded under the cross and the banner, a revolution that will need only a little help to set the corners of the world on fire.

Let each act of your life tend then to discover the Philosopher's Stone. The alchemists of the middle ages lost their time and the gold of their dupes in the quest of this dream. That of the secret societies will be accomplished for the simplest of reasons, because it is based on the passions of man. Let us not be discouraged then by a check, a reverse, or a defeat. Let us prepare our arms in the silence of the lodges, dress our batteries, flatter all passions the most evil and the most generous, and all lead us to think that our plans will succeed one day above even our most improbable calculations.

Both Versions of the Secret of La Salette

Secret of Our Lady of La Salette to Mélanie (1851 Version)

1. "Secret given to me by the Blessed Virgin on La Salette Mountain on September 19, 1846"

2. Secret

3. "Mélanie, I'm going to tell you something you will not tell anyone:

4. "The time of God's wrath has come!

5. "If, when you have told the people what I told you earlier, and what I will tell you to say again, if, after that, they do not convert (if we do not do penance, and if one does not stop working on Sunday, and if one continues to blaspheme the Holy Name of God), in a word, if the face of the earth does not change, God will take revenge against the ungrateful and slave people of the devil.

6. "My Son is going to burst his power!

7. "Paris, this city soiled with all sorts of crimes, will perish infallibly.[180]

[180] The 1870 Siege of Paris was followed by widespread destruction in the city, during which much of its historical heritage was lost.

8. "Marseille will be destroyed in a short time.[181]

9. "When these things happen, the disorder will be complete on the earth.

10. "The world will surrender to its impious passions.

11. "The Pope will be persecuted on all sides: he will be shot at, he will be put to death, but nothing will be done to him. The Vicar of God will triumph again this time.

12. "The priests and nuns, and the true servants of my Son, will be persecuted, and many will die for the faith of Jesus Christ.

13. "A famine will reign at the same time.

14. "After all these things have come, many people will recognize the hand of God on them, will convert, and will do penance for their sins.

15. "A great king will ascend the throne, and reign for a few years.

16. "Religion will flourish and spread through all the earth and fertility will be great, the happy world to not miss anything will start its disorders, abandon God, and indulge in his criminal passions.

17. "Among the ministers of God and the Brides of Jesus Christ, there will be those who will indulge in disorder, and that is what will be terrible.

18. "Finally, hell will reign on the earth. It will be then that the Antichrist will be born of a nun: but woe to her! Many people will believe him, because he will say he came from heaven, woe to those who believe him! The time is not far; it will not happen twice 50 years.

19. "My child, you will not say what I just told you. (You will not tell anyone, you will not say if you have to say it one day, you

[181] The Germans systematically destroyed the old industrial sector and port of Marseilles in 1944.

will not say what it concerns), finally you will not say anything until I tell you to say it!

20. "I pray Our Holy Father the Pope to give me his holy blessing."

21. Mélanie Mathieu, bergère of La Salette

22. Grenoble July 6, 1851

Secret of Our Lady of La Salette to Mélanie (1879 Version)

1. "Melanie, what I am about to tell you now will not always be a secret. You may make it public in 1858.

2. "The priests, ministers of my Son, the priests, by their wicked lives, by their irreverence and their impiety in the celebration of the holy mysteries, by their love of money, their love of honors and pleasures, and the priests have become cesspools of impurity. Yes, the priests are tempting vengeance, and vengeance is hanging over their heads. Woe to the priests and to those dedicated to God who by their unfaithfulness and their wicked lives are crucifying my Son again! The sins of those dedicated to God cry out toward Heaven and call for vengeance, and now vengeance is at their door, for there is no one left to beg mercy and forgiveness for the people. There are no more generous souls; there is no one left worthy of offering a spotless sacrifice to the Eternal for the sake of the world.

3. "God will strike in an unprecedented way.

4. "Woe to the inhabitants of the earth! God will exhaust His wrath upon them, and no one will be able to escape so many afflictions together.

5. "The chiefs, the leaders of the people of God have neglected prayer and penance, and the devil has bedimmed their intelligence. They have become wandering stars which the old devil will drag along with his tail to make them perish. God will allow the old serpent to cause divisions among those who reign in every society and in every family. Physical and moral agonies will be suffered. God will abandon mankind to itself and will send punishments which will follow one after the other for more than thirty-five years.

6. "The society of men is on the eve of the most terrible scourges and of the gravest events. Mankind must expect to be ruled with an iron rod and to drink from the chalice of the wrath of God.

7. "May the Vicar of my Son, Pope Pius IX, never leave Rome again after 1859; may he, however, be steadfast and noble, may he fight with the weapons of faith and love. I will be at his side.

8. "May he be on his guard against Napoleon: he is two-faced, and when he wishes to make himself Pope as well as Emperor, God will soon draw back from him. He is the mastermind who, always wanting to ascend further, will fall on the sword he wishes to use to force his people to be raised up.

9. "Italy will be punished for her ambition in wanting to shake off the yoke of the Lord of Lords. And so she will be left to fight a war; blood will flow on all sides. Churches will be locked up or desecrated. Priests and religious orders will be hunted down and made to die a cruel death. Several will abandon the faith, and a great number of priests and members of religious orders will break away from the true religion; among these people there will even be bishops.

10. "May the Pope guard against the performers of miracles. For the time has come when the most astonishing wonders will take place on the earth and in the air.

11. "In the year 1864, Lucifer together with many demons will be loosed from hell; they will put an end to faith little by little, even in those dedicated to God. They will blind them in such a way that, unless they are blessed with a special grace, these people will take on the spirit of these angels of hell. Several religious institutions will lose all faith and will lose many souls.

12. "Evil books will be abundant on earth and the sprits of darkness will spread everywhere a universal slackening of all that concerns the service of God. They will have great power over nature: there will be churches built to serve these spirits. People will be transported from one place to another by these evil spirits, even priests, for they will not have been guided by the good spirit of the Gospel which is a spirit of humility, charity, and zeal for the glory of God. On occasions, the dead and the righteous will be brought back to life. Everywhere there will be extraordinary wonders, as true faith has faded and false light brightens the people. Woe to the Princes of the Church who think only of piling riches upon riches to protect their authority and dominate with pride.

13. "The Vicar of my Son will suffer a great deal, because for a while the Church will yield to large persecution, a time of darkness and the Church will witness a frightful crisis.

14. "The true faith to the Lord having been forgotten, each individual will want to be on his own and be superior to people of the same identity. They will abolish civil rights as well as ecclesiastical; all order and all justice will be trampled underfoot

and only homicides, hate, jealousy, lies and dissension will be seen without love for country or family.

15. "The Holy Father will suffer a great deal. I will be with him until the end and receive his sacrifice.

16. "The mischievous will attempt his life several times to do harm and shorten his days, but neither he nor his successor will see the triumph of the Church of God.

17. "All the civil governments will have one and the same plan, which will be to abolish and do away with every religious principle to make way for materialism, atheism, spiritualism, and vice of all kinds.

18. "In the year 1865, there will be desecration of holy places. In convents, the flowers of the Church will decompose and the devil will make himself like the King of all hearts. May those in charge of religious communities be on their guard against the people they must receive, for the devil will resort to all his evil tricks to introduce sinners into religious orders, for disorder and the love of carnal pleasures will be spread all over the earth.

19. "France, Italy, Spain, and England will be at war. Blood will flow in the streets. Frenchman will fight Frenchman, Italian will fight Italian. A general war will follow which will be appalling. For a time, God will cease to remember France and Italy because the Gospel of Jesus Christ has been forgotten. The wicked will make use of all their evil ways. Men will kill each other, massacre each other even in their homes.

20. "At the first blow of His thundering sword, the mountains and all of Nature will tremble in terror, for the disorders and crimes of men have pierced the vault of the heavens. Paris will burn and Marseilles will be engulfed. Several cities will be

shaken down and swallowed up by earthquakes. People will believe that all is lost. Nothing will be seen but murder; nothing will be heard but the clash of arms and blasphemy. The righteous will suffer greatly. Their prayers, their penances, and their tears will rise up to Heaven and all of God's people will beg for forgiveness and mercy and will plead for my help and intercession. And then Jesus Christ, in an act of His justice and His great mercy will command His Angels to have all His enemies put to death. Suddenly, the persecutors of the Church of Jesus Christ and all those given over to sin will perish and the earth will become desert-like. And then peace will be made, and man will be reconciled with God. Jesus Christ will be served, worshipped, and glorified. Charity will flourish everywhere. The new kings will be the right arm of the holy Church, which will be strong, humble, and pious in Its poor but fervent imitation of the virtues of Jesus Christ. The Gospel will be preached everywhere and mankind will make great progress in its faith, for there will be unity among the workers of Jesus Christ and man will live in fear of God.

21. "This peace among men will be short-lived. Twenty-five years of plentiful harvests will make them forget that the sins of men are the cause of all the troubles on this earth.

22. "A forerunner of the Antichrist, with his troops gathered from several nations, will fight against the true Christ, the only Savior of the world. He will shed much blood and will want to annihilate the worship of God to make himself be looked upon as a God.

23. "The earth will be struck by calamities of all kinds (in addition to plague and famine which will be widespread). There will be a series of wars until the last war, which will then be

fought by the ten Kings of the Antichrist, all of whom will have one and the same plan and will be the only rulers of the world. Before this comes to pass, there will be a kind of false peace in the world. People will think of nothing but amusement. The wicked will give themselves over to all kinds of sin. But the children of the holy Church, the children of my faith, my true followers, they will grow in their love for God and in all the virtues most precious to me. Blessed are the souls humbly guided by the Holy Spirit! I shall fight at their side until they reach a fullness of years.

24. "Nature is asking for vengeance because of man, and she trembles with dread at what must happen to the earth stained with crime.

25. "Tremble, earth, and you who proclaim yourselves as serving Jesus Christ and who, on the inside, only adore yourselves; tremble, for God will hand you over to His enemy, because the holy places are in a state of corruption. Many convents are no longer houses of God, but the grazing-grounds of Asmodeus and his like.

26. "It will be during this time that the Antichrist will be born of a Hebrew nun, a false virgin who will communicate with the old serpent, the master of impurity, his father will be B. At birth, he will spew out blasphemy; he will have teeth; in a word, he will be the devil incarnate. He will scream horribly; he will perform wonders; he will feed on nothing but impurity. He will have brothers who, although not devils incarnate like him, will be children of evil. At the age of twelve, they will draw attention upon themselves by the gallant victories they will have won; soon they will each lead armies, aided by the legions of hell.

27. "The seasons will be altered; the earth will produce nothing but bad fruit; the stars will lose their regular motion; and the moon will only reflect a faint reddish glow. Water and fire will give the earth's globe convulsions and terrible earthquakes which will swallow up mountains, cities, etc.

28. "Rome will lose the faith and become the seat of the Antichrist.

29. "The demons of the air together with the Antichrist will perform great wonders on earth and in the atmosphere, and men will become more and more perverted. God will take care of His faithful servants and men of good will. The Gospel will be preached everywhere, and all peoples of all nations will get to know the truth.

30. "I make an urgent appeal to the earth. I call on the true disciples of the living God who reigns in Heaven; I call on the true followers of Christ made man, the only true Savior of men; I call on my children, the true faithful, those who have given themselves to me so that I may lead them to my divine Son, those whom I carry in my arms, so to speak, those who have lived on my spirit. Finally, I call on the Apostles of the Last Days, the faithful disciples of Jesus Christ who have lived in scorn for the world and for themselves, in poverty and in humility, in scorn and in silence, in prayer and in mortification, in chastity and in union with God, in suffering and unknown to the world. It is time they came out and filled the world with light. Go and reveal yourselves to be my cherished children. I am at your side and within you, provided that your faith is the light which shines upon you in these unhappy days. May your zeal make you famished for the glory and the honor of Jesus Christ. Fight, children of light,

you, the few who can see. For now is the time of all times, the end of all ends.

31. "The Church will be in eclipse; the world will be in dismay. But now Enoch and Eli will come, filled with the Spirit of God. They will preach with the might of God, and men of goodwill will believe in God, and many souls will be comforted. They will make great steps forward through the virtue of the Holy Spirit and will condemn the devilish lapses of the Antichrist.

32. "Woe to the inhabitants of the earth! There will be bloody wars and famines, plagues and infectious diseases. It will rain with a fearful hail of animals. There will be thunderstorms which will shake cities, earthquakes which will swallow up countries. Voices will be heard in the air. Men will beat their heads against walls, call for their death, and on another side, death will be their torment. Blood will flow on all sides. Who will be the victor if God does not shorten the length of the test? All the blood, the tears and prayers of the righteous, God will relent. Enoch and Eli will be put to death. Pagan Rome will disappear. The fire of Heaven will fall and consume three cities. All the universe will be struck with terror and many will let themselves be led astray because they have not worshipped the true Christ who lives among them. It is time; the sun is darkening; only faith will survive.

33. "Now is the time; the abyss is opening. Here is the king of kings of darkness; here is the Beast with his subjects, calling himself the Savior of the world. He will rise proudly into the air to go to Heaven. He will be smothered by the breath of the Archangel Saint Michael. He will fall, and the earth, which will have been in a continuous series of evolutions for three days, will open its fiery bowels; and he will be plunged for all eternity with all his followers into the everlasting chasms of hell. And then

water and fire will purge the earth and consume all the works of men's pride and all will be renewed. God will be served and glorified."

Mélanie Calvat, *Apparition of the Blessed Virgin on the Mountain of La Salette* (Lecce, Imprimatur by Msgr. Bishop of Lecce, 1879).

Timeline of Liturgical Changes

1859: Pope Pius IX institutes Marian prayers to be recited after all Low Masses within the Papal States (three Hail Marys, Salve Regina, and Prayer for the Church).

1886: Pope Leo XIII adds his own Saint Michael prayer to the prayers recited after all Low Masses.

1911: Pope Pius X introduces a new arrangement of the Psalter for use in the breviary.

1949: Pius XII gives permission to the Chinese to celebrate the vernacular Mass except that the Roman Canon had to remain in Latin.

1955: Pius XII issues a thorough liturgical reform of Holy Week. Changes include that the priest is assigned more to the chair and less to the altar. On Holy Saturday, the triple candle (trikirion) is abolished. The Maundy Thursday and Easter Vigil Masses are moved from the morning to the evening.

1957: Pius XII reduces the Eucharistic fast to three hours before Communion.

1958: Pius XII gives permission (months before he died) to bishops of Germany, Austria, and the German parts of Switzerland to proclaim the Lesson/Epistle and Gospel of the Mass in the vernacular from the altar.

1959: In the missal, John XXIII removes the word *perfidis* (Latin: "faithless") from the Good Friday prayer for the Jews and adds the name of Saint Joseph to the Canon of the Mass.

1960: Pope John XXIII changes the liturgical calendar and removes the feast of the Circumcision from January 1.

1962: Vatican II opens under John XXIII.

1963: Vatican II passes *Sacrosanctum concilium*, the Constitution on the Sacred Liturgy, calling for the vernacular and more lay participation.

1964: Pope Paul VI reduces the Eucharistic fast to one hour before receiving the Communion.

1964: The Leonine Prayers are suppressed by the instruction *Inter oecumenici*.

1965: Vatican II closes under Paul VI.

1965: A provisional missal is issued. The changes include these: use of the vernacular is permitted; freestanding altars are encouraged; the psalm Judica at the beginning and the Last Gospel and Leonine Prayers at the end are omitted.

1966: National episcopal conferences are ratified by Pope Paul VI's motu proprio *Ecclesiae sanctae*.

1967: Priestly concelebration is allowed, and Communion under both species is allowed to the laity.

1967: Married deacons are allowed by Pope Paul VI in *Sacrum diaconatus ordinem*.

1968: Pope Paul VI changes the Rites of Ordination for bishops, priests, and deacons.

1969: Paul VI grants an indult for Holy Communion in the hand to nations where it is "already the custom" (Holland, Belgium, France, and Germany).

1969: Pope Paul VI promulgates the *Novus Ordo Missae* with his Apostolic Constitution *Missale Romanum* of 3 April.

1970: The *Novus Ordo Missale* of Pope Paul VI is published.

1970: The Society of Saint Pius X (Fraternitas Sacerdotalis Sancti Pii X) is founded by Archbishop Lefebvre in order to allow priests to celebrate the 1962 Mass.

1971: Paul VI bars cardinals over eighty years old from voting in papal elections.

1972: The minor orders of porter, exorcist, and subdeacon are abolished by Pope Paul VI in *Ministeria quaedam*.

1973: Extraordinary lay Eucharistic ministers are allowed.

1975: Pope Paul VI expands number of cardinal electors from the traditional 70 to 120.

1977: An indult to receive Communion on the hand is granted to United States.

1988: SSPX Archbishop Lefebvre consecrates four bishops at Écône.

1988: The Priestly Fraternity of Saint Peter (FSSP) is created.

1992: Altar girls are allowed by John Paul II.

2007: The option to celebrate the Latin Mass is granted to all priests by Pope Benedict XVI in *Summorum Pontificum*.

Dates of Indults for Communion in Hand

On the following dates, the indults for Communion in the Hand were granted by Pope Paul VI:

Holland, Belgium, France, and Germany, 29 May 1969
South Africa, 3 February 1970
Canada, 12 February 1970
Rhodesia (Zimbabwe), 2 October 1971
Zambia, 11 March 1974
New Zealand, 24 April 1974
Australia, 26 September 1975
England and Wales, 6 March 1976
Papua and New Guinea, 28 April 1976
Ireland, 4 September 1976
Pakistan, 29 October 1976
United States, 17 June 1977
Scotland, 7 July 1977
Malaysia and Singapore, 3 October 1977

Timeline of the Life of Ex-Cardinal McCarrick

July 7, 1930: Theodore E. McCarrick is born to Theodore E. McCarrick and Margaret McLaughlin. When McCarrick is three, his father dies. As a child, McCarrick attends Catholic elementary school.

1946: McCarrick is expelled from Xavier High School.

September 1947: McCarrick begins at Fordham Prep.

May 1949: McCarrick graduates from Fordham Prep with honors.

1949–Aug 1950: McCarrick in Sankt Gallen from ages nineteen to twenty.

20 July 1950: At a Carthusian monastery in Switzerland, McCarrick receives his calling to be a priest.

September 1950: Twenty-year-old McCarrick returns to New York to study at Fordham University.

31 May 1958: Francis Cardinal Spellman ordains McCarrick to the priesthood in the Archdiocese of New York.

1958–1963: McCarrick earns a second master's degree in social sciences and a Ph.D. in sociology from the Catholic University of America.

1963–1965: McCarrick is assistant chaplain, dean of students, and director of development at the Catholic University of America.

1965: McCarrick becomes a monsignor and the president of the Catholic University of Puerto Rico.

1969–1971: Terence Cardinal Cooke brings McCarrick to New York, where McCarrick serves as associate secretary for education and assistant priest at Blessed Sacrament parish from 1969 to 1971.

1971-1977: McCarrick serves as secretary to Terence Cardinal Cooke.

During this time in 1971, McCarrick assaults a sixteen-year-old altar boy while measuring his inseam. This claim was found to be credible by Cardinal Dolan of New York.[182]

In 1972, the same sixteen-year-old student was in the bathroom, where McCarrick grabbed him, and shoved his hand down his pants, trying to get into his underwear. This claim has been found to be credible.[183]

1977: Pope Paul VI appoints McCarrick as an auxiliary bishop of the Archdiocese of New York. He is the vicar of East Manhattan and the Harlems.

1981: Pope John Paul II appoints McCarrick the first bishop of Metuchen, New Jersey.

1986: Pope John Paul II appoints McCarrick archbishop of Newark, New Jersey.

[182] Laurie Goodstein and Sharon Otterman, "American Cardinal Accused of Sexually Abusing Minor Is Removed from Ministry," *New York Times*, 20 June 2018.

[183] Ibid.

1997: Archbishop McCarrick, a founding member of the Papal Foundation, begins serving as its president.

2000–2014: McCarrick serves as a board member of Catholic Relief Services.

22 November 2000, Fr. Boniface Ramsey, O.P., a professor at a diocesan seminary in Newark from the late 1980s to 1996, writes a letter at the request of Nuncio Gabriel Montalvo about a recurring rumor in the seminary that McCarrick "shared his bed with seminarians, inviting five at a time to spend the weekend with him at his beach house ... [and] that he knew a certain number of seminarians, some of whom were later ordained priests for the Archdiocese of Newark, who had been invited to this beach house and had shared a bed with the Archbishop." The diocese had purchased the beach house at McCarrick's request in 1984.

2 January 2001: Pope John Paul II appoints Archbishop McCarrick archbishop of Washington.

February 2001: Pope John Paul II elevates McCarrick to the College of Cardinals.

Fall 2001: Cardinal McCarrick opens Redemptoris Mater, a new seminary to educate diocesan missionary priests.

2002: Cardinal McCarrick announces the Vatican's new policy on sexual abuse by priests, by which an accused priest will be put on "administrative leave" and removed from clerical duties while his case is investigated. The procedures also include providing church pastoral services to victims and psychiatric treatment for the accused priest.

April 2005: Cardinal McCarrick votes in the conclave that elects Pope Benedict XVI.

16 May 2006: McCarrick retires as archbishop of Washington, D.C.

In 2005 and 2007, the New Jersey Metuchen and Newark Dioceses paid settlements to two men, Mr. Robert Ciolek and an unnamed former priest, for allegations of sexual abuse by McCarrick that occurred at Mount Saint Mary's in Maryland.

2006: Archbishop Viganò reports that Nuncio Pietro Sambi transmitted an indictment memorandum against McCarrick to the cardinal secretary of state, Tarcisio Bertone.

20 June 2018: The Archdiocese of New York announces that an allegation of sexual abuse by Theodore Cardinal McCarrick has been found to be "credible and substantiated."

19 July 2018: The *New York Times* reports the allegations of James Grein, who says that McCarrick serially abused him beginning in 1969, when Grein was eleven years old.

28 July 2018: Pope Francis accepts the resignation of McCarrick from the College of Cardinals and suspends him from the exercise of any public ministry.

25 August 2018: Archbishop Carlo Maria Viganò releases a testament claiming that Pope Francis knew about sanctions imposed on McCarrick by Benedict XVI but chose to repeal them. The next day, Pope Francis on an airplane states that in response he "will not say one word."

28 September 2018: The Dioceses of Salina and Washington announce that Archbishop McCarrick has begun his life

of prayer and penance at Saint Fidelis Capuchin Friary in Victoria, Kansas.

5 December 2018: McCarrick's victim James Grein is interviewed by Dr. Taylor Marshall in a one hour, forty-two-minute YouTube video, in which he discloses the details and dates of his abuse, along with the shocking connections of McCarrick to Grein's family in Sankt Gallen, Switzerland.

27 December 2018: James Grein testifies in a canonical deposition by the Archdiocese of New York, stating he was molested by McCarrick, beginning when he was eleven years old and also within the context of sacramental confession.

11 January 2019: McCarrick is removed from the clerical state.

13 February 2019: McCarrick appeals the decision against him, and the appeal is rejected on 15 February. His removal from the clerical state stands.

Photo credits

29 Pope Pius IX, 1877: Wikimedia Commons, public domain

35 Pope Leo XIII, ca. 1898: Wikimedia Commons, public domain

46 Pope Pius X: Sueddeutsche Zeitung Photo / Alamy Stock Photo (C47PP0)

53 Pope Benedict XV, ca. 1915: Wikimedia Commons, public domain

57 Lúcia Santos, Jacinta and Francisco Marto, 1917: Attributed to Joshua Benoliel (http://www.santuario-fatima.pt) in Ilustração Portuguesa no. 610, 29 October 1917, *Wikipedia*, public domain

72 Page from Ilustração Portuguesa, 29 October 1917, showing the crowd looking at the Miracle of the Sun: *Wikipedia*, public domain

78 Pope Pius XI, 1939: Wikimedia Commons, public domain

92 Pope Pius XII, 1950: Everett Collection, Inc. / Alamy Stock Photo (BTJRH5)

129 Assembly of the Second Vatican Council, Saint Peter's Basilica, Rome, Album / Alamy Stock Photo (P2HWMK)

167 Michele "the Shark" Sindona: Keystone Press / Alamy Stock Photo (E10WYA)

205 Theodore McCarrick and James Grein, 1974: courtesy of James Grein

Index

About the Author

Dr. Taylor Marshall is the best-selling author of nine books, including *The Eternal City: Rome & the Origins of Catholic Christianity*, *Thomas Aquinas in 50 Pages: A Layman's Quick Guide to Thomism*, and *The Catholic Perspective on Paul*. He is also the author of the popular historical fiction *Sword and Serpent Trilogy* about the Roman persecution of the Catholic Church.

Dr. Marshall earned his Ph.D. in philosophy at the University of Dallas with his dissertation "Thomas Aquinas on Natural Law and the Twofold Beatitude of Humanity." He is the founder of both the New Saint Thomas Institute and the Troops of Saint George. He and his wife live in Texas with their eight children. Please learn more at taylormarshall.com.

CRISIS Publications

Sophia Institute Press awards the privileged title "CRISIS Publications" to a select few of our books that address contemporary issues at the intersection of politics, culture, and the Church with clarity, cogency, and force and that are also destined to become all-time classics.

CRISIS Publications are *direct*, explaining their principles briefly, simply, and clearly to Catholics in the pews, on whom the future of the Church depends. The time for ambiguity or confusion is long past.

CRISIS Publications are *contemporary*, born of our own time and circumstances and intended to become significant statements in current debates, statements that serious Catholics cannot ignore, regardless of their prior views.

CRISIS Publications are *classical*, addressing themes and enunciating principles that are valid for all ages and cultures. Readers will turn to them time and again for guidance in other days and different circumstances.

CRISIS Publications are *spirited*, entering contemporary debates with gusto to clarify issues and demonstrate how those issues can be resolved in a way that enlivens souls and the Church.

We welcome engagement with our readers on current and future CRISIS Publications. Please pray that this imprint may help to resolve the crises embroiling our Church and society today.

A Special Thanks to Our Launch Team

A special thanks to our *Infiltration* Launch Team who read this book before publication and also helped us with promotion. Thank you for your time, input, and enthusiasm.

Godspeed,
Taylor

Davis Aasen, Colette Marie Abascal, Sharon Abrahamson, Matthew Abrameit, Patti Abruzzo, Antonio Acosta, Alberto Adame, Mary Jane Adams, Jeremy Adams, Sylvia Ador, Jose Aguilar, Omar Aguilar, Dina Aguilar-Franks, Peter Akomanyi Tawiah, Rawad Al Feghali, D. C. Alan, Sergio Alaniz, George Alcantara Martinez, Emily Alcaraz, Armando Alderete, Anil Alexander, Marilyn Alexieff, Junius Alfonsus, Juliano Aliberti, Raymond Aliganyira, Lance Allen, Nancy Allen, Theresa Allen-Caulboy, Linda Allison, Sergio Almeida, Nelson Almeida, Dr. Mikhail Alnajjar, Alberto Alsina, Bernardo Altamirano, Robert Amann, Amelia Schade, Paula Amicarelli, Fr. Raphael Amor, Andre Amorim, Catherine Anderson, Jason Anderson, Mike Andrew, James Andrews, Aaron Andzel, Janet Aniello, Matthew Luis Antero, Tony Appleton, Barbara Aquilon, Tina Araujo, Aaron Arehart, John Arellano, María Cristina Ariza-Gómez, Samantha Armentor, Dr. Eladio Jose Armesto, Mark Arminio, Julie Arnold, Dwight Arnott, Luke Arredondo, Gabriela Arriaga, Michelle Arriaga, Jonathan Arrington, Paulo Arruda, Marie-Claire Arseneau, Nathene Arthur, Scott Artigue, Antonio Arvesu, Matthew Ashburn, Zach Aszalos, Robert Atkinson, Richard Attar, Michael Atwood, Abe AuBuchon, Gerald Augustine, Louise Aussant, Ronald Austin, Doug Austreim, Robert Auten, Giuseppe Avola, Jose Azurdia, Ani B., David Babb, Christopher Baca, Jacqueline Badolato, Isabella Baeten, April Bailey, Clint Bain, Christopher Baker, Peter Baker, Bruce Balconi, Linea Baldwin, Suki Baldwin, Michael Balog, Kristina Baran, Charles Baran, Daniel Barbaglia, Barbara Mancuso, Barbara Svatek, Kristina Barber, Catherine Barbercheck, Carlos Bárcenas, Lynn Bares, Matt Barhorst, Taylor Barranco, Marc Barrera, Joseph Barrett, Duane Barth, Michael Bartkoski, Jacob Barton, Jennifer Barton, Barbara Basgall, Eliot Bassett, Margo Basso, Chris Bates, Thomas Batiancela, Jeremy Bauer, Madeline Bauer, Lawrence Bayer, Adriana Beaumont, Ruben Eduardo Becerril Guzman, David Bedford, Toby Bedford, Larry Bednarz, Laurelee Beduhn, Peter Beerse, Meredith Beery, Linda Beiscoe, Paul Bell, Mark Bell, Melinda Bell, Phillip Bellini, Joshua Belokur, Jonathan Benefiel, Marjorie Benke, Elaine Bennett, Robert John Bennett, Jacob Bennett, Mary Benz, Brennan Bergeron, Dave Bergeron, Patrick Bergin, Ralph Bergmann, James Berkon, John Bertolozzi, Roberto Bertran, Barbara Bertsch, Linda T. Besink, Suzanne Betendt, Spencer Beverly, Kathryn Bevis, Gerard Biagan, Carol Bianchi, Nicholas Bianco, Aaron Biard, Steven Bien, Yvette Bingley, Sean Binkley, Andrea Bird, Annie Blackburn, Kate Blair, Eric Blair, Dana Blanchard, Jocelyne Blanchette, Charles Blankenship, Aleksandra Blaszczyk, Johnathan Blauw, Mark Bleil, Brett Bloch, Donald Bloom, David Blyth, Joseph Boateng, Robert Boatwright, Janet Bodell,

Harvey Boersma, Peggy Boese, Nicholas Boettler, Mari Boland, Richard Bole, Rev. Kenneth Bolin, Nancy Boll, Aliziris Bombino, Carmine Bonavita, Lydia Bond, Derek Bonenclark, Thomas Bonin, Jeffrey Boozer, Natalie Borda, Matthew Borders, Mary Bordi, Paul Born, Robert Borys, Jackie Boshers, John Boslem, Anthony Bossoletti, Luke Boston, Richard Boterf, Vince Bottoni, Michael Bounds, Cynthia Bounds, Jacquelynn Bourdeau, Debbie Bourgault, Todd Bourgeois, Eric Boutin, Randall Bowers, Michele Boyer, Karen Boyle, Sherry Bradl, Matt Braman, Steve Branch, Cahlen Brancheau, Deann Brandel, Stephen Brash, Robert Brassil, John Braun, John A. Bray, Brian Brecheisen, Chase Breedlove, William Breen, Joseph Bremer, Matthew Brend, Gisela Bresler, Max Brewington, James L. Brewster, Cindy Brickel, Bridgit Bellini, David Bright, John Briones, Zachary Brissett, Andrew Broniewski, Greg Bronson Bronson, Finn Brooke, Courtney Cogan Brooks, Forest Brooks, Gregory Broussard, Emile Broussard, M.D., John Brower, Graham Brown, Christopher Brown, Jacob Brown, John Paul Brown, Carolyn Brown, Simon Brown, James Brown, Bob Browning, Levi Broyles, Jonathan Brunk, Donna Brunk, Scarlet Brunstetter, Christine Brusnahan, Zachary Bryan, Jeff Buchholz, Edward Bucnis, OFS, JoAnne Budi, Jan Bugaj, Paul Burdett, Johnathan Burke, Patrick Burke, Aisling Burke, Mrs. Meredith Burl, Joyce Ann Burns, Aaron Burns, Matt Burrill, Christopher Burrows, David Buskey, Kathi Buskey, Roger Bussell, Tamara Buterbaugh, Todd Byrd, Matěj Čadil, Ryan Cafferty, Lisa Caicedo, Joe Calato, Chris Caldwell, Sister Mary Brigid Callan, Ben Callicoat, Kyrby Caluna, Paul Camarata, James Camden, William Camirand, Marc Cammarata, Deb Campano, Lindsay Campbell, Barbara Campbell, Ruth Campbell, Philip Campbell, Brian Campbell, Kathleen Campos, Jacqueline Candello, Diana Cangelosi, Kamau Canton, Teresa Cantu, Vincent Capuano, Jay Caracciolo, Fernanda Caranfa, Kris Cardella, Teresa Cardinez, Mary Carey, Amelia Carlson, Michael Carr, Roxanne Carrasco, Donna Carret, April Carter, Andrew Carter, Sam Carter, Pat Carvalho, Corwyn Carver, Darren Cary, Cyprian Casadaban, Dominic Casanova, Ethan Case, Mark Casey, Paul Casey, Ruth Cassin, Anton Casta, Christopher Castagnoli, Andrew F. Castaneda, David Castillo, Vince Cavanaugh, Robert Cella, Christopher Ceniceros, Sarah Cervantes, Cecilia Chai, Tom Chambers, Edward Chandler, Fr. Paul Chandler, Karen Chapman, Lisa Chappell, Patrick Charles, Joshua Charles, Monica Chaves, Kim Chavez, Myrna Chavez, Alejandra Chavez, Kenny Cheah, Lonnie Cherryholmes, Fr. David M. Chiantella, Rose Chiechi, Pascal Chimezie, Catherine Choi, Andy Chong, Alex Choong, Charlotte Chow, Mark Christianson, Christopher Becker, John Church, Samantha Cifelli, Leo Cintron, Rosemary Circo, Sharon Clair, Katina Clark, Effie Clark, Susan Clark, Alexandra Clark, Ierma Clark, Raphaelle Clark, Fr. Karl A. Claver, Fr. Laurent Cleenewerck, Sean Cloonan, Patricia Coffin, Joseph Coicou, Kevin Coleman, Dr. Tim Collins, Juan Colón, Jr., Robert Colquhoun, Bonnie Comar, Justin Combs, Matthew Commons, Emer Condit, Stephen Conlon, Kevin Conlon, Wesley Conn, Mike Connell, Maria Conner, Simon Consalvo, Simon Consalvo sfo, Kevin Conway, Grace Cooke, Patricia Cooper, Joseph Coote, Patrick Copeland, Debra Corcoran, Cleider Cordero Guzmán, Janssen Cordova, Christopher Corleone, Marie Correa, Frank Corsi, Carlos Cortez, Wayne Costello, Lisa Cothran, Thomas Cotner, Marie Cotter, Paul Coupe, Katherine Cowen, Emily Cowley, John Cox, Gregory Cravetz, Marco Crawford, Myles Creek, Wayne Crenwelge, Teresa Crichton, Rossa Croce, Kristy Crosby, Linda Crowley, Kaitlyn Croyle, Angel Croyle, Margaret Cruz, Alfredo Cruz, Thomas Cullor, Fr. Fergal Cummins, Sean Cunningham, Angela Cusack, Rudi Cvelbar, Michael Czabala, David D'Alessandro, Cristina D'Averso Collins, Gerri Daigle, Douglas Dall'Agnol,

Thomas Daly, Philip Damiani, Chris DaSilva, Marla Daugherty, Jim Davenport, Kevin Davey, Vicent David, Oliver Davidson, Deric Davidson, Sarah Davis, Matt Dawson, Christopher Dawson, Austin Day, Donald DCruz, Felipe de Araujo Ribeiro, Roberta de Jager, Ramón De Meer, Eduardo De Varona, Viola De Velasco, Ms. Deb De Vries O.P., Matthew DeBerry, Andrew DeCelles, Susan Dedow, Michele Deering, Joseph S. DeFranco, Deborah DeGraw, Ryan Dehaan, Andrew DeJoseph, Robin DeLage, Edward DelaHoussaye, Austin DeLaRosa, Rev. Mr. Armando deLeon, Jennifer Delgado, Hugo Delgado, Edgardo Delgado, Gabriel Dell'Aira, Rexcrisanto Delson, Libby DeMattia, Catalino Demetria, Michael DeSandre, Jim DeSart, Joe Deschler Deschler, Regina DeSpain, Vincent DeStefano, Christine Deters, Becky Dever, Kent Devine, Patricia Devine, Marc Devoid, Mike DeWitt, Antonia Dey, Steve Di Mauro, Sebastian Diaz, Dan DiBiase, Steve Dicarlo, Brad DiCarlo, Andrea Dick, Olga Dickieson, Michelle DiEnno, Kimberley Dierdorf, Thomas DiGiuseppe, Lisa Diller, Joseph Dillett, Casey Dillon, Kevin Dillon, Amado David Dimal, Mary Dimmel, Claire Dion, Debra DiPace, Damon DiPietro, Mark DiSciullo, Jim Disimoni, Michael Do, Matthew Dober, Vedran Dodig, Rebecca Doherty, Eileen Doherty, Sean Dollahon, David Dollman, Kathy Dominique, Joe Donahay, Bobby Donahoo, Kevin Donohue, Michael Dooley, Linda Doran, Darius Doria, John Andrew Dorsey III, Norine Dowd, Melanie Dowell, Trevor Downey, Roger Downey, Keith Downey, Gregory Doyle, Nathan Draper, Dylan Drego, Lloyd Dsouza, Johann du Toit, Carol Dubeansky, Jamie Dugan, Scott Dunn, Chris Dupree, Drew Durbin, Aaron Durocher, Melissa Durow, adam durst, David Dusek, Brian Dvorak, Pam Dwyer, Kate Dyson-D'Onofrio, Shawna Dziedziak, Rick Eagan, Sylvia Earnst, Teresa Earp, Stephen Eastepp, Darren Easterday, Sterling Eckert, Shirley Eckert, Karl Edmond, Douglas Edwards, Samuel Edwards, John Egerer, Elizabeth Gregorius, Gregory J. Ellermann, Valerie Ely, Jared Emry, Ronald Endoma, Molly Ennis, Laurie Ensworth, Tongay Epp, Daniel Erb, John Ericson, Erin Hames Erin Hames, Sean Esposito, Tauna Esslinger, Ray Etter, Richard Evans, Keith Evans, Edward Evans, Michelle Evert, Des Eyden, Peter Ezetta, Gerard Fagan, Angela Fairbairn, Michael Fakult, Mary Fala, Joseph Falciano, Celina Falck-Cook, John Fallens, Nolan Farkas, Stephen Farlow, Beth Farmer, Susan Farnum, Amanda Farnum, Brenda Farrell, Alan Fassina, Gregory Fast, Tanya Favantines, Paul Fedele, Nancy Fehner, Simon Feil, Amber Feist, Catherine Felicien, Anthony Ferch, Agnello Fernandes, Mayur Fernandes, Agnes Fernandez, Fred Fernandez, Adrian Fernandez, Alfred Ferrante, Davide Ferrara, Stacie Ferry, Mary Feryan, Albert Fiedeldey, John Fiffick, Bonjello Figueroa, Jeff Finkbonner, Diane and Anthony Fiore, S.C. Fischer, Richard Fisher, Andrea Fisher, Ann Fitch, Flo Fitch, Rebecca Fitzmaurice, John Fitzsimmons, Sharon Fitzsimons, Sean Flanagan, Derrick Flannigan, Andy Flattery, Eric Fleming, Edna Flores, Francis Fogarty, Julia Fogassy, Marianne Fogelson, Ryan Foley, Charlene Fong, Adrian Fonseca, Carla Fontanilla, Martin Forbes, Matthew Forget, mark Forkun, James Foronda, Fred Forthofer, Rick Fortune, Peggy Foster, Nicholas Foster, Denise Fouracre, Randall Fox, Robert Fox, Patricia Fraide, Fr. Mason Fraley, Paul Francis, Kirk Francis, Alisa Franco, Frederick Frankel, Charles Fraune, Ron Fredericks, Emily (Harder) Friedl, Kari M. Froelicher, Gerald Frost, Norbert Fuchslehner, Howard Fulks, Pamela Fuller, Jocelyne Furtado, Laura Fusco, Roderick Gabbert, Patrick Gabriel, Lucas Gabrielson, Katherine Gabryel, Lynne Gaffey, Owen Gagliardo, Peter Gagnon, Rose Gallardo, Randy Gallegos, George Galloway, Joseph Galvan, Ayanda Gamana, Rachel Gamarra, Denise Garcia, Julio Garcia, Edgar Garcia, Maria Garcia, Luis Garcia Laurent, Bryan Gardner, Joseph Garza, Jason Gates, Jennifer Geaghan, Teresa Geiselman, Brendan Gendhar,

Roberta Genini, Sharon Geppert, Geraldine Dobson, Neven Gerich, John Germain, Anthony Giangiulio, Nathan Gibson, Rebecca Gibson, Emily Gibson, Valerie Giggie, Lou Gigliotti, Annemarie Gillan, Joseph Gillespie, Mary Gillett, Ellen Gillis, George Gillon, Becky Gilmore, Jim Giordano, Mark Girardeau, Michelle Givan, Janice Givens, Bonnie Goard, Susan Gockowski, Dan Goddu, Thomas M. Goethe, Russell Goff, Jared Gogets, Thomas Goh, Peter Gojcaj, Angela Gole, Jonathon Gomez, Sherry Gonzales, Cristina Gonzalez, Joshua Gonzalez, Margarita González, Magdalena Good, Fr. Richard Goodin, Colin Gordon, Randall Gough, Renee Graceffa, Reuben Gracia, Sharon Grant, Jodi Grant, Ed Graveline, Nikki Graves, Christopher Gray, Lois Grebosky, Gloria Greenup, Jane Greenwood, Liz Gregorius, Kate Gregory, Gay Lynn Gremmel, Joe Gressock, Chimene Griego, Giselle Griffin, Joel Grissom, Robert Groppe, Jon-Mark Grussenmeyer, Lorenz Gude, Matthew Guerreiro, Marty Guerrero, Arthur Guillaume, Christopher Gutierrez, Ricardo Gutierrez Jr, Alice Guzman, Tamara Haas, Alex Haggard, Nathaniel Haire, Maryann Hajduk, Anne Hajek, Virginia Hajovsky, Joyce Hale, Michael Hall, Kennedy Hall, Ryan Hall, Roseanna M. Hallman, Cindy Hamer, Hilary Hammett, Paul Hammond, Sheelagh Hanly, Ken Hann, Renee Hannam, Tony Hansen Hansen, Jacob Hanson, Mike Harder, Joseph Hardy, Kent Hare, Michael Hargadon, Bill Harkins, Christine Harrington, Pam Harris, Adam Harrison, Kevin Harrison, Chris Harrison, Andrea Hart, Mary Hart, Annmarie Hart, Todd Hartch, Mary Harter, Dustin Harvey, Joseph Hatcher, Christopher Haukom, Patrick Hawkins, Vicki M. Hayden, Matthew Hayes, Trish Hebert, Georgia Hedrick, Rosanne Heiliger, Kimberly Heilman, Michelle Heiring, Jeff Helbling, David Helle, Steven Helm, Tonya Hembree, Teresa Hemphill, James Henderson, Paul Hepperla, Gilbert G. Herbig Sr., Megan Hermosillo, Jose Hernandes Hernandes, Victor Hernandez, Aida Hernandez, Gino Hernandez, Eladio Hernandez, Caleb Hernandez, Linda Hernandez, Amanda Herrick, Jay Hershberger, Fr. Thomas Hickey, Thomas Hickey, Donna Marie Hickman, Stephen Higgins, Robert Hill, William H. Hill, Wes Hill, Fr. Graham Hill C.Ss.R., Diana Hilmer, David Himes, John Hindery, Darlene Kostelac Hinman, Isaías Hipólito, Susan Hirst, Matthew Hisscock, Mari Hobgood, John Hoehn, Suzi Hoen, Julie Hoerle, Daniel Hoff, Michael Hoff, Michael Hoffman, Christopher Hoffman, Brian Hoffmann, Linda Hoffstetter, Laraine Hofmann, Shane Hollandsworth, Andrew Hollingsworth, Dan Hollowell, Peter Holm, Michael Holmes, Frances M. Holmes, John Holmstadt, Fred Holtslag, Timoteo Saldaña Honesto, Caroline Honn, Sonia Hooper, Bryan Hooper, Patricia Hooten, Darin Hopegood, Susan Hopkins, Jean Hosier, Richard Housey, Carol Howard Howard, Roman Hrynyszyn, Brian Hubacek, Kathleen Huddleston, Scott Hudecki, Sean Hudson, Randall Hulstein, OFS, Trever Humphres, Maria Hunter, Tom Hunter, Celeste Hupert, Brian Hurley, Michael Hurley, Andrea Huza, Steve Hyatt, Gannon Hyland, William Hynd, David Ibarra Hernandez, John-Camillus Igboanusi, Luciano Imbo, Chad Ingling, Paul Ingrassia, Olivia Ingrassia, Joan Italiano, Kevin Jackson, Will Jackson, Kevin Jacque, Nancy Jaeger, Ivan Jagas, Flo Jakobeit, Arkadiusz Jakubczyk, Mark Jakubiec, Jennifer Jalette, Louis-Benedict Aykhan Jalilbayli, Susan Jankowski, Anthony Jankowski, Stephen Janowski, Annie Jansen, James Jansen van Vuuren, Heather Jaracz, Larry Jaramillo, Karlo Jelincic, Jenifer Jenkins, W. Scott Jenken, Jerry Jenkins, Lauren Marie Therese Jenkins, Nora Jensen, William Jerome, Jeff jimenez, Alejandro Jimenez, David Jividen, Peter Johansen, Darryn Johnnie, Christian Johnson, Dale Johnson, Angela Johnson, Patricia Johnson, Galen Johnson, Teri Johnson, Jared Johnson, Brian Joly, Kristoffer Jonasson, Ray Jones, Walter Jones, Thomas Jones, Richard Jones, Maria Jones, Nicole Jones, Jessica Jones-Carson, Amanda Jordan,

Julie Jordan, Sjoerd Jorritsma, Renju Jose, John Josefsberg, Thomas Joseph, Tom Joseph, Stephen Joseph, Joseph Martin, Sharon Joyce, Randy Juanta, Chad Judice, Kelvin Jukpor, Claude Julien, Rachel Jurado, Janeann Kakalecz, Austen Kalin, Mary Kalls, James Kanning, Rossano Kapauan, Delane Karalow, Joseph Karanja, Glenn Karhoff, Victor Karlak, Denise Karmody, Alexander Karzon, Jonathan Kash, Anita Keahey, Louise Keanr, Megan Kearney, Mary Keck, Steven Keedle, Victoria Keens, David Kelch, Esq., Thomas Keller, Kristine Keller, Maurice Kelly, Marie Kelly, Debbie Kelly, John Kemna, Adam Kemper, Sylvia Kendall, Pamela Kaye KendLl, John Kennedy, Keith Kennedy, Tim Kennedy, Angela Kennedy, Michael Keogh, Jill Kerekes, Dolorese Kershaw, Dan Ketelle, Mike Key, Jeffrey Keyes, Alex Kilates, Lucy Kildow, Ellen King, Michele King, Diana Kinnaird, Luke Kippenbrock, Robert Kirby, Gary Kirsch, Ed Kise, helen kish, Maureen Klecker, Leo Klump, Patrick Kniesler, Eric Kniffin, Stacey Knoch, Christopher Koechig, Karen Koehle, Michael Koeniger, Kathleen Kois, Patricia Koranda, Patti Koski, William Koszelak, Sunita Kottoor, James Kovats, Emi Koyama, Frank Kramer, Rev. Edward Krause, Jerry Krebs, Mark Kristine, Christopher Kruchten, James Kubu, Barbara Kubu, Daniel Kuehn, Matthew Kuizon, Kateri Kullman, Bonnie Kuntz, Stephen Kunz, Dr. Kenneth Kuzdak, David Kwiecinski, Elizabeth L'Esperance, Patricia La Barbera, Cheryl La Follette, Debra Lacas, Dana LaCombe, Pete LaFave, Eric Lafferty, Cynthia Laforty, Kevin Lally, Kyle Laluces, Katherine Lamb, Catherine Lambert PA-C, Brad LaMorgese, Allen Landes, Josh Lane, Fr. Jeffrey Langan, Elisabeth Langenkamp, Robert Lapaz, Carol Lara, Fr. Nicholas Larkin, Brenda Laronde, Michael Larson, Miguel Lasaga, Christopher Laurence, Kathleen LaValley, Mary Lawrence, Thanh Le, Paul Leader, Yecenia Leal, Will Leatherwood, James LeBert, Joseph LeBlanc, Claude LeBlanc, Lawrence Leconey, Chris Lee, Alexander Lee, H.S. Lee, Joshua Lee, Thomas Lee, Cathy Lees, Andrea Lefebvre, Kara Leger, Wellington Lemmer, maria lenzen, Alex Lessard, David Letendre, Heather Leuci, Nicole Leung, André Levesque, Christopher Levis, Laurie Lewandowski, Chester Lewandowski, Debra Lewis, Valerie Lewis, John Lewis, Robert Lewis, Alwyn Lewis, Alan Liang, Benjamin Licciardi, Braden Licciardi, Joseph Lichtenwalner, Chris Lim, Teresa Limjoco, Julie Linares, Linda M. Solis, Cathy Lins, Rose Anne Livingston, Beth Locricchio, Margie Loesch, Catherine Loft, Joshua Logan, Sheila Logue, Jim Logue, Jeff Logullo, Lois Tucci, Cristobal Longton, Francisco Lopez, Elisa Lopez, Jaime Lopez, Carl Lordi, Rod Lorenz, Ian Carlo Lositaño, John Lowman, Lucy Lozano, Brian Lucero, James Lucier, Carmela Lukacs, Laura Luster, Louise Lutz, Heather Luzzi-Miller, Michael Lynch, Corey Lyon, Joe Lyon, June Mabry, Matthew Mach, Jovi Macholowe, Raul Macias, Eugenia Macias, John MacIsaac, Joseph Mack, Michelle MacKellar, Sharon MacKenzie, Catherine MacMullin, Katherine Maddox, Justin Maderer, Emeka Maduekwe, Trevor Mahan, Joie Maida, Darko Majdic, Marty Major, Michael Maker, C. Malan, Daniel Malone, Sean Maltbie, Gregory Mandt, Joseph Maniaci, James Manley, Denise Mantei, Julie Maravilla, Gregory Marco, Robert Marcuccio, Margaret Leiberton, Maria Thrift, Mrs. Morag Marinoni, Mark Power, Paul Market, Brian Marks, Charles Marks, Kristen Marquis, Douglas Marr, Patrick Marron, Ryan Marsh, Thomas Marshall, Maryann Marshall, Scott Martell, Chris Martens, Robert Martin, Linda Martin, Michael Martinez, Martin Martinez, Martha Martinez, Rafael Martinez, Drew D. Martinez, Andriya Martinovic, Lawrence Martone, Bob Marts, Fr. Anthony Mary, F.SS.R., Michael Massey, Marco Mastromonaco, James Mata, Mary Mateer, Elizabeth Mathew, Bob Matters, Brandon Mauch, Neal Maxwell, Brigidetteñ McAnea, Kim Mcbride, Joseph McCallion, Trapper McCammon, Marie McCammon,

Jennifer McCarthy, Katie McCarthy, Brett McCaw, Mark McComish, Joanne McCourt, Michele McCoy, April McCullough, Jay McCurdy, John McDevitt, Elizabeth McDonald, Michael McDonnell, Daniel McDowell, John McGinnis, Teresa McGlasson, Thomas McIntyre, Jeff McKay, Julie McKee, Patrick McKinney, Lisa McKinnon, Joseph Mclaughlin, Kyle McLemore, Peter McNally, Terry McNellis, Rosaria McNierney, Dina McNulty, Seth McQuillan, Bret McVeigh, Jennifer Meade, Jorge Medina, Andrew Medina, Elizabeth Mejia, Miguel Melendrez, Alexander Melhorn, Richard Melvin, Damyan Mendoza, John F. Mercer, Marisa Merkle, Kathleen Merry, Fr. Andre Metrejean, Auguste Meyrat, Benoit Meyrieux, Michael Bonin, Piotr Mietus, James Miguez, Laura Miller, Paul Millington, Dennis Minnice, Timothy Misencik, William Missavage, Dolores Mitchell, Quinton Mitchell, Jonathan Mittiga, Jill Mizen, Diane Moen, Anne Mohanraj, Dan Mohler, Dennis Mohr, Doreen Moisey, Erik Mojica, Alvaro Molina, Jason Molitor, Jon Mollison, Lynn Momboisse, Carol Monaco, Michael Monahan, Al Mondejar, Jonathan Charles Valentine Monge, Patricia Monroe, Ana Maria Monte Flores, Michael Monteforte, James Mooney, Jason Mooney, Philip Moore, Christine Moore, Mary Moore, Joseph Moore, Thomas J. Moore, Xavier Morales, Ximena Morales, Kevin Moran, Matthew Moreau, Crislee Moreno, Briana Morgan, Donald Morgan, Andy Morgan, Dean Morra, Kevin Morris, Olivia Morris, Mary Helen Morrow, Christian Mortensen, Christopher Moser, Thomas Mosser, Matthew Moucha, Maureen Mourt, Michele Mroczek, Abraham Mudrick, Debbie Mueller, Mike Muglia, Mike Mulcahy, Patrick Mullan, Brendan Muller, Paolo Munoz, William Murat, Andrew Murdison, Cristian Murillo, Mary P. Murphy, James Lee Murphy, Brian Musha, Felix Mutuc, Scott Myers, Eric Myers, Alex Nagel, Leslie Najm, Carlos Naranjo, Chris Nash, Bro. Harold Naudet, CSC, Joseph Ndu, Ross Neill, William Nelligan, Kristina Nellis, Mary Nelson, Keith Nelson, Erik Nelson, Paul Nelson, Norma Nelson, Luigi Neri, Timothy Neubauer, LeAnn Neubauer, Brian Newberry, Deborah Newell, Sandra Newton, Theresa Newton, Emmanuel Ngabire, Michael Nguyen, Joseph Nguyen, Stefanie Nicholas, Aimee Nickolas, Michael Nielsen, Michael Nielson, Nathan Niemann, Cort Niemi, Charles Nieves, Katherine Nini, Dalia Nino, Patricia Nisbet, Christopher Nnamani, Seaghan Nolan, Amber Nold, John Nolen, Arash Noori, Alexander Norris, Didier Nuncio Morales, Linus Nworie, Michael Nyoagbe, Eamon O'Brien, Mary Elizabeth O'Connor, Tim O'Flaherty, Jason O'Neill, Mark O'Rosky, Stephanie O'Rourke, Andrew O'Shaughnessy, Tom O'Brien, Lady Mary Ellen O'Brien, LGCHS, Valerie O'Doherty, Slobodan Obrenovic, Joshua Ochoa, Brian Ocurran, Lydia Ogoc, Stanford Oliver, Barbara Oliverio, Mark Olivero, Elaine OMalley, Timothy ONeil ONeil, Greg Onyango, Luís Raúl Oquendo, Bill Orsborn, Christopher Ortega, Sebastian Orth, Raymond Ortiz, Aileen Osias, Elizabeth Ovidia Osland, Carol Osteen, John Ott Ott, Sharon Otto, Ryan Owens, Therese Padilla, Nick Padley, Rebecca Padley, Damon Palestra, Tami Palladino, Theresa Palmer, Deborah Palumbo, Theresa Palumbo, Pam Brubaker, Michael Pant, Laura Paradis, Pete Parcs, Juan Martin Pardo van Thienen, Deborah Paris, Judith Park, Michael Parrett, Matthew Parsons, Colleen Pasnik, Joseph Pastorek, David Paterson, Joann Patras, Casey Patterson, Albin Paul, Joe Paul, Paul Pekarek Paul Pekarek, Joe Pausa, Amy Pavey, Marina Pearson, Vanessa Pehl, Martyn Pękala, Ernesto Pelayo, Vicky Pelegrin, Marco Antonio Pellens, Richard John Pelo, Emilio Perea, Nativedade Pereira, Manuel Pereira, Andy Perez, Melissa Perez, Jason Perez, Wendell Perez, Benjamin Perry, Marla Perry, Patrick Perusse, Kevin Peteres, Fran Peterson, Phil Petrucci, Pamela Pettibone, Paul Pettie, Amanda Pflanz, Mitzi Phalen, Philip Thoma, Sarah Louise Phillips, Theresa Phillips, Joseph Piccirillo, George Piccone, Nicholas Picini,

John Picone, Victor Pidermann, Thomas Piegsa, Brent Pierce, Joshua Piersall, Diane Pietras, Theresa Pilkerton, Alain Pilote, Melissa Pimentel, Maureen Pinho, Ashton Pinto, Stephen Pistorius, Amanda Pizzo, Christopher Plessner, Kyle Pociask, Gavan Podbury, Marija Podniece, Bridgette Poitras, Sean Patrick Pokall, John Pollard, Jakob Pollard, Fr. Jeff Pomeisl, Matthew Pommier, Regina Pontes, Bradley Poole, Fr. Mark Porterfield, Paulette Portz, Jared Pottkotter, Mark Potzick, Eric Poulsen, Aurelio Prahara, John Pramberg, Donna Prather, Phil Pratt, Linden Predy, Terra Marie Presotto, Emily Prest, Chris Prieto, Kathleen Principe, Emily Principe, Kent Purdy, Glenn Purpura, Mark Quaranta, Ed Quigley, Daniel Quigley, Ron Rack, Lukas Radmann, Jurgita Radziunaite, Kate Raeder, Gordon Rafool, Jacob Rainey, Michael Rakaczewski, Frank Ramirez, John Ramirez, Lino Ramirez, Renacito Ramos, Maggie Ramshaw, Richard Randall, Paul Raney, Juni Ranillo, Nicholas Rankin, Chantelle Rantucci, David Rantucci, Joe Rappa, Ann Rastorfer, James Rauch, Jeff Ravenscroft, Wenceslaus Raymond, Jennifer Raymond, Antone Raymundo, Heath Rayne, Joshua Reagan, Dawna Reandeau, Edward Rebholz, Donna Rebre, Vinicius Rebuli, Robin Reed, Marcy Reese, Nathan Reffitt, Kevin Reginald, Donal Reid, Jeremy Reidy, Michael Reilly, Anthony Render, April Reneau, Lisa Renne-Kent, Gerald Renville, Rev. Fr. Richard Carr, Paolo Reyes, Rudy Anthony Reyes, Matthew Reynolds, Jayne Rheinhardt, Damian Rhodes, Zulema Richards, Joshua Richards, Nathaniel Richards, Linda Richardson, Carissa Ridenour, Caleb Rider, DeAnne Ridge, Geraldine Ridgway, Erich Riedel, Kevin Rilott, Michael Riopel, Mary Lynne Riopel, Kristina Ripka, Joyce Riske, Joan Risley, Ramona Rita, William Ritter, Eugenio Rivera, Joseph Roach, Zachary Robb, Amanda Robben, Donald Roberts, Chris Roberts, Aaron Roberts, Neil Robertson, Terry Robinette, Darren Robinson, Barbara Robinson, Vince Robles, Mabel Robles, Edwin Rocabado, Fabio Rocha, Marie Roche, Sébastien Rock, Ciara Rodgers, Theresa Rodrigues, Christine Rodrigues, Gretchen Rodriguez, Carlos Rodriguez, Tony Rodriguez, Gil Rodriguez, Carlos Rodriguez-Lampon, Alex Roerty, Bob Roesser, Matthew Roessner, Robert Roetting III, Melani Roewe, Steve Rogers, Eva Rohr, Robert Roll, Damon Roman, Michele Rooney, Dana Roraback, Charles Jone Rosales, Sandra Rosas, Laura Roscoe-Griffin, Heather Ross, Jeff Rosser, Ksy Rossiter, Derek Roush, Peggy Rowe-Linn, Roland Roy Roy, Terri Roy, Scott Roy, Ron Royer, Andrea Ruccolo, Richard Ruesch, Jane Ruggiero, Fernando Rui, Cesar Ruiz, Sarananda Ruiz, Raul Ruiz Jr., Rose-Ann Rumpus, Michael Rund, Adrian Rusch, Alexandra Russell, Allison Russo, Antonio Ruvolo, Nowellyn Ryan, Brendan Ryan, Phyllis Ryan, Bruce Sabatino, Greg Sabourin, H. William Safford, Mitchell Sager, Andrey Saiz, Ethan Salazar, Humberto Saldana, Juan Saldivar, Mary Salmond, Sharon Saltzman, Audry Salvador, Gaurav Salvi, Lito Samaniego, John Sammons, Janine Samz, Amy San Filippo, Lindsey Sanchez, Christopher Sanchez, Bill Sanchez, Carlos Sanchez Bonano, Maria Sánchez-O'Brien, Teresa Sando, Nikki Sanner, Maryanne Santelli, Patricia Santy, Austin Sarabia, Deacon Greg Sass, Jeremy Sauer, Fr. Timothy Sauppé, S.T.L., Lori Sautter, James Savage, Anthony Scarpantonio, Jeffrey Schack, Kevin Schad, Adam Schaefers, Cathy Schaffer, Mary Schaub, Patricia Schauble, Lou A. Schell, Brad Schepisi, Ron Schexnaydre, Eduardo Schiavon, Paul Schiller, Tom Schirra, Cheryl Schlimpert, Sherry Schlosser, Michael Schmidt, Christopher Michael Schmitz, Richard Schneider, Timothy Schomburg, Danielle Schott, Rick Schrader, Daniel Schreck, Levi Schroer, Daniel Schuler, Adam Schwankl, Brent Schwartz, Michael Schweigert, Ryan Schweitzer, Heather Schweitzer, Diane Schwind, Bryan Scibelli, Jeffrey Scott, Timothy Scott, Grant Scott, Thomas Scott, Susanne Scott, Mark Scott, Andrew Seamans, Paul Seco, David Seefeldt, Curtis Seelhammer, Paul Sefranek,

F. Scot Segesman, Gail Seiler, Krystian Sekowski, Noah Sell, Robin Sellers, Benjamin Varle Semah, James Senecal, Dominic Sepich, Carl Sergeant, Paul Serwinski, Janette Sessions, Jenny Seymour, Matthew David Shaddrix, Loretta Shalosky, Sharon Pry, John Sharry, James Shaw, Genie Shaw, Robert T. Shea, Fran Shea, Elizabeth Sheehy, James Sheflin, Paulette Sheldon, Dutch Shenefield, Ann Sheppard, Thomas Sheridan, Diana Shertenlieb, Oriane Shiroma, Carleen Short, Ronald Shpakoff, Adam Shrives, Kathryn Sibley, Janey Sibson, Althea Sidaway, Edward Sidleck, Peter Sierra, Anderson Macedo Silva, David Silva, Suzanne Silvir, Cheryl Simanek, Eddy Simon, Emmanuel Simon, Leila Simonsen, Francesco Sinagra, Jeffrey Singer, Asher Sircy, Clinton Sites, Ashley Sivertson, Ric Sjostrom, Jordan Skog, Ante Skoko, Brian Slaby, Dennis Slavik, Jesse Smaldone, Jeffrey Small, Alyssa Smeltzer, Julie Smith, James A. Smith, Melinda Smith, Jay Smith, Karen Smith, Barbara Smith, Samantha Smith, Charles Smith, David Smither, Valerie Smyder, Tim Sniffen, Gregory Snyder, Elaine Sobozenski, Liz Soliz, Alexander Soltysik, Josh Somerville, Hugh Somerville Knapman OSB, John Sommer, Herbert D. Sommerfeld, Julian Sommers, Siegfred Sornito, Peter Sorrentino, Nicholas Sosa, Steve Souza, Joseph Sparandera, Karen Spaziante, Jeff Spiegelhoff, SharonRose Spiers, Charles Spivak, Doug Spriggs, Louise Springer, Jennifer Spurgin, Burke Squires, Andrew Stahl, Jennie Stanbro, John Standifird, Karen Stanford Bonvecchio, Jim Stanislawski, Paul Stark, Benjamin Starnes, Jayden Stauffer, Martha Stefanchik, Jenifer Steffel, Eileen Steng, Richard Stevens, Kristopher Stickney, Charles Stiebing, Anthony Stine , Theresa Stiner, James Stocks, Chad Stolly, Logan Stolly, Noah Stolly, Vincenzo Stone, Patrick Stoops, Dan Stover, William Stowe, Eleanor Stowell, Mark Straub Sr., Judith Strausbaugh, Michael Strauss, Joan Strayham, Donna Sullivan, Alex Sullivan, Karen Sullivan, Bret Sunnerville, Patrick Suter, Donna Swager, Janet Swallow, Edward Swann, Philip Swanson, Thomas Swartz, Margie Sweeney, Nekeya Sylvester, Steve Szabo, Jan Szafrański, David Tambellini, Mary Tanberg, Celeste Tanodra, Patrick Taylor, Michael Taylor, Timothy Taylor, Guadalupe Tenpenny, Sasha Tesija, Erin Teter, Jennifer Tewell, Roger Theobald, Jessica Therriault, Sue Thibodeaux Ph.D., Curtis Thoene, Leigh Thomas, Coe Thomas, Ellen Thomas, John Thompson, David Thrower, Michael Ticich, Kyle Tillotson, Dave Timmerding, William Timmerman, Cindy Titus, James Tobin, Jeff Todd, Gregory Todd, Matthew Toenjes, Deborah Tofflemire, Anna Tognaci, Paul Tognetti, Joseph Tolin, Elizabeth Tomlinson, Derek Tonkin, Ryan C. Toups, Brad Toups, Bill Townsend, Nathan R. Towsley, Stephen Trabanino, Kathleen-Marie Tracey, Brandan Tran, David Trana, Nicholas Trandem, Joe Trassare, Jennifer Traughber, Jeffrey Traughber, Catherine Traugott, John Trausch, John Trautwein, Janice Travasso, Susan Treacy, Vaughn Treco, Justin Trefney, Reynaldo Trejo, Ernest Trevino, Caroline Trimble, Dave Troupe, Charles Trujillo, Andrea Trujillo, Ronaldo Tuazon, Tim Tubilewicz, Nancy Tucker, James Tucker, Forrest Tucker, Jose Tumbaga, Phil Tureau, Teresa Turner, Maryrose Turner, Joseph Turner, Jeffery Turner, Karly Tuttle, Dianne Uhler, Cutter Uhlhorn, Stephan Ulm, Bernard Untalan, Chris Urban, Jeremy Urban, Katherine Urquidi, Lima Vadakara, David Valdez, Mark Valencia, Jean Valerga, Dayle Van Alstine, Teo Van der Weele, Richard Van Kirk, Rik Johannes Franciscus Maria van Steenoven, Jaime Vanchura, Samuel VanDeest, Dana VanDorsselaer, Brenda VanWeezel, Scott Varga, Benjamin Vasko, Joanne Vavoso, Giona Vazhappilly, Lotus Vele, Michael Velosa, Michael Verceles, Adam Verheyen, Benjamin Verhovsek, Rich Vetrano, Deborah Victory, Maria Vida, Matthew Viergutz, Joseph Vigneri, Ted Villalon, Cindy Villarreal, Gerald Villaver, Janice Vinson, Stephen Volk, Daniel Volpato, Charles Volz, Dr. William von Peters, Amber Vowels, Diana Vredeveld, Thomas

Wachtel, David Wagner, Deacon Brooke Wagner, Matt Wagner, Angela Wagner, M.K. Waiss, Marye Waite, Jesse Waitz, Leslie Wakeman, Matthew Walczak, Mark Waldecker, Carol Walenga, Alexander Walker, Jonathan Walker, Jennifer Walker, Travis Walker, Craig Walkins, Peggy Wall, Colin Wallace, Nigel Wallace, David Wallace, Mary Grace Wallsten, Karen Walsh, Catherine Walton, Todd Wannemuehler, M.D., Stephen Ward, Hazel Ward, Sean Warfield, David W. Warner, Kenneth Warnshuis, Mitchum Warren, Victoria Warren-Mears, Chris Washington, John Wasko, Dennis Waszak, Gordon Watson, Gregory Watson, David Watts, Chris Watts, Rosalind Weeks, Tim Weiland, Russ Wenzel, Alfred West, Ernie West, Neil Weston, Daniel Westrick, Fr. Alan B.Maria Wharton, John Whattam, John Whibley, Leonard White, Jessamyn White, Morgan White, Tanner Whitham, Lauren Whittaker, Steve Wiberg, Adam Wiederman, Kelly Wilbur, Avit Wilderness, Gary Wiley, Theresa Wilhelm, David Williams, Ronny Williams, Fredrick Williams, Rick Williams, Ryan Williams, Natalie Williams, Joan Williamson-Kelly, David Wills, Steven Wilson, David Wilson, Gerard Wilson, Hilda Wilson, James Wilson, Yvonne Wince, Steven Windey, Blake Winn, Christopher Winner, Aaron Winter, Pierre Wirawan, James Wiscott, Courtney Wissinger, Lynn Wofford, Tim Wolfe, Janet Wolfe, Kurt Wolfe, Tres Wolfford, Debbie Womack, Christopher Wong, Jennifer Woo, Benjamin Wood, David Woodby, Sara Jane Woods, Jeffrey William Woods, Joel Woods, Gilbert Wright, Sandra Wright, Rene Wu, David Wurst, Pieter Wycoff, Darek Wyrzykowski, Patrick Yanke, Gerald Yeakula, Harry Yonemura, Kristin Young, Joshua Youngblood, Tyler Younghouse, Jerome Ypulong, David Yung, Christopher Yurkanin, Aidan Zaballero, Colin Zak, Sandra Zanni, Royce Zant, Marilyn Zayac Zayac, Kale Zelden, Adam Zerger, Rose Zingleman, Thomas Ziolkowski, Amy Zizzi, David M. Zuber, Sam Zummo, Leo Zupan, Waldemar Zurek